HA

The Journal of the
Hannah Arendt Center for
Politics and Humanities
at Bard College

The Journal of the Hannah Arendt Center for
Politics and Humanities at Bard College

hac.bard.edu

©2019 Bard College

Published by
The Hannah Arendt Center for Politics and Humanities at Bard College
Roger Berkowitz, Editor
Samantha Rose Hill, Managing Editor

Editorial Board
Jerome Kohn
Patchen Markell
Wyatt Mason
Thomas Wild

Produced by
Bard College Publications Office
Mary Smith, Director
Barbara Ross, Copy Editor
Karen Spencer, Designer

Cover: ©Estate of Fred Stein, fredstein.com

ISSN: 2168-6572
ISBN: 978-1-936192-64-9
Bard College, PO Box 5000
Annandale-on-Hudson, NY 12504-5000
bard.edu

Foreword

This seventh volume of the *Hannah Arendt Center Journal* includes a series of talks from our 2018 conference "Citizenship and Civil Disobedience." If one focuses on the fact of disobedience, civil *disobedience* might appear a dereliction of the first duty of citizenship: to obey the laws. But when we focus on the civil aspect, *civil* disobedience is something else entirely. Our English word "civil," which comes from the Latin *civis*, has a dual association. On the one hand, it is connected to the city, the *civitas*, and names the ideal of citizenship—what it means to belong to the city. On the other hand, it describes the action of a citizen as one that eschews violence and acts in a mild and civilized way. Civil disobedience is that kind of lawbreaking that is at once civilized and aimed at the protection and reinvigoration of the city rather than its destruction.

We are living through a moment of increased bipartisan civil disobedience. From antifa, Occupy, #metoo, Black Lives Matter, and sanctuary cities, to the Tea Party, Patriots, #fakenews, and fundamentalist bakers in Colorado, the tradition of American civil disobedience is being reinvigorated as form of mass political citizenship. The outbreak of civil disobedience today manifests the fraying of a consensus around questions of economic and racial equality as well as social discrimination, immigration, and the uses of American power abroad. So many various minorities are dissenting from the established way of doing things that we ask whether there is still something that holds our diverse and divergent nation together. In raising the questions of citizenship and civil disobedience, we ask if and how a new democratic American ideal can emerge.

Civil disobedience can be uncivil. But Hannah Arendt knew that being an active citizen is dangerous. She famously wrote, "Whoever entered the political realm had first to be ready to risk his life, and too great a love for life obstructed freedom, was a sure sign of slavishness. Courage therefore became the political virtue par excellence."[1] As dangerous as political action is, it is also the lifeblood of democratic political change. Arendt saw the tradition of active disobedience by citizens in the name of reviving the republic as a key feature of American democracy. In her essay "Civil Disobedience," she writes (citing Alexis de Tocqueville):

> "As soon as several inhabitants of the United States have taken up an opinion or a feeling which they wish to promote in the world," or have found some fault they wish to correct, "they look out for mutual assistance, and as soon as they have found one another out, they combine. From that moment, they are no longer isolated men but a power seen from afar, whose actions serve for an example and whose language is listened to." It is my contention that civil disobedients are nothing but the latest form of voluntary association, and that they are thus quite in tune with the oldest traditions of the country.[2]

Civil disobedience succeeds when it expresses new ideas that inspire the majority. Arendt criticized the student revolutionaries of the 1960s because they lacked new ideas that could transform the revolutionary situation into a political revolution. Without ideas, the violence of so-called revolutionaries is nothing more than protest. The creation of a new, meaningful politics is the challenge of movements like Black Lives Matter, the Resistance, and the Tea Party. To become revolutionary political movements, these associations must imagine a more legitimate and just world.

The Arendtian tradition of citizenship and civil disobedience involves not individual acts of conscience but political movements that mobilize organized minorities. Civil disobedience is an act of citizenship by which minorities can change the minds of majorities. Thus, disobedient minorities—those groups who collectively dissent from majority opinion—are not traitors or rebels but are part of the fabric of democratic government.

In this volume we collect essays based on talks given at the Hannah Arendt Center conference "Citizenship and Civil Disobedience." We include essays by Theda Skocpol, Marion Detjen, Seon-Wook Kim, Allison Stanger, Mark Bray, David Bromwich, Sarah Jaffe, Christopher Schmidt, Kenyon Victor Adams, Amy Schiller, and Thomas Chatterton Williams, and Roger Berkowitz. In addition, we publish a reflection on the conference by Arendt Center Associate Fellow Nikita Nellin.

We also include three essays by Libby Barringer, Joshua Plencner, and Joshua Foa Dienstag from the workshop "Heroic Politics on Screen" exploring the political backdrop of our fascination with superheroes. At home and abroad, questions about the limits of representation, sovereign authority, and democratic action have defined a political world that, simultaneously, has become saturated with superheroic narratives. These essays ask what kinds of political life, and what kinds of citizens, these big-screen superheroic stories imagine—and whether they foster, or impede, democratic ends.

Finally, we publish some of your favorite essays by Arendt Center Fellows and colleagues that appeared over the past year. We include essays by John Douglas Macready, "Hannah Arendt on the Oasis of Friendship"; Jana Schmidt, "The Kids Are Responsible"; Thomas Bartscherer, "'Swift as a thought,' as Home Used to Say"; Ken Krimstein, "Hannah Arendt and the Miracle of the New"; Max Feldman, "The Fundamental Chord: Remembering Carl Heidenreich"; and Katherine Bermingham "Time for Arendt: Political Temporality and the Space-Time of Freedom."

—Roger Berkowitz

---

1. Hannah Arendt, *The Human Condition* (Chicago: University of Chicago Press, 1958), 36.
2. Hannah Arendt, "Civil Disobedience," in *Crises of the Republic* (New York: Harvest/HBJ Books, 1969), 95.

About the Hannah Arendt Center

The Hannah Arendt Center for Politics and Humanities at Bard College is an expansive home for thinking in the spirit of Hannah Arendt. The Arendt Center's double mission is first, to sponsor and support the highest-quality scholarship on Hannah Arendt and her work, and second, to be an intellectual incubator for engaged humanities thinking at Bard College and beyond, thinking that elevates and deepens the public argument that is the bedrock of our democracy. The Arendt Center cares for and makes available the Hannah Arendt Library, with nearly 5,000 books from Hannah Arendt's personal library, many with marginalia and notes. Visit hac.bard.edu for more information.

VOLUME 7 *HA*

Citizenship and Civil Disobedience

Reflections on Civil War and Civil Disobedience

Roger Berkowitz

In the years leading up to the Civil War, there were more than seventy violent clashes between Representatives and Senators in Congress. In her book *Field of Blood: Violence in Congress and Road to Civil War* Joanna Freeman tells a story of a raucous antebellum Congress replete with bullying, dueling, and fistfights.[1] Even amidst the bitter animosity that pervades Washington, D.C., in the era of President Donald Trump, it takes some effort to imagine our elected officials engaging in regular canings, duels, and fistfights; it is bracing to learn that congressmen were brandishing pistols and knives and even flinging the occasional brick in the Capitol building. But all this was happening in Congress in the two decades before the Civil War.

The fighting culture in the antebellum Congress reflected the country at large. In four months during 1835 alone there were 109 riots across the United States. The murderous battles of "Bloody Kansas" in 1850 actually played out a mini civil war between proslavery Missourians and antislavery Kansans from the North. And John Brown's raid on Harper's Ferry unleashed a tide of anger on both sides of the national divide over slavery.

The violence in Congress began with Southern Democratic congressmen intimidating Northern abolitionists; however, something changed in 1856. Suddenly, a new class of Republican congressmen decided to fight back. The abolitionists stood up to intimidation from the South and met threat with defiance and force with force. As a result, the 34th Congress was the most violent in history and culminated in the barbaric caning of Massachusetts Senator Charles Sumner after his "Crime against Kansas" speech. The speech insulted Southern slaveholders by name, insinuating that they were holding on to slavery at least partly for reasons of sexual mastery. This led Representative Preston Brooks—a relative to one insulted senator—to walk up to Sumner and cane him mercilessly until Sumner was carried away bloody and barely conscious.

I bring up this history of the pre–Civil War period not to suggest we are about to have a second civil war—although we should not rule out that possibility. Last year, *Foreign Policy* magazine asked a group of national security analysts to evaluate the chances of a civil war in the United States over the next ten to fifteen years. The answers ranged from 5 to 95 percent. The average was 35 percent. And this was before the Unite the Right March in Charlottesville. Keith Mines, a Special Forces officer turned diplomat, estimated the probability of war at 60 percent. He said:

Violence is "in" as a method to solve disputes and get one's way. The president modeled violence as a way to advance politically and validated bullying during and after the campaign. Judging from recent events the left is now fully on board with this, although it has been going on for several years with them as well—consider the university events where professors or speakers are shouted down and harassed, the physically aggressive anti-Israeli events, and the anarchists during globalization events. It is like 1859, everyone is mad about something and everyone has a gun.[2]

In our time, speakers are shut down. Antifascist groups justify violence against fascists. Black parishioners are killed in churches. Jews are murdered in synagogues. Muslims are beat up in subways and shot in bars. Across the country and on both sides of the political divide, there is an extraordinary polarization. The very idea of a common American culture and a shared American way of life flickers like a specter from a nostalgic era. And yet, the polarized atmosphere today pales when compared to the political violence of the 1850s.

Hannah Arendt reminded us not to see too much wisdom in history. She warned repeatedly that the present is always unprecedented and we must look upon it fresh. But in her essay "Civil Disobedience," Arendt writes that history can teach us about the causes of revolution.

If history teaches anything about the causes of revolution . . . it is that a disintegration of political systems precedes revolutions, that the telling symptom of disintegration is a progressive erosion of governmental authority, and that this erosion is caused by the government's inability to function properly, from which spring the citizens' doubts about its legitimacy. This is what the Marxists used to call a "revolutionary situation"—which, of course, more often than not does not develop into a revolution.[3]

It is fair to say that we are today in at least some version of a revolutionary situation, one in which large numbers of citizens reject the legitimacy of our established institutions. Lasting authority persists in institutions that earn our respect. But the post–World War II institutions that built modern America have failed. Above all, it is the elite—the academics, businesspersons, and governors—who have betrayed the trust placed in them. As Martin Gurri writes, the basic fact of our current political moment is the failure of our elites and our elite institutions. The fact underlying the crisis of authority "was failure: the painfully visible gap between the institutions' claims of competence and their actual performance."[4]

This week in the *New York Times* Emily Badger offered an insight into the depth and breadth of the popular anger against the establishment.[5] Even today, two years into the Trump presidency, 47 percent of Trump supporters feel like strangers in their own country. At the same time, 44 percent of those who disapprove of Trump report they feel like strangers in their own country. It is not simply that people disagree; an overwhelming majority of Americans—people in power and people out of power, persons of color and white people, women and men—all feel alienated, rootless, and powerless in their own country.

We are at one of those rare moments at which the country sits on a pivotal point amidst a conflict of fundamental values. With the failure of the elites and the loss of authority, the result is not the emergence of a new consensus. Paralyzed by distrust, the country is engaged in a frantic embrace of ideological extremes. At such moments, as in the 1850s, violence and even civil war are very real possibilities.

• • •

We should not be shocked that violence is a possibility in America today. One of the most prescient observers of America, Hannah Arendt well understood how the United States is a fertile ground for violence. In her essay "Is America by Nature a Violent Society?" Arendt writes:

> It seems true that America, for historical, social, and political reasons, is more likely to erupt into violence than most other civilized countries.[6]

American propensity to violence coexists with the country's deep respect for law. The paradox between violence and lawfulness is rooted in the American traditions of political activism and freedom of assembly, which, for Arendt, are "among the crucial, most cherished, and, perhaps, most dangerous rights of American citizens." Precisely because of our constitutionally guaranteed rights of assembly, speech, and political activism, the United States is perennially threatened with disunity and fundamental dissent:

> Every time Washington is unreceptive to the claims of a sufficiently large number of citizens, the danger of violence arises. Violence—taking the law into one's own hands—is perhaps more likely to be the consequence of frustrated power in America than in other countries.[7]

Violence emerges as a real possibility at those moments when diverse constituencies feel themselves abandoned and disempowered. To the extent we are in a revolutionary situation, it is because a majority of Americans from multiple backgrounds feel like strangers in their own land.

If Arendt is right that in the United States such situations can lead easily to political activation and violence, it is also the case that history is not fate.

Our situation today is not the same as the 1850s. A civil war and widespread political violence are not inevitable.

The question before us is how to reempower the citizens of American democracy. Doing so means restoring the possibility of and faith in citizen action mattering in our shared political community. And one distinctive way that citizens can and do matter in America is through the American tradition of civil disobedience. Is it possible, therefore, that civil disobedience is the kind of active citizenship that has, and might again, bring about revolutionary change without a civil war?

• • •

Arendt's prime example of how civil disobedience can bring about revolutionary political change that refounds a body politic is the civil rights movement. The Fourteenth Amendment passed after the Civil War guaranteed to all Americans equal protection of the law. The Fourteenth and Fifteenth Amendments were "meant to translate into constitutional terms the change that had come about as the result of the Civil War."[8] But the South resisted that change and developed the system of Jim Crow laws that evaded racial equality through the vastly unequal implementation of "separate but equal." In Arendt's telling, the Amendments failed to bring about the promised revolutionary refounding of America; that revolution, to the extent that it happened, was a product of civil disobedience.

Of the leaders of the civil rights movement in the 1960s, one of the most central in defining a strategy of civil disobedience that aimed at a political revolution was Bayard Rustin.[9] In 1963, in the wake of Bull Connor's attacks on civil rights demonstrators in Birmingham, Alabama, Rustin was instrumental in organizing the March on Washington for Jobs and Freedom. The march is best known today for Martin Luther King Jr.'s "I Have a Dream" speech. Rustin is one of those leaders of the movement who is too often overlooked. But it was Rustin who traveled to Montgomery in 1956 to help organize the bus boycott; it was Rustin who introduced King to Gandhi's thinking on nonviolent resistance, and Rustin who was one of the first to expand the civil rights movement politically by demonstrating against nuclear testing in North Africa. It was also Rustin who was forced to resign from the Southern Christian Leadership Conference because of controversy over his sexual orientation. As a gay, communist, African American man who believed passionately in a nonviolent revolution, Rustin is one of the great if unsung heroes of the civil rights movement's strategy of civil disobedience.

In 1965, Rustin wrote a seminal manifesto, "From Protest to Politics: The Future of the Civil Rights Movement."[10] He argues that the destruction of legal racism is only the first phase of the civil rights struggle. To bring about true civil rights, the movement would have to morph from fighting legal racism to bringing about political equality. He writes, "The minute the movement faced this question, it was compelled to expand its vision beyond race relations to economic relations." What this means is that the revolution in civil rights could no longer be a matter of protesting unjust laws; it must transform itself from a protest movement into a political movement; it must become, he argues, "a conscious bid for *political power.*"

In this second stage of the movement, the struggle for civil rights is essentially revolutionary. Rustin writes:

> I believe that the Negro's struggle for equality in America is essentially revolutionary. . . . The term revolutionary, as I have been using it, does not connote violence; it refers to the qualitative transformation of fundamental institutions, more or less rapidly, to the point where the social and economic structure which they comprised can no longer be said to be the same.[11]

The struggle for civil rights, Rustin claims, will not stop moving until either it has been utterly defeated or it will win substantial equality. In his words, [this struggle] can only be won when it achieves a revolution that brings about full employment, the abolition of slums, the reconstruction of our educational system, and new definitions of work and leisure. He continues: "Adding up the cost of such programs, we can only conclude that we are talking about a refashioning of our political economy."

• • •

What Rustin calls a revolution, Hannah Arendt calls politics, and she names that revolutionary politics civil disobedience. For both Rustin and Arendt, civil disobedience is a revolutionary form of politics.

The core of Arendt's argument about civil disobedience is that it is a means of active and collective political dissent:

> Civil disobedience arises when a significant number of citizens have become convinced either that the normal channels of change no longer function, and grievances will not be heard or acted upon, or that, on the contrary, the government is about to change and has embarked upon and persists in modes of action whose legality and constitutionality are open to grave doubt.[12]

As an activity of dissent, civil disobedience has the political capacity to reenergize democratic citizenship and free it from its corruption. The great threat to democracy is the atrophy of active citizenship. Democracy, or at least American constitutional democracy as Arendt understands it, is founded upon the principle that multiple and diverse communities with unique value systems can coexist within a government of freedom. Freedom, however, is not simply a negative absence of power. It is the power to act together with others to build a public world. To be free and to act, she writes, are the same.

Arendt worries that large bureaucratic states will over time detach the power to act from the people and lead to the loss of freedom:

> Representative government itself is in crisis today, partly because it has lost, in the course of time, all institutions that permitted the citizens' actual participation, and party because it is not gravely affected by the disease from which the party system suffers: bureaucratization and the two parties' tendency to represent nobody except the party machines.[13]

Because large and bureaucratic democracies tend toward centralization of power and the disempowering of citizens, democracies will need to experience perennial episodes of refoundation.

Such moments of refounding are central to the democratic spirit of the United States. And Arendt (citing Alexis de Tocqueville) finds in the civil disobedience of the civil rights movement a modern reemergence of the American tradition of political action:

> As soon as several inhabitants of the United States have taken up an opinion or a feeling which they wish to promote in the world, or have found some fault they wish to correct, "they look out for mutual assistance, and as soon as they have found one another out, they combine. From that moment, they are no longer isolated men but a power seen from afar, whose actions serve for an example and whose language is listened to." It is my contention that civil disobedients are nothing but the latest form of voluntary association, and that they are thus quite in tune with the oldest traditions of the country.[14]

Civil disobedience is an act of citizenship by which minorities can change the minds of majorities. Thus, disobedient minorities—those groups who collectively dissent from majority opinion—are not traitors or rebels, but are part of the fabric of democratic government.

The rise in civil disobedience is a sign of a revolutionary situation. But revolutionary situations rarely lead to revolution. More often, they lead to counterrevolution, or to nothing at all.

• • •

For Arendt, civil disobedience must be nonviolent for the simple reason that civil disobedience, unlike a revolution, seeks to revolutionize the world, but it ultimately accepts the frame of established authority and the system of laws. Violence can change the world; but violence, as one of the West Point cadets said in our debate last night, opens a Pandora's box of unpredictable and uncontrollable evils. Or, as Arendt writes, violence may change the world. But more often, violence leads to more violence. "The civil disobedient shares with the revolutionary the wish 'to change the world,' and the changes he wishes to accomplish can be drastic."[15] But in the end, the civil disobedient affirms that shared world.

The challenge in our particular moment is that so many concurrent organized minorities are battling to have their own view of fundamental American values prevail. From #antifa, Occupy, #metoo, Black Lives Matter, and sanctuary cities, to the Tea Party, Border Patriots, #fakenews, and fundamentalist bakers in Colorado, the tradition of American political association is being reinvigorated as form of mass political citizenship.

Amidst this struggle of opposing yet concurrent minorities there is a tendency to turn political adversaries into political enemies. I want to suggest this is a mistake.

I am not arguing that we need a centrist politics of compromise. Nor am I calling for the discovery of a rational consensus that somehow resolves and mitigates the real differences that define the various communities of opinion that comprise the present United States. The aim of an Arendtian democracy is not one that produces a thick consensus on fundamental values. Instead, I am arguing for a political democratic ideal of active citizenship.

1. Joanna Freeman, *Field of Blood: Violence in Congress and Road to Civil War* (New York: Farrar, Straus and Giroux, 2018).

2. Keith Mines, "Will We Have a Civil War?" *Foreign Policy*, 10 March 2017.

3. Hannah Arendt, "Civil Disobedience," in *Crises of the Republic* (New York: Harvest/HBJ Books, 1969), 69–70.

4. Martin Gurri, *The Revolt of the Public and the Crisis of Authority in the New Millennium*, 2nd ed. (San Francisco: Stripe Press, 2018), 175.

5. Emily Badger, "Estranged in America: Both Sides Feel Lost and Left Out," *New York Times*, 4 October 2018. nytimes.com/2018/10/04/upshot/estranged-america-trump-polarization.html.

6. Hannah Arendt, "Is America by Nature a Violent Society?" in *Thinking without a Banister: Essays in Understanding, 1953–1975*, ed. Jerome Kohn (New York: Schocken Books, 2018), 355.

7. Ibid., 356.

8. Arendt, "Civil Disobedience," xx.

9. See Henry Louis Gates Jr., "Who Designed the March on Washington?" pbs.org/wnet/african-americans-many-rivers-to-cross/history/100-amazing-factswho-designed-the-march-on-washington/.

10. Bayard Rustin, "From Protest to Politics: The Future of the Civil Rights Movement," *Commentary* 39 (February 1965): 64ff.

11. Ibid., 65.

12. Arendt, "Civil Disobedience," 74.

13. Ibid., 89.

14. Ibid., 95.

15. Ibid., 75.

Saving America Once Again: Comparing the Anti-Trump Resistance to the Tea Party

Theda Skocpol

Good morning, everyone. I'm very grateful for the invitation to speak at Bard College—this is my first visit—and at a conference in honor of a remarkable thinker, Hannah Arendt. And I'm very appreciative of the introduction from Professor Peter Rosenblum and the chance to hear Dean Deirdre d'Albertis and Professor Roger Berkowitz speak before me.

What I'm going to do today is to talk about two remarkable upsurges of self-organized citizen activity that have spread across the United States in just the last decade. I'm going to be talking about the Tea Party from 2009 to 2011—although there are still some Tea Parties meeting—and the anti-Trump grassroots resistance that has self-organized across many communities in the country since the November 2016 election.

I want to begin with two quotations my colleagues and I heard from organizers of local groups in the Tea Party and the anti-Trump resistance. Notice the remarkable similarities. An Arizona Tea Party husband and wife that my coauthor and colleague, Vanessa Williamson, met in 2011 explained to her:

> We've always voted, but being busy people we just didn't keep up, keep as involved as maybe we should have. And now we're at the point where we're really worried about our country. I feel like we came out of retirement. We do Tea Party stuff to take the country back to where we think it should be.

That's the kind of message we heard from all of the grassroots Tea Party participants and organizers we met and interviewed and observed in different parts of the country in 2011—in Arizona, Virginia, and New England.

More recently, I've been traveling around the country to study what's happening in counties that went for Trump in North Carolina, Ohio, Pennsylvania, and Wisconsin; and one of the Wisconsin organizers of a local resistance group that I met told me in 2017,

> I had always been a consistent voter and donated to my party and some select candidates; but I had not been super-involved. Then the presidential campaign of 2016 became more and more ridiculous and frightening, and our very worst nightmare happened.

My life changed overnight. My peace of mind was robbed from me. I was called to action. I feel like a soldier in a war trying to save this country, my children's future, the climate, and the list keeps growing.

The anti-Trump resister is a little more wordy than the Tea Party people, but it's very much the same message of being called to action by a startling national electoral event.

Before I proceed, let me just say to everybody here that protest and civil disobedience are important, but voting is the single most important thing a democratic citizen can do. I read in the *New York Times* today that only one-third of young people are getting ready to vote in the November 2018 election. It is perhaps the most important election in my lifetime, and I've been around for a while. Vote as you choose, but make sure you're registered and make sure you vote, and tell all your friends and relatives across this country to do the same.

What I'm going to do today is to compare the Tea Party upsurge after 2008 to the anti-Trump grassroots upsurge that happened after 2016. I'll talk a little bit about what we've learned, my colleagues and I, about the scope and the type or organizing that happened in the grassroots Tea Party and in the grassroots resistance; I'll talk about who leads and participates in the local groups that have been formed by the thousands around the United States; and I'll mention a little bit about Presidents Obama and Trump as focal points of the organizing on the two sides, as well as the centrality of battles over health-care reform, the relationship between bottom-up and top-down forces in these two loosely connected upsurges of organizing activity, and their relationship to the two parties at the two ends of the political spectrum. I'll be drawing on a whole series of studies. A lot of the work right now, including some I think you'll be hearing about at this conference, talks about the current resistance situation in terms of national movements and nationally organized advocacy efforts.

The research that my colleagues and I have done—particularly Leah Gose, a graduate student in sociology at Harvard who has worked with me on this work—looks at locally organized voluntary groups, not professionally run advocacy operations or even national internet operations; so that's what makes our research different. The evidence we have answers the question: how widespread is the grassroots anti-Trump resistance beyond big cities and liberal places? The evidence is based on field observations and interviews, most of which I've conducted as part of a study that was launched by three female professors at Harvard right after the election.

Within days of the November 2016 election we got together and decided that we would regularly visit eight pro-Trump counties, one a medium-size city area, a swing area; the other, a smaller, more conservative place—two apiece in North Carolina, Ohio, Pennsylvania, and Wisconsin. My part of that work involves traveling to those places, staying in Quality Inns or Comfort Inns, and getting to meet with local newspaper editors, the heads of the Democratic and Republican county parties if they exist, any surviving Tea Party heads. Also with business group leaders and civic leaders of various kinds. In addition, somewhat to my surprise, as my husband (who's a retired physicist) and I drove thousands of miles across the country, I discovered in all of these places self-organized, anti-Trump, grassroots resistance groups and got to meet their leaders and organizers. In some cases, we attended meetings just as Vanessa and I had attended meetings of local Tea Parties eight years before.

In addition to that, Leah Gose and I have gotten to know the organizers of a kind of umbrella group, Pennsylvania Together, which has dozens of resistance groups affiliated with it across the pivotal state of Pennsylvania. We persuaded them to fill out questionnaires about the origins of groups and the reasons people participated. So that gives us one entire state where we're not just looking at pro-Trump areas but all kinds of areas, including the suburbs around Pittsburgh and Philadelphia.

The last part of the research is to compare our experiences with the resistance groups with the work that Vanessa Williamson and I did when we visited local areas around the country in 2011, when we observed Tea Party meetings and sat down for face-to-face interviews with the leaders and key participants in self-organized local Tea Parties.

Let me just start by reminding us about the events then and now. Barack Obama was elected the first African American president in 2008, with a surge of liberal Democratic support, youthful support, support by minorities; and it was only six weeks into his presidency when a nationwide Tea Party protest organized and kicked off. It actually started a month into his presidency. In many ways the national spark event was the CNBC commentator Rick Santelli calling for Tea Party protests against, of all things, the mortgage assistance programs of the fledgling administration. But that was picked up by Fox News, by right-wing talk radio hosts, by various advocacy groups, who spread the idea of holding Tea Party protests far and wide. When I met local Tea Partiers a year later, many of them told me they heard about it on the radio or simply by watching television, and then started taking action themselves without anybody actually telling them what to do in any detail.

By April, tax day, of 2009, there were protests involving half a million to a million protestors in 542 counties around the country. Some of these were major regional demonstrations; those were the ones that got the most coverage, particularly on Fox, but also on the main networks at that point. But you can see how widespread the Tea Party self-organizing was at that point.

And it didn't stop just with protests, with older people dressed in colonial costumes and carrying signs denouncing President Obama as a fascist or a communist, or both. From 2009 through 2011, at least 900 regularly meeting local Tea Parties—this is really the innovation in this period—were created. Our research since then suggests that we may have underestimated by about four or five hundred. There were regularly meeting Tea Parties, meeting once a month, sometimes as often as once a week, all over the country in those crucial first years of the Obama presidency.

Eight years later, in 2016, another controversial president is elected, and in fact the anti-Obama: Donald Trump. It didn't even take a month in this case for citizen organizing to spread. Instead the organizing started right away after the November 2016 election, and on January 21st, the day after the inauguration, there was a massive women's march in Washington, D.C. More to the point and of more interest to me, there were six hundred marches across the country, including in very small and conservative parts of the country, joined by more than an estimated 4.2 million people—so an even quicker and more massive response eight years later.

Immediately after the 2016 election Democrats started saying that they were going to become more politically active than they had been before. And I don't have a comparable slide for Republicans after the Obama election, but I think the same was true back then.

In the case of the anti-Trump resistance, interestingly enough, some commentators started appearing MSNBC or in publications like the *Nation* talking about the lessons that anti-Trump resisters could learn from the Tea Party organizers eight years before. So there's a certain amount of learning across time, imitation of tactics, and we know that several congressional staffers who organized the Indivisible effort sat down and wrote a guide that went online in late 2016, and that guide explicitly referred back to local Tea Party organizers. It delivered a message that liberals really needed to hear in the United States: if you want change, don't just contact Washington. At that point there wasn't really anybody to contact in Washington. Organize locally and start doing things like community events, contacting the local office of your elected representative to express your views.

There are some very important parallels in the process by which these two upsurges emerged. But a big question in our research, especially for me, has been whether in our partisan, polarized country the anti-Trump resistance would simply organize in already liberal areas. Would it be concentrated around the big cities that gave overwhelming margins to Democrats in 2016 but absent in other parts of states where Hillary Clinton lost by massive margins, much more massive than Obama did? Or would it be spread out like the Tea Parties were spread out? And so we're looking closely at the four states—and these are some results from two states—just looking to see how many counties in these states had one or more Tea Parties and one or more resistance groups listed on that Indivisible map that was put together as a guide for people to figure out what was going on in their area.

You can see that in both Pennsylvania and North Carolina these had both been very widespread voluntary grassroots mobilizing efforts. It's not exactly the same counties, but it certainly isn't a situation where all the organizing for the Tea Parties is outside the big cities and all the organizing for the resistance is in the big cities plus a few college towns. That's not the way it is. Both upsurges are widespread.

Let me talk a little bit about how grassroots resistance groups have formed, as I learned in detail in my visits to the eight pro-Trump counties. It's a fascinating process, and we asked people—I asked people—to reconstruct exactly how they went about organizing a local group, same as I did for the Tea Party when I talked to Tea Party organizers eight years before, because one of the big questions is, do Americans organize regularly meeting groups anymore? The political scientist Robert Putnam and others have argued that it happens much less than it used to. Since it has happened in both of these cases, how did that happen?

There were ten resistance groups formed in these eight relatively conservative-leaning counties—and in every case two to five leader initiators were the ones who took the call in hand to start organizing. Two of the groups split off from previously organized ones, but all of the originally organized groups started right after the 2016 election and their founding meetings were held in libraries or local restaurants, usually by March of 2017 at the latest. They got going pretty quickly. And of interest to me is that the organizers often met for the first time after the election; they weren't necessarily friends already, although they've since become close friends. They might have met because they contacted each other through the Facebook group Pantsuit Nation, where a lot of people, mostly women, had signed up to celebrate Hillary Clinton's election; then it turned into a mourning and support group operation right after the election, and the site added a feature that allowed people to find out who was in their area. Some people met that way. Others met (just as Tea Party organizers often did years before) on buses or trains on the way to regional or national marches and protests.

A lot of the groups that formed did take some tactical advice from the *Indivisible Guide*. They didn't necessarily get any directions from a Washington, D.C., office. Indivisible staffed up and got millions of dollars and formed an office in Washington, D.C., by March of 2017; but most of the effect of Indivisible was through that guide that was online that people simply read and emailed or Facebooked to each other in the early weeks after the November 2016 election. A lot of the local groups did take some tactical pointers from that online guide.

They were all up and running by the spring of 2017. They had leaders, plans, projects, Facebook pages, and sometimes periodic newsletters, all led by leaders committing their time voluntarily and members coming to meetings on their own time. And when we collected the questionnaires for the thirty-six groups across all different types of communities in Pennsylvania, we found very similar patterns. Here's what some of the groups look like in the smallest, most heavily conservative counties—I love these pictures. In Catawba County, North Carolina, you see them meeting for their founding meeting in the library. In Licking County, Ohio, you see them in the basement of the one liberal Protestant church in the town, and they are reciting for a YouTube video a credo, a citizen's credo, that resembles the credo that liberal Protestants recite in church, but it's adapted to politics. And in tiny farming-oriented Monroe County, Wisconsin, that's a doctor leading the founding meeting.

Well, our questionnaires enabled us to pin down exactly who the people are that have organized this widespread voluntary grassroots resistance. I don't want to disappoint some of the people in the audience who think that everything progressive comes from the young and people of color. The counties I'm visiting are overwhelmingly white places, so it shouldn't be a surprise that the organizers are white. But two-thirds to 90 percent of the leaders and participants in these grassroots groups are women, overwhelmingly white women, and usually older, from their fifties to their seventies; although it is the case that sometimes local anti-Trump resistance groups have mothers in their thirties or forties, sometimes with their children in tow. We never saw that in Tea Party meetings eight years before; we saw only grandparental-generation men and women, and sometimes they had a couple of unhappy grandchildren with them for the meeting; but the middle working-aged group was absent.

In today's resistance groups, 80 to 90 percent of the participants and organizers are college educated, and about half of them have advanced degrees. They are teachers, or sometimes they're professors or adjuncts at local or regional universities and colleges. They are health-care providers or service managers, and a fair number of businesswomen and nonprofit managers. Now, there are men in all of these groups, but they are usually the partners or husbands of the women who are kind of front and center. That is different from the Tea Party situation where the Tea Partiers were usually husband-and-wife couples. Often, we saw women taking the lead in organizing voluntary activities in Tea Parties, so the idea that Tea Parties are all male is not right; but there was certainly a higher proportion of male presence in the Tea Parties.

Just like Tea Partiers in the early Obama years said they were Republican-leaning or Independents who were to the right of the Republican Party, most of the resisters today say that they are Democratic identifiers of varying degrees of enthusiasm. They include certainly some Independents and the occasional disgruntled Republican, and there are Bernie supporters as well as Hillary supporters in these local groups; but they're not spending any time arguing about the kinds of things that the Democratic National Committee is arguing about.

We asked people to say what their reasons were for participating in organizing and populating these local resistance groups. You can see that opposition to Trump is a very important reason: forty percent of the respondents to all of our questionnaires in both the eight counties groups and the groups across Pennsylvania—there were 436 respondents over all; we allowed them to give more than one reason, or we coded more than one reason—40 percent of them certainly mentioned opposition to Trump. But notice that saving or improving the country and American democracy is also very frequently mentioned by people. And the barred lines give the percentage of all of the 765 reasons that we coded; and once again, saving American democracy is very prominent in the motivations.

People are also finding community with others—that's especially important in very conservative places where the desire to reach out to like-minded other people when you're in a sea of red is very motivating for the women and men who participate in resistance groups. Electing Democrats and Progressives is there, but it's not the most prominent reason; and you can see some of the others. And you can read some of the detailed reasons that people give in their own words.

I'd like to make a series of comparisons of these two upsurges starting in 2009 and 2016. They were both triggered by an event that is actually pretty rare in American democracy but doesn't seem rare these days, and that's the election of a president who's backed by his own political party winning both houses of Congress at the same time. That is a particularly frightening event to partisans on the other side. I mean, I remember how frightened everybody was in Cambridge, Massachusetts, when George W. Bush was, I don't know, declared the victor—I'm not going to say "won"—the 2000 election. Suddenly people woke up and realized that an Evangelical Christian conservative from Texas backed by his own party was going to be controlling Washington. In Cambridge, Massachusetts, that's a deeply shocking event. So people did what many of the Tea Partiers told me they did after Barack Obama was elected with Democrats: yelled at the TV a lot.

But the Tea Partiers went further. They self-organized. And the same thing has happened in the Trump presidency after the shock of Trump's victory happened at the same time that Republicans remained overwhelmingly in control of the House and the Senate. The anti-Trump resistance emerged, self-organized, as much out of fear and loathing, I would say, as out of hope.

Now, what the controversial presidents exactly connote to the people who have organized in opposition to them is a little different in these two cases. Based on my face-to-face listening to Tea Party people in the past and even now, Barack Obama symbolized un-Americanness. You know, in an interview nobody is going to tell a Harvard professor right out, "I hate him because he's black," or, "I hate him because he's an immigrant." They do say they hate him because he's a Democrat—there's no hesitation there—and that they fear him because he might have a Muslim father. That's for sure. But he simply symbolizes un-Americanness, or as one gentleman said to me, "There's something that doesn't add up there." Obama was scary to Tea Partiers because of all of the things that he represented—his race, his immigrant father, his urban background, the fact that he's a professor. Being a professor is a very bad category in Tea Party land. And, of course, his Democratic Party affiliation.

To resisters, Donald Trump is equally horrifying, but I think for slightly different reasons. He's seen as lacking the character and the qualifications to be president, and he represents disrespect and hatred in their minds toward women, minorities, and immigrants. And above all, I think, he activates people because he represents a selfish disregard for the public good. So that's very much tied to that sense of saving American democracy that is a prominent reason many resisters give for organizing.

These presidents resonate with what each party, each movement, represents. The Tea Party, Vanessa and I found in our discussions with activists, was not mainly about economic suffering. They were mainly middle class, older white people who were not suffering the most in the economic downturn of 2009. They resented the changes, the sociocultural changes, happening in the country and feared them, not just the racial and ethnic changes but also the arrival of immigrants—that was the top issue everywhere we talked with people and why, even in 2011, many of the Tea Partiers who we interviewed were fascinated by Donald Trump because he had emerged on the public scene challenging Barack Obama's citizenship.

But Tea Partiers also worried about young people and the direction the country was going with young people, including young people in their own families. They were fiercely opposed to the idea not just that Democrats and Barack Obama would accomplish changes that they found frightening, but that the Republican Party, which they also resented at the time, might compromise too much with Democrats in Washington and the states.

Today's resistance thinks in terms of threats to good government, rolling back of policy gains in the Obama presidency. There's a difference here because most resisters actually liked the Obama presidency; most Tea Partiers disliked the George W. Bush presidency by the end and were not so enthusiastic about John McCain either by the end of the election. So resisters see Trump and all that's happening as a threat to previous good government, to democracy, and to public policies that include diverse and less privileged people, even if they themselves are white and relatively privileged.

Despite the different beliefs of activists, the local groups have a lot of similarities across these two periods. I've already talked about how they were formed by organizers who often met for the first time, sometimes at rallies or on the way to marches. A couple of Tea Party organizers back then met when one of them read an op-ed by another one and looked her up in the local area; but they didn't know each other before they started organizing together.

The internet and social media mattered in both cases; but it was the Meetup internet site that was used by Tea Parties, and it's Facebook that's used by today's older resisters at the grassroots.

Tea Party groups usually met monthly, and their programs usually featured speakers provided by outside advocacy groups, with often people sitting there with remarkable patience through lectures that I considered to be incredibly dull. But they sat right there. As for resistance meetings, at least at the beginning they also happened about once a month, and even now continue to be pretty regular in most places. But they have a different feel from Tea Party meetings. They're a little bit more like sort of let's-get-down-to-business; people say, "Here are reports from the various subcommittees, let's decide how we're going to take the next steps." There's less listening to outside speakers, but there is some of that in the resistance group meetings.

Resistance groups are now meeting less frequently than they were at first, and that is probably a reflection of their greater willingness to form subcommittees and task forces to focus on different issue areas or different challenges in what they see as a constant barrage of challenges coming from Washington, D.C. In addition, the resistance groups now are much more interested in federating with other groups around the Democratic Party in their area, not necessarily with the party but with unions, with the NAACP, with churches, with immigrant-protecting groups or refugee-serving groups; whereas the Tea Parties were often kind of focused on themselves. Maybe they federated a little bit with each other, but mostly they were stubbornly autonomous and self-assertive in their own terms.

Both the Tea Party back then and the resistance now fought long battles over the Affordable Care Act that passed in 2010. The Tea Partiers were mobilized to oppose the Affordable Care Act as it was being debated in Congress, and they also fought very hard against a cap and trade and other efforts to deal with global warming. The first year of the resistance, probably the single policy struggle that was most consistently mobilizing for local grassroots groups was the fight over whether the Affordable Care Act would be repealed in Washington. And I think that was pretty important, because it kind of resonated with the concerns about the community and about health care that so many of the women organizing these groups had. This fight to save the health-care law gave them things to do – for example, they would send delegations once a week to congressional offices, almost always Republicans in most of the areas, usually with some cupcakes to give to the staff, very polite to staff people but with a constant message: don't repeal the Affordable Care Act. In addition, they would hold community protests, they would hold various die-ins—look at the die-in there in North Carolina using pro-life language to fight the Affordable Care Act's repeal, and in the Action Together Stark meeting you see them at a GOP representative office near Canton, Ohio. And you see a street demonstration in Hazelton, Pennsylvania, of various local resistance groups.

Obviously, in the end the grassroots resisters didn't persuade very many Republicans to back off repeal. Repeal almost happened. But what did happen during the course of that year was American public opinion went from being negative about the Affordable Care Act to being in favor; and so I think all that local organizing managed to finally do what Democrats had not done for eight years, which is to communicate to ordinary people what was in the Affordable Care Act and why they and their neighbors had a stake in it. So it made a huge difference in my view. This is what happened with public opinion. You can see that in the early years of the implementation of the Affordable Care Act in 2013 and 2014, public opinion in the country was negative. Most Americans didn't know what was actually in the law, and Democrats never talked about it. Their consultants told them not to talk about it because it wasn't popular. But in the last year, as these local groups talked in detail about the stakes, public opinion shifted.

Many of you may be thinking, well, didn't those Tea Parties get organized by the Koch brothers? The answer is no, they didn't. And I can prove it. I won't bother you with the statistics, but my research group studies the Koch network. We know how they operate, we know what a tremendous effect Koch efforts have had. But we have not found close correlations between Koch efforts and the growth of Tea Parties. These were two separate forces. Top-down funding and activist-manipulating operations intersected with bottom-up self-organized groups, and the bottom-up and the top-down leveraging each other to push the Republican Party. You cannot collapse one into the other, and if you do, you will not understand what is going on out there.

Similarly, the resistance against Donald Trump is composed of top-down operations, some of which have been professionally organized or beefed up since the Trump presidency, others of which have received millions of dollars from liberal and progressive donors to staff up at the regional and national levels. But a lot of the action is more bottom up, in these self-organized voluntary grassroots groups. They, too, the grassroots groups like the Tea Parties of yore, are taking bits and pieces of ideas, and resources, and speakers, and maybe some help from the top-down forces. But the local groups are kind of choosing from a menu and taking whatever they want from different places.

Meanwhile, the top-down groups both then and now put themselves in front of the cameras on Fox News or on MSNBC and tell us all that they're in charge. Well, they're not actually in charge. They don't control nearly as much as they think they control, and they don't control nearly as much as they tell their big donors they control. There are real tensions between top-down and bottom-up groups about policy priorities. For example, Tea Partiers back then cared mostly about resisting immigration into the United States and cracking down on law and order issues. And if they were Christian Right people they also cared about fighting abortion access and gay rights. The top-down groups in the Koch network and beyond that said they were orchestrating the Tea Party went on TV and told us that the Tea Party was about cutting Social Security and Medicare. I can assure you, it was about no such thing. The Tea Party activists were all *on* Social Security and Medicare! And they considered them, like most Americans consider them, to be earned benefits that are their right. . . .

Similarly, some of you maybe remember that there was a big fuss about the DACA protections in the fall of, I believe it was 2017, and there was a lot of pressure from MoveOn.org and national advocacy groups tied to the resistance on Democratic Senate Minority Leader Chuck Schumer to supposedly go to the wall to shut down the government over DACA funding. As a political scientist I can tell you, the Senate Democrats had no such power really, but that was what the top-down groups were pushing. And the national Indivisible organizers, who usually don't make this mistake—I think they understand that they are sitting on top of a self-organized collection of grass-roots groups—they put somebody on TV to claim that Indivisible around the country, all the groups were demanding the closing down of government over DACA funding. Well, I checked in with my fellow researchers, and we went back to all our local groups' Facebook pages, and not a single one of them was demanding any such thing. In today's resistance, just like in the Tea Party, there are tensions between top-down and bottom-up organizations, and it's best to think of both of these movements as mutually jostling sets of organizations, not as one big organization or one big authoritative effort.

Finally, I'll talk about the two major U.S. political parties. We asked the resistance groups across Pennsylvania to tell us about their relationships with the local Democratic Party. Now, I need to point out that in some places there was no local Democratic Party in 2017. One of the counties I visited, nobody had been able to get the local Democratic chair to return an email, a phone call, a message—I mean nobody, not even the local newspapers. And, of course, he didn't respond to me either when I tried to set up an interview. The one time I did get him on the phone I'm pretty sure he was in a Trump rally. So there might not have been an actual local Democratic Party in a lot of these places in the sense of an office and a set of people that could be contacted, and groups of people who were actually doing things.

But to the degree that there were, the relationships with the self-organized resistance groups ran the entire gamut. In some cases, particularly where pairs of women were in charge of both the party and the resistance, they might just join each other's efforts and push in the same direction. In no place did the local resistance groups want to collapse into the Democratic Party. That's partly because they were trying to reach out to people who didn't think of themselves as regular Democrats, either to the left or to the middle. But often in those cases there was a lot of cooperation between the local parties and the local resistance groups, particularly around things like registering voters or fighting to save the Affordable Care Act.

But in other cases, especially if local Democratic parties were led by old-boy establishments that were mainly there to make sure that in low-turnout elections they were reelected to local government offices, they were outright hostile to these new groups. Now, that was then. By this spring, I would say across Pennsylvania many of those old-guard people have been swept out of office in the local Democratic parties, or local Democratic parties that had not much of a presence have had their committee people replaced, in many cases by resistance organizers. The parties and resistance groups continue to be separate efforts, overlapping separate efforts; but I think there's real change coming to the Democratic Party at the grassroots, at least in the places I know about.

Yet the impact of the grassroots anti-Trump resistance on the Democratic Party and its governing agendas is going to be, I suspect, quite different this time around from the impact of the Tea Party on the GOP some time ago. The Tea Parties were organized by activists who considered themselves solidly to the right of the Republican Party establishment at the time, and were angry at Republicans for any kind of governing compromises. Over time, many of those Tea Party groups studied the rules of the Republican Party at their local and state levels and took over offices; so in some cases, the Republican parties now are Tea Party people. In other cases, they're not. There are surviving Tea Parties in two out of the eight counties I'm visiting, and I've gotten to know their leaders; but the Republican Party itself has changed a lot in the interim, and is now much less compromise oriented and has moved far to the right on the issues of concern to Tea Partiers.

Resisters are not consistently on the left side of the Democratic Party. They are not Bernie Sanders, Our Revolution organizers. I didn't find a single piece of Our Revolution in the places I visited. People would say, "Oh yeah, there's a Bernie guy who stands up in our meetings and gives speeches." But for the most part, individual Bernie and Hillary people are simply getting on with it, and in a fairly pragmatic way that is not necessarily going to drag the Democratic Party as a whole to the left.

Now, let me be clear here: I think most of these resistance groups—they're liberals, they're unabashed liberals or progressives, and they are prodding the Democrats to become more grassroots oriented and to run candidates even in places where they have not run candidates. And in most places you could say those candidates are to the left of what was there before, because what was there before is, in most places, Republican. But over all it's not going to be like the impact of the Tea Party on the Republican Party, which was to drag it further to the right, particularly on social- and immigration-related issues, in the process of remaking it. In today's resistance, I think there'll be a remaking, and perhaps a new rooting, local rooting, of the Democratic Party through the efforts of these approximately two thousand resistance groups across the country. But the outcome will not necessarily push the Democratic Party consistently to what on a national level or in a conference like this we would consider to be "the Left."

There's no question that voting was already being stressed by the time the second Women's Marches occurred in 2018. You can see, "Grab 'Em By the Ballot, Grab 'Em By the Midterms "was another very common theme. And we've seen out of both of these movements, the Tea Party and the resistance, a remarkable upsurge of people running for office. These offices are not just the U.S. House but local and state legislative positions as well. For the resistance groups, this is something new, because Democrats had tended to neglect running for office at the local and state level in many of the states I'm visiting.

There was an upsurge of people running for office around 2010 on the Republican side, and a comparable upsurge this year on the Democratic side. What's different is that on the Democratic side it's overwhelmingly women running for office—not only women, because in many cases it's men backed by these women going door-to-door, knocking on the doors, like for Anthony Delgado, going door-to-door. So it's not as if men are excluded or in any way discriminated against; it's just that there are more women who are organizing and more women saying, "If they won't do it right, we'll do it." I think that's very much like somebody—one of the articles I read drew an analogy to the housework: if your husband can't fold the laundry right, you'll just do it. You'll roll your eyes and do it instead. And I think this is very similar. It's a pragmatic upsurge. We'll see how many of these women win. Many of them are going to lose. But losing is also important as long as there is a presence, and as long as there's somebody there to organize around and to make the arguments. Hopefully it will persist (I say that speaking in my citizen capacity).

The November 2018 midterm elections will be pivotal. They'll help us begin to answer the question of whether the widespread resistance that has emerged since Donald Trump and his fellow Republicans took over Washington will help the Democrats overcome what for them is a very different problem from what the Republicans faced in 2010, because Democrats usually don't turn out in midterm elections. It's a higher mountain to climb to see whether this resistance upsurge will help Democrats overcome their usual midterm turnout decline. And not only will they have to overcome it; they'll have to overcome it by a lot to take enough seats in the House, and enough seats in state legislatures, and enough governorships, to really make a difference.

I'm not sure what the impact of the recent Kavanaugh struggle will be. I do know that most of the women organizing in the local groups I talked about were not doing it mainly around #MeToo issues or mainly around abortion access issues. Like women have throughout American history, they were organizing around the full array of policy issues. And I think it may turn out that the Kavanaugh struggle has less of an immediate impact than we think.

Will grassroots voluntary resistance groups remain active if Democrats win the House and make state and local gains? Equally important, will they remain active if Democrats lose, as they will in many places? We don't know yet. It remains to be seen. My research group will be continuing to monitor the situation, and we'll see whether the impact of this round of citizen organizing is comparable to the last round that the Tea Party sparked in 2009 to '11. The Tea Party persisted, and it remains to be seen whether today's resistance will too.

Discussion and Audience Q&A

Peter Rosenblum: Thank you very much. The ground covered was extraordinary. So many of my questions you answered along the way. I guess I'll just ask one very quick question, and then turn to the audience.

You gave what comes across as what could be seen as an extraordinarily optimistic picture of the capacity in American society for self-organized grassroots groups that continue to operate in a way that is unaffected somehow in their core by the influences of power and money, whether it's Fox News, or the Kochs, or—you didn't say Soros, but we've been hearing that a lot. And in passing you mentioned someone like Robert Putnam, who told us years ago that this capacity was diminishing, or the sustainable capacity for this was gone. If there aren't bowling leagues, is it possible to maintain this kind of structure, or will it come and go? What does Robert Putnam say to you? Does he look at you and say, "Oh my God, yes, this is a flash in the pan. We no longer have that capacity and a meaningful ability to sustain it."

Theda Skocpol: Well, actually, he's come around. But look, both Professor Putnam and I, Bob and I, have documented in different ways and explained in different ways a long-term decline in ongoing civic organizations. In my case, I documented that they were usually multilevel—national, state, and local—where people just, through thick and thin and often not for political purposes as much as social purposes, continued to meet face-to-face. And there's no question that those classic voluntary federations are mostly gone. I mean, persistent groups are now usually professionalized, usually have a lot of money, or spend a lot of time in fundraisers trying to raise more money. Furthermore, my research group has documented the activities of millionaires and billionaires who are organized on both the left and the right to give a lot of money to some of these professionally run groups.

So the Tea Parties and the local resistance groups -- as electorally sparked citizen upsurges—are really pushing against the grain of the way in which organized American civic life has evolved since the late twentieth century; but they're fascinatingly against the grain. They show that there's something in America's DNA that remains there. For one thing, the meetings are remarkably similar. And on the right, the Tea Parties start the way civic associations always started, with the Pledge of Allegiance and a prayer. There are no prayers or pledges of allegiance on the resistance side, but there is that kind of a shared civic faith that "we can do it," we can organize, we have to organize and assert our active citizenship if the country is to be saved. That kind of thing has swept the United States again and again throughout our history, starting in Colonial times. This kind of citizen self-organizing is part of our national character. So I do think that there's a similarity to the past.

There's also a difference. Today's upsurges rarely result in one big organization or set of organizations with an ongoing federated structure. And I think in many ways the activity is through or upon the two major political parties, which still have, at least in principle, federated structures, because they have to contest elections at all levels of government.

Q: My name's Mark Bray from Dartmouth College. Thank you for that very interesting presentation; it's fascinating research. My question is about language. So there is a photo from the original Women's March that's gone around the internet where the sign says, "If Hillary Had Won We'd Be At Brunch." And a lot of organizers who've been doing work around the issues that Trump has exacerbated recently said, "Yes, exactly, that's the problem: if Hillary *had* won, you'd be at brunch."

So the response to a lot of the hashtag resistance in organizing circles among people who've been doing work on incarceration or police violence for decades was, "Oh, there's this group of middle-class liberal white people who think they're the resistance; but we've been doing this work for years, and when Trump gets voted out of office and there's another Democrat in, they'll go to brunch, and we'll still be doing this work."

So I think it's really interesting to do your research on this specific cross-section of the resistance, but you often speak about it as *the* resistance, but it's just a cross-section of the resistance.

TS: I said it was the grassroots resistance, and I used that phrase repeatedly.

Q: You called it *the* resistance. On your sheet it says *the* anti-Trump resistance. I would encourage you—it's super-important—to talk about it as the middle-class, white liberal, rural resistance. This is not *the* resistance. And you didn't mention on your sheet J20, which is one of the most important moments of resistance recently: January 20th, the two hundred people who were charged with decades in prison, which got no solidarity from the hashtag resistance—oh, maybe a few small things. So please, be precise. This is one cross-section of the resistance.

Thank you.

TS: All right. Well, I said that there were many organizations organizing and jostling with one another. And if you look at my handout, it mentions some of the others.

The United States, like it or not, is a federated political system. That means that political and governmental power has to be won by networks of organizations that have a presence across many places. Let me say that again: political power is not won in the United States except by networks, by organizations or movements that have a presence across many places. You don't see me talking in broad demographic categories, or in ideological categories that refer to demography, because if the United States were one big demographic pile of people, Hillary Clinton would be president of the United States. And if Hillary Clinton were president of the United States, your movement would have a lot more possibilities for moving forward, not because she necessarily stands for all you want but because even moderate liberals in governmental power create more openings for organizing, and leverage, and policy change on the left.

In my opinion, we face right now the possibility of a permanent, minority authoritarian right-wing government. And as for violence, violence will be used on the right; not very much or to any good effect on the left.

So the reason that my colleagues and I are trying to understand the spread of the grassroots, boringly white middle-class women-led part of the resistance, is because we want to know whether they're going to be allies for Black Lives Matter, for immigration activists, for refugee activists, for anti-incarceration activists. Now, that doesn't happen automatically. And I'll grant you that when a Democratic president is elected, hopefully with Democratic legislatures, because Congress and state legislatures are more important than presidents and governors, a lot of times the Left has had a tendency to look for invitations to the White House or to argue who is the real resistance. What a ridiculous argument that is rather than taking advantage of the political levers to protest and to get change that even moderate left power opens up.

You may not agree with my analysis, but that's my analysis, and that's why I'm talking about the geographical spread of these groups, not simply trying to reduce their activities, or their outlooks, or their impact to their biological demography. I think the Left is too tied to biographical demography in this country. We gotta get over it, or we're not going to get very far in recapturing and redirecting American democracy.

Q: My name is Miranda Kerrigan. I'm a sophomore here at Bard. I have one general observation and then one substantial question. During the whole presentation, specifically about the Tea Party, I realized very quickly that in 2009 I was nine years old and that there's probably a divide between the students and the academics who are here and who remember what the Tea Party was like. I am just thinking about how the people that are in college right now grew up with the Tea Party and with the Tea Party's criticism of Obama, and how that might have affected us as the youth in the way that we've tried to effect change now—or haven't, because maybe we don't remember what the Tea Party was like because we were so young. And I'm not really sure which one of those is right, but just a thought.

As an actual substantial question: I think something that really struck me was the similarities between Obama and Trump as presidencies, specifically the fact that when they were elected, the entire Congress was one political party or the other, and the fact that both presidents were unique in their elections. But what also struck me was that this isn't something that was divided by time. They were right next to each other—both presidencies were one right after the other—and I wonder what the future is going to be, because there are a lot of Democrats that I know who think that we *must* take Congress back and we *must* have a Democratic president all at the same time. I'm wondering if we're not going to have a counterrevolution to that again in the future, and what your thoughts are about that.

TS: There's no question that the Obama presidency ended up sparking—and this is not anything about blaming Obama, so I'm not talking in blame terms—but his presidency absolutely activated ethnonationalist fears and anger among a large proportion of older white people, particularly outside of metropolitan areas—not among all white people; white people are divided in this country, very divided. But his presidency, I think precisely because of the happenstance that it coincided with Democratic takeovers in the House and the Senate, and with an economic downturn, and with what looked to many people on the right like a bold set of policies, even if they looked to people on the left like timid policies—that really sparked that kind of fearful pushback.

But, you know, it's not only that. It also coincided with a decade and a half of Koch donor-funded national ultraright organizing. I didn't talk about that part of my research today, but the ground was prepared for the popular and voter reaction to Obama on the right by a very different kind of top-down, money-fueled organizing that my—if you want to read about it, it's in the September 2016 issue of *Perspectives on Politics*, we have a paper called "The Koch Network and Republican Party Extremism." It was about the way in which organized millionaires and billionaires organized by the Kochs and funding a political party–like operation on the far right actually pulled the Republican Party toward tax cutting, opposition to environmental policy, the kind of extremism we've now seen installed on the Supreme Court—all of that. So that was already there when this popular upsurge on the right occurred, and it was able to leverage that popular upsurge, even though they're often at cross-purposes about what to care about.

You don't see anything quite like that in the same way on the left in the United States. There are lots of Left movements around important causes, but they tend not to have the kind of resources and organizational reach that that right-wing organizing attained throughout the 2000s. So if you do have a president and a Congress elected that are all Democrats, that opens the possibility for policy changes and, you know, I don't want to upset too many people in the room, but actually some important policy changes did occur during the first two years of the Obama presidency, and more was done through executive action after that. But it isn't as if there's a longstanding powerful juggernaut on the left that can take advantage and push that further in the same way. So these moments—a lot matters about the moment against the backdrop of which they come in, and that's not all based on voters and popular protesters, or even organizers of local groups.

As for your point about not remembering the Tea Party, that's why you need to read about it.

Historical memory is two things: it's people's remembrance of their lives and what they hear from their parents, and their grandparents, and their friends, and their teachers; it's also reading. And so read about it, because there are similarities and differences, and for people on the left, some horrifying lessons to learn, but also some organizing lessons to learn. That's why the *Indivisible Guide* actually helps some of the center-to-left organizers, because it taught them some principles that the Tea Partiers had done before. And the fact of the matter is that the local Tea Partiers who organized were good citizens in the sense that they recognized that in America we have the right to organize, we have the right to say what we think, we have the right to press for what we want. I personally happen to think they were pressing for terrible things, and interviewing them was often a—I had to go back and have a Tylenol before I went to bed because I would meet people that in many ways were personally admirable, who were organizing as citizens in ways I had to respect, and at the same time they were saying horrifying, hateful, and factually mistaken things. So nevertheless, I learned more from that than from almost any other research I've ever done.

Q: My name is Gary. There are similarities between these two movements. But it seems to me that at the heart of the Tea Party movement is racism, is fear of the other; whereas at the heart of the anti-Trump movement is a fear for the ideals of American democracy. Is that simply my knee-jerk liberal opinion, or do you get a sense of that?

TS: Well, I think that's pretty much what I said.

Q: Allison Stanger, Middlebury College. Thanks so much for that fascinating presentation. I thought what I would do is maybe ask a variant of the previous questions in a slightly different way, and just say that when I looked at the qualitative and quantitative data that you presented about both resistance movements I saw some significant gender divides and significant class divides. So I wondered if you might comment a little bit on the importance of racism and sexism in explaining some of the differences we see today in our country.

Q: My name is Margaret Rubin. I'm a middle-class college-educated white woman, and I don't teach here. My question is that—I'm in Pantsuit Nation, I'm in my local Indivisible group, and the thing that struck me with your comments and also with the basis of the conference here is that in both of those we have been told to play nice. And I'm wondering to what degree that is a differentiation. For example, in the original Indivisible pamphlet/booklet, whatever you want to call it, we were told, "Here are the things the Tea Party did that worked; but don't do the mean, icky things. Do take cake cupcakes, be nice, don't yell when you go to offices, don't threaten." And on Pantsuit's Facebook platform, moderators are constantly screaming to keep things sometimes despairing, but upbeat-ish.

So those are notable differences, and given the theme of whether civil disobedience will have violence, should have violence, might have violence, I'm curious about your thoughts about that.

Q: My name is Awa Cherry, and I'm an eleventh grader in high school. I thought a similar question might have already been asked, but based on your research do you think that people actually despise Obama because of his political or presidential decisions, or was it that they didn't like his race and they would kind of be mad at that, so they directed their rage toward his political decisions.

TS: Okay, this is a wonderful set of questions.

Let me start by saying that maybe I didn't stress enough that the goals and understandings of these two manifestations are quite different. When I was discussing what the president that they opposed symbolizes to each side, I agree with the proposition that Tea Partiers, grassroots Tea Partiers, many of whom have become hardcore Trump voters, are sparked by anger and fear about ethnic, and cultural, and racial changes in the country.

Now, I want to be careful about that. Of course, in my interviews people were not going to say overtly racist things to a professor from Harvard University—first of all, not everyone will talk to a professor from Harvard University, but I'm very good at worming my way into almost anyone. Since my grandfather would have been a Tea Partier—he was a farmer in Michigan—I can relate to people who are conservatives. I can also talk about football, and I do not faint if a Bible verse is quoted to me—I was raised a Methodist. I can relate to people and I can treat them with respect. And when you treat people with respect, they will talk to you.

So what I heard from people on the right was more complicated than crude racism. I heard fear and anger about changes in the country. Now, they certainly will say they hate Obamacare; but the interesting question is, *why* do they hate Obamacare? And people hate Obamacare because they thought it was giving people something for nothing, because they thought immigrants, which really are their biggest worry—immigrants, not African Americans—were taking advantage of it, and because it was sponsored by Obama, who in their mind was a world-striding tyrant. Imagine what it was like to go from Cambridge, Massachusetts, where people think Obama is a milquetoast, to talk to people who think he's the demon. But it's fundamentally a matter of fear and anger about changes in the country that seem to be taking it away from the America they know and love. That's what I heard.

Now, what I hear from resisters—and of course I agree with them a lot more in my citizen capacity, so I'm probably not hearing the same things that a conservative interviewer would hear—I hear their anger about what is happening to government and democracy in this country, and their desire to do something about it, and their sense that Trump violates all that.

So these are very different in their purposes. However, their demography is remarkably similar. They are middle-class white movements. And I just have to say, the United States is a country where middle-class white people, particularly women, have organized again and again throughout our history. They may not be the glamorous ones, and they may not be the most-left ones; but they often are the ones who actually do things when it comes to voluntary action. No question that on the Tea Party side there were many more men, but they were more often the couch potatoes. It was often a woman who was leading a meeting that we saw, or arranging for the cupcakes to be sold to raise the money, or the Sarah Palin biographies to be sold—I mean, you know, like a church meeting. So gender is an imperfect divide. There's no question that conservatives and conservative activists lean more male and have different conceptions of male and female roles; that's quite clear. Gender's very important in that regard. But it is not important in the sense that only men lead on the right and only women lead on the left. They are both involved in activism and leadership in both cases.

As for race, it's just a fact that at the grassroots level—and frankly in liberal places as well as more moderate and conservative places—the voluntary group organizers in the current grassroots resistance are overwhelmingly white women. A lot of people have gone out and looked who didn't want to find that, and they found the same thing. There's a new book out called *The Resistance*, and they found some of the same things that we found. I'm an empirical scholar. If the facts are the facts, the facts are the facts. That's the way it is. It might not be the way we want it.

But at the same time, attitudes toward race and toward the United States as a racially inclusive country and a country that welcomes immigrants couldn't be more different in these two movements.

I guess I'll just conclude by saying that I think—I want to talk about the violence thing, too—that I think it's very important not to reduce people's attitudes and interests to their individual demography. Values, and outlooks, and things people aspire to learn and do matter as well. Because the United States is still an overwhelmingly white country, the civil war among white people is pretty important to nonwhite people, how it turns out. It's also important to the country. I'll speak personally and say that I think the very nature of America is at stake in our time in a way that I only remember being true back when I was young, when it was the civil rights movement. Is the United States going to continue to be a country that weaves together so many different kinds of people into a powerhouse of innovation, inclusiveness, and fairness; or is it going to be one more authoritarian tribe in a world full of them? That's what's at stake—very much at stake.

Now, on violence: I think it's possible to be a very tough-minded civil moderate in manner. I think this is a time for enormous tough-mindedness on the part of people who think of themselves as liberals or centrists in American democracy. But yelling and insulting are not necessarily signs of strength. And the use of violence, which is pervasive in all aspects of American society, mostly nonpolitical, is not a sign of strength either. I don't think we're in a period where there's going to be a militarized civil war. The negative outcome for Americans who care about an inclusive country will be a cynical, privatized, increasingly unequal country that simply continues its decline. It won't be violence except against some of the people who try to speak up against that.

So I don't think violence is a good tactic, and I don't think it's necessary to yell at congressional staffers when you go in to protest what the representative stands for. After all, the secretary and the staff assistants might not even completely agree with the boss, and they certainly aren't going to come around to thinking about the argument the messenger is delivering if you come in there while the boss is away and scream at them. It's just not necessary, and I think it's not tough-minded.

I think tough-minded means for citizens to work together to organize, to argue, to assert, to vote, and to keep holding politicians accountable after you elect them into office. That needs a lot of tough-mindedness, but it doesn't need insults or violence.

"We are more" and "We can do it": Political and Moral Claims of Civil (Dis)obedience in the German Refugee Crisis

Marion Detjen

I am aware of the fact that the last German who stood here in a Hannah Arendt conference to speak to you about Germany was Marc Jongen, the so-called party philosopher of the AfD, the German extreme right-wing party. While I am not going to apologize for my bad English, one could easily get the impression that Jongen and I represent the two opposing and conflicting camps which these days challenge and strain the cohesion of German society, each claiming to fight for the "true" Germany, the "good" Germany, the "other" Germany, appropriating the tradition of the emigrants and resistance fighters of the Nazi period.[1]

On some fundamental questions Marc Jongen and I are indeed symmetrically opposed: there exists a deep rift in German society over the question whether Germany should be an immigration country or not; whether citizenship and belonging in Germany have to be ethnically and culturally defined or not. In these questions, Marc Jongen and I have a harsh political conflict. He wants ethnicity and "culture," whatever that is for him, as the decisive criteria for being German. I want civil and political rights and duties as the decisive criteria. This can be a matter of negotiation and public debate, and I am prepared to discuss this with everyone, even with extreme right wingers.

But here the symmetry ends, because the far right usually does not argue with negotiable goals but with unnegotiable alleged realities, insisting that the ethnocultural identity of the German people is a given. This is simply not true. The Basic Law, our constitution, is ambiguous and full of tensions with regard to who belongs and who doesn't belong.[2] It does have an ethnonational dimension, but it also and more effectively opens up to multiple ways of belonging that work with our common humanity and human dignity, with civic and political rights, with social and material contributions, apart from the fact that ethnoculturalism is highly contradictory in itself when it has to determine the ethnos and culture that it pleads to. In the face of these ambiguities it is more important than ever to keep up the distinction between our negotiable differences in what we want, and our nonnegotiable differences in how we treat reality.

Let me now (1) first give you a personal account of how I experienced the "pro-refugee" movement in Germany that I consider myself part of in

2015–16; its political agendas and maybe protorevolutionary impetus; then (2) analyze two claims of that movement and why they are so ambivalent and even futile in the current political situation in Germany; and (3) conclude with a suggestion on how to read Hannah Arendt and what to take from her thinking into the future.

1) The "summer of welcome" in Germany 2015, when thousands and thousands of asylum seekers poured into the country every week and met a wave of solidarity and willingness to help, has long passed. While German society and government are taking a more and more anti-immigrant stance, it has now become customary to belittle the solidarity movement of those days as naive, and to discredit the helpers as "Gutmenschen," goody-goodies who didn't really know what they were doing. There is a denial of the fact that the solidarity movement in 2015 was broadly perceived as a novum in history, a big surprise, a new spirit to acknowledge global realities and to finally embrace the immigration society. More than 10 percent of the grown-up population in Germany were actively involved in a huge volunteer struggle; around fifteen thousand initiatives and projects emerged.[3] I myself got involved with an NGO organizing private sponsorships for family reunifications,[4] and then quickly moved on to activities more in my professional field,[5] until I ended up at Bard College Berlin, where we have up to this moment achieved thirty-two full scholarships for displaced students in the liberal arts.[6]

In 2015 and even 2016 there was an overwhelming optimism. History seemed to be on our side. We seemed to bring into completion what we had left incomplete and flawed in the previous "refugee crisis" more than twenty years ago, in the mid-1990s. Then, there had already been a huge humanitarian engagement, an engagement which had not managed to articulate itself in political terms though. While we—I was a student then—were volunteering as German teachers in refugee camps, we had not been prepared to fight for consequential, rational, and fair political solutions to the migration and asylum issues. We stood by helplessly and eventually withdrew as the government under Helmut Kohl, with the support of the Social Democrats, changed the constitution and installed their infamous "asylum compromise," cutting down the refugee numbers with the introduction of so-called safe third countries and making it impossible to ever find a fair European solution.[7] Twenty years later, in 2015, we were determined not to make that mistake again. Our activities were humanitarian, but we brought them into the political arena— we had a political agenda.

Another cause for our optimism was that in the twenty years between these "crises" the relationship of the German public to the Nazi past seemed to have undergone a fundamental change: while in the 1990s a toxic memory discourse about the uniqueness or comparability of the Holocaust and the role of the Wehrmacht obstructed any attempts to reach an inclusive understanding of what it means to be German, in 2015–16 the memory discourse on flight and expulsion after the Second World War actually helped to create or allow empathy. A lot of people related to family experiences and traumas of having been a refugee oneself when getting involved, and the media were full of comparisons between the refugee situation in Germany after the war and today.[8]

The political activism of the "pro-refugee" mass movement of 2015–16, its political agenda, even if it wasn't always explicit, played out on three levels.

The first level was internal German politics. There was a strong impetus to give the finishing blow to Germany's self-denial of not being an immigration country. With 20 percent of the German population nowadays having a so-called immigration background, either born or with one or two parents born as foreigners, and Germany suddenly showing such surprising generosity as a nation, it seemed possible to get rid of the ethnonational dimension of the German state construction altogether and to base the country on a new, inclusive identity.[9]

The second level was European and international: without really offering alternatives, the "pro-refugee" movement implicated a protest against the EU border regime, the illegalization and criminalization of migrants, the horrible dying in the Mediterranean, and the unfair system that puts most of the burden of unregulated migration to the southern states of Europe, where they arrive with their dinghies. The life-saving and refugee aid activities of young people like Sara Mardini, the Bard College Berlin student who was imprisoned in Greece, manifested a moral and political claim that the EU member states forcing the migrants to do such dangerous journeys and risk their lives is inacceptable. Projects, organizations, and coalitions like the "Seebrücke" demanding safe routes and safe havens for people who are forced to flee not only challenge the Dublin system but also address the erosion of the entire postwar international refugee order of the Geneva Convention.[10]

The third level for politicization is most far-reaching. It emerged in the conviviality with what we then called "newcomers" from the Middle East, once they had arrived and we got to know each other. They brought their own realities, their own knowledge, and getting close to them, befriending them, meant that we started to connect to these realities. The causes and consequences of the Arabellion and especially the Syrian revolution suddenly became real to us: the dictatorships, the crimes, the murdering, the torturing, the misery, the persecutions, the bravery of the people in their battle for freedom, and the complicated reasons for people to flee. Suddenly we realized how near the Middle East is to Europe and felt the postcolonial connections. This new sense of transnational and global responsibility was threatening for many, but for others to discover it and share it in public settings like demonstrations, cultural events, and volunteer activities created a profound happiness, a special kind of public happiness that I have only found described adequately in Hannah Arendt's descriptions of the revolutionary experience.

But what does it need for such political activism to qualify as civil disobedience? Did the movement violate laws for the purpose of testing their constitutionality, which is the main criteria of civil disobedience according to Arendt? There was, and still is, definitely a preparedness, a negotiation of the possibilities and necessities to break the law. Projects like the International Conference of Traffickers and People Smugglers in Munich, Fluchthilfe & Du (Refugee Help and You), and the Peng Collective developed strategies against the criminalization of migration in the German residency law, calling for breaking the law but in an artistic context. But in 2015 we had parts of the authorities on our side, and all of these projects received public funding. Since then, with the dramatic political shift going on, I think that we have drifted into a situation of uncertainty and suspense. Right now, politics and the authorities are definitely pressed toward a course that contradicts the human rights and human diginity principles of the German constitution and the European Convention on Human Rights—for example, by limiting the right to family reunification for refugees who only received subsidiary protection even though they will never be able to return to Syria without a regime change there.[11] The protest against this development is still very much focused on advocacy, on using legal loopholes and finding solutions for individual cases. It remains to be seen what will happen when the situation aggravates further and measures against refugees are being tightened—whether the movement altogether falls back into a purely humanitarian mode, giving up on its political potential, or whether parts of it will cross the line to break inhuman and unconstitutional laws and turn into true civil disobedience.

What about another criterium set by Hannah Arendt to qualify civil disobedience: did the movement claim to represent the majority of the German people? Its complicated and unresolved relationship to the majority society has to be analyzed in two different claims:

First of all, the movement had a strong connection to Angela Merkel's famous sentence: "Wir schaffen das"—"We can do it," or "We can work on it," "We can manage." The NGO I myself got involved in called itself Wir Machen Das—"We are doing it"—to enforce Merkel's claim in an avangardist approach: "We are doing it anyway." The verb used by Merkel, "schaffen," literally means "to accomplish." It has the notion of working hard, and once you have finished the job, then you can rest. That you work so hard, that you show sweat and really lean into it while being confident in your abilities, is part of the moral justification of what you do. It has the intrinsic value of Protestant work ethics.

The "wir schaffen das," to be able to do it and work for it, referred to the challenge of housing and feeding and clothing and providing an income for the one million refugees in 2015–16. But it also connected to a much larger challenge, the challenge of transforming Germany into an immigration country—that first-activism level that I mentioned before. The immense struggle to achieve and acknowledge this transformation had been going on for decades. The years between 2000 and 2014, with new citizenship laws and new residency laws, could be seen as a breakthrough. But that acknowledgment and that change were heavily conditioned. The 2005 law providing for immigration is, strictly speaking, not an immigration law at all; it is an integration law, putting all immigration under the condition of integration. Without integration, no immigration.[12]

What does integration in the German context mean? It implies that you start off with a unified, whole community. Then a new, a foreign, element enters, and then this element as well as the entire community have to change and to assimilate to each other and to merge until you can't tell the difference anymore, until the foreignness is gone and the wholeness and unity are reestablished. The enigmatic "it" in Merkel's sentence "We can do it" can be specified as integration. We can "do" the integration of all these refugees, and once that is done we will enjoy German wholeness again.

I and my fellow activists never subscribed to this integration concept. We are inclusionists, not integrationists. We want citizenship and belonging based on political and social rights and duties, and we find the cultural notions of integration dubious and unsatisfactory. But in the situation of 2015–16 we aligned with the integrationists, and were to a certain degree grateful for the Merkel government. We thought that we could work with that approach, that we were allies.

Now with the hindsight of more than two years and confronted with an ever-rising AfD, the problems of this alliance between integrationists and inclusionists are starting to show: driven by that shift in immigration politics in 2000–5, an ethnopluralist-cultural-racist movement had formed that differed from former racists and Nazis by allegedly not claiming genetic superiority over other "races" but insisting on the existence of distinct ethnocultural circles and identities. These people were able to make use of the integration paradigm by taking it dead seriously. They said goodbye to the former Germanic exclusionism, expanded their understanding of what it means to be German to what they call the "Christian-Judeo community of tradition," and made cultural integration the main criteria. They claimed that Muslims can never be integrated simply because they are Muslims, creating a self-fulfilling prophecy, and then they grabbed all the racist notions floating around and attached them to Muslimhood and to the alleged "Muslim Kulturkreis," the parts of the world where the refugees come from.

Now—even if you don't want to share the plain and obvious racism, but do share the integration paradigm and believe in cultural integration, it's hard to deny that it won't be possible to melt all these newcomers into that alleged Christian-Judeo community of tradition. The dominance of the integration paradigm shifts the whole discourse about refugees and immigration to a field where we can only lose. More and more people in the political center now also believe that Merkel was wrong and that Germany actually cannot "do it," no matter how good or bad the economic and social situation is.

By arranging ourselves with the integration concept and jumping onto the "Wir schaffen das" mantra of the chancellor, we failed to develop the political ideas needed to create the political and social conditions for the inclusion—not the integration—of the newcomers. We failed to problematize those parts of the German constitution that legitimize ethnonationalist and culturalist concepts of belonging. We shuffled ourselves into a corner where we now seem like naive "Gutmenschen," stupid and irresponsible agents and accomplices of an immigration experiment that was bound to fail, and find ourselves entangled in all kinds of absurd discussions, like whether Islam belongs to Germany or not.

The other claim made by us has only recently found its slogan in the anti-AfD demonstrations in Chemnitz: "Wir sind mehr"—"We are more." In 2015–16 we were absolutely sure that the inclusionists together with the integrationists formed a majority, an impression also based on the media discourse that, with the yellow-press *Bild Zeitung* leading from the front, was almost unanimously pro-refugee in those days. But the right wingers put another claim against it which extracted legitimacy exactly out of being the minority: "Wir sind das Volk"—"We are the people"—became their slogan. You have to know about the iridescent meaning of that term, the *Volk*, in German history, to understand that. "We are the *Volk*" appeals to the people as the ruled against the rulers, but also to the *volonté générale*, the will and the essence of the nation, and that can be represented by an avant-gardist minority. The far right took a new pride in being marginalized. They sucked coolness out of being at the fringe, and gave their position a pseudorevolutionary veneer. They hijacked all the scarce tradition of revolution, civil disobedience, and resistance that we have in Germany to bolster their struggle against Merkel, the "system," the "mainstream," the "establishment," which in their ideology betrays the *Volk*. In the latest polls, the AfD has an 18.5 percent approval rate—a terrifying number, but still very clearly the minority. Nevertheless, the majority-minority relationship is shifting and shaking these days. The *Bild* and parts of the governing coalition have long adopted positions that very tragically do the business for the AfD. And we now have to face the paradoxical situation that, on the one hand, our majority claim makes us look boring, while on the other hand, we are not sure anymore whether we still really are the majority, as more and more former integrationists are now adopting anti-immigration positions.

Now, my conclusion:

Revolutions fail when and because they cannot institutionalize. The pro-refugee movement has failed in many respects and will surely fail more in the future. We need to get a lot better in developing convincing ideas about how inclusion can work, and reconceptualize the nation state and international system. But reading Hannah Arendt can help us on another level. Rereading *On Revolution* I realized that she was probably at least as preoccupied with the failings of revolutions as with their success. Failed revolutions have one thing that can live on even when the revolution dies: they can create traditions. On the penultimate page of the text Arendt writes:

> There is nothing that could compensate for this failure or prevent it from becoming final, except memory and recollection. And since the storehouse of memory is kept and watched over by the poets, whose business it is to find and make the words we live by, it may be wise to turn in conclusion to two of them.

And she turns to the poet René Char to explain what could be remembered as the lost treasure of the revolution:

> The treasure was no more and no less than he himself. That he had "found himself," that he no longer suspected himself of "insincerity," that he needed no mask and no play-acting to appear, that he, whereever he went, *appeared* to others and to himself as who he was, that he could afford "to go naked."[13]

One of my Syrian students said it in other words: "Freedom is a way of life." And this discovery will survive, no matter what happens.

---

1. "The other Germany" originally was the title of a pacifist-republican magazine forbidden by the Nazis in 1933, and then served as a title for various anti-national-socialist publications by German emigrants like Erika and Klaus Mann (1940), Heinrich Fraenkel (1942), and Bertolt Brecht (1943–44). Recently, two authors from the extreme right, Erik Lehnert and Wiggo Mann, appropriated it for a book that claims to describe nine phenotypes of nationalist opposition against the German "red-green mainstream": Erik Lehnert and Wiggo Mann, *Das andere Deutschland: Neun Typen* (Schnellroda: Verlag Antaios, 2017).
2. See Douglas B. Klusmeyer and Demetrios G. Papademetriou, *Immigration Policy in the Federal Republic of Germany: Negotiating Membership and Remaking the Nation* (Oxford: Berghahn Books, 2009).
3. Werner Schiffauer, *So schaffen wir das—eine Zivilgesellschaft im Aufbruch. 90 wegweisende Projekte mit Geflüchteten*, ed. Anne Eilert and Marlene Rudloff (Bielefeld: Transcript Verlag, 2017).
4. fluechtlingspaten-syrien.de/.
5. wirmachendas.jetzt/en/.
6. berlin.bard.edu/program-for-international-education-and-social-change/.
7. See the historical account in Marcus Engler and Jan Schneider, "German Asylum Policy and EU Refugee Protection: The Prospects of the Common European Asylum System (CEAS)," *Focus Migration*, no. 29 (May 2015), published by the Institute for Migration Research and Intercultural Studies of the University of Osnabrück. For the proponents' perspective, see Kay Hailbronner, "Asylum Law Reform in the German Constitution," *American University International Law Review* 9, no. 4 (1994): 159–79.

8. See Mathias Beer, "Die 'Flüchtlingsfrage' in Deutschland nach 1945 und heute. Ein Vergleich." *Zeitgeschichte-online* (April 2016). zeitgeschichte-online.de/thema/die-fluechtlingsfrage-deutschland-nach-1945-und-heute.

9. For the numbers of Germans with a "migration background," see destatis.de/DE/Themen/Gesellschaft-Umwelt/Bevoelkerung/Migration-Integration/Tabellen/migrationshinter-grund-geschlecht-insgesamt.html. For the changing attitudes, see Orkan Kösemen, "Bürgersinn in der Einwanderungsgesellschaft. Was Menschen in Deutschland unter einem guten Bürger verstehen," published by the Bertelsmann Foundation, December 2018. bertelsmann-stiftung.de/fileadmin/files/Projekte/Migration_fair_gestalten/IB_Buergersinn_in_der_Einwanderungsgesellschaft_2018.pdf.

10. See the Seebrücke's political statement: seebruecke.org/en/startpage-2/.

11. See the overview by the Informationsverbund Asyl und Migration, "Country Report: Germany," last updated April 2018, asylumineurope.org/reports/country/germany/content-international-protection/family-reunification/criteria-and.

12. Ulrike Davy, "Integration of Immigrants in Germany: A Slowly Evolving Concept." *European Journal of Migration and Law* 7 (2005): 123–44.

13. Hannah Arendt, *On Revolution* (1963; London: Penguin Books, 1990), 280. The passage on René Char is clearer and better understandable in the German version, translated by Hannah Arendt herself for publication in Germany in 1965, and I therefore retranslated it into English here; see Hannah Arendt, Über die Revolution (Munich: Piper Verlag 1974), 361.

Korean Candlelight Rallies from an Arendtian Perspective

Seon-Wook Kim

Korea experienced a most remarkable political phenomenon between 2016 and 2017, and many Koreans like to call it the Candlelight Revolution. It is a revolution in the Arendtian sense, according to which the essential element of revolution is that it brings about a new political order—*novum ordo seclorum*.

To illuminate the significance of the event, it is instructive to start with the North Korean issue. Since Donald Trump won the presidential election, U.S. relations with North Korea have seen extreme ups and downs. In his speech at the U.N. General Assembly of 2018, Trump said, "I would like to thank Kim [Jung-un, the North Korean Leader] for his courage and for the steps he has taken." At the previous year's U.N. General Assembly, however, Trump mocked Jung-un Kim by calling him a "rocket man," and said, "We will have no choice but to totally destroy North Korea." In June of 2018 there was a summit between the U.S. and North Korea in Singapore, and again in February of 2019 in Hanoi, Vietnam. The Hanoi summit ended with no consensus, and yet the situation is very different from the one before 2017.

At the center of this tremendous change, there is South Korean President Jae-in Moon, who initiated dialogues for the peace in the Korean Peninsula and an acceptable solution on the North Korean nuclear issue. More importantly, there is strong support from the Korean people, which appeared during the Candlelight Rallies between October of 2016 and March of 2017—the Korean Candlelight Revolution. People democratically impeached a corrupt government and its president, Park Geun-hye, and elected Mr. Moon as the new president and empowered him politically as well as morally.

The first Candlelight Rally occurred on the evening of 29 October 2016. This, along with the twenty-two consecutive rallies that followed, occurred on a Saturday. The first rally brought in about twenty thousand participants, but the numbers grew and grew, and by the sixth rally, which was the largest, [there were] more than 2.3 million.

The average number of [people at] the twenty-three rallies was 730,000, and the cumulative number reached 16.85 million. The rallies were held during the winter: the coldest rally day was 14 January 2017 and the number was still one hundred fifty thousand. Considering that the whole population of Korea is about fifty million, these numbers mean quite a lot. According to a survey, about 23.6 percent of respondents answered they participated at least once, and 49.8 percent answered that they wanted to participate but couldn't

Candlelight Rallies in South Korea, 2016–17

Rally	Date	Number of Participants (millions)	
1	29 October 2016	0.02	President Park's approval vs. disapproval rating: 17 percent (25 percent the previous week) vs. 74 percent (64 percent)
2	5 November	0.2	5 percent vs. 89 percent
3	12 November	1.0	5 percent vs. 90 percent
4	19 November	0.95	5 percent vs. 90 percent
5	26 November	1.9	4 percent vs. 93 percent
6	3 December	2.32	4 percent vs. 91 percent
7	10 December	1.04	5 percent vs. 91 percent
8	17 December	0.77	Rally after the congressional proposal to impeach Park is passed
9	24 December	0.702	Christmas Eve day
10	31 December	1.104	Number of rally participants to date: 10.006 million
11	7 January 2017	0.7	One thousandth day following the sinking of the *Sewol* on 16 April 2014
12	14 January	0.146	Bitterly cold, with temperatures below 19°F
13	21 January	0.3535	Temperatures below 32°F, with snow
14	4 February	0.4255	No rally held on 28 January, the Korean New Year holiday
15	11 February	0.806	Cumulative number of rally participants exceeds 12.436 million
16	18 February	0.84486	
17	25 February	1.07	Fourth anniversary of Park's inauguration
18	1 March	0.3	Independence Movement Day; Yellow Ribbon Campaign honoring victims of the *Sewol* ferry disaster
19	4 March	1.0	Last weekend rally before the impeachment verdict
20	11 March	0.2	Impeachment announced at the Constitutional Court on 10 March; cumulative number of rally participants: 16 million
21	25 March	0.1	Arrest and examination of Park; investigation of the *Sewol* ferry disaster begins
22	15 April	0.1	Rally marking the third anniversary of the *Sewol* disaster
23	29 April	0.05	Final rally; presidential election campaign begins

due to personal reasons. So 62.1 percent of the Korean public strongly favored the rallies.

There were various slogans for the rallies, but two were particularly popular. They were "Is this a state, really?" and "Resignation of Park Geun-hye." They clearly showed what the people wanted: the impeachment of the incompetent and corrupt president. There were also longer slogans that were made into songs. One was made of sentences from the Korean Constitution: "The Republic of Korea shall be a democratic republic. The sovereignty of the Republic of Korea shall reside in the people, and all state authority shall emanate from the people." People wanted to have a country that practices the spirit of the Constitution. To reach that goal, legal institutions such as the police, public offices, the National Assembly, and judicial institutions had to incarnate the constitutional spirit. But most of them did not. Another longer slogan was "Darkness cannot defeat light. Lies cannot defeat truth. Factual truth will never sink. We will never give up." This was a reaction to what was seen as the extreme malfunction, corruption, and lies of the government during President Park's term.

The direct cause of the Candlelight Rallies was the discovery of President Park's secret helper and the evidence of their misconduct.[1] At that time, many rumors roamed around. A news reporter from a major TV news station found the so-called "smoking gun": a tablet PC that contained national secrets and emails that contained communications between the confidant and government officers. This discovery was reported on national television and made public. President Park was forced to make a public apology and attempted to quell the outrage, but that same night the same news program revealed additional facts that proved the president's apology was dishonest.

According to Korean law, the term of presidency is [limited to] five years. Park became president in 2013. Many people were excited by her election because they expected that she would bring back "the good old days," the days of her father Park Chung-hee's rapid economic growth. Her father was also notorious for his brutal political oppression. Soon, however, people faced her inability to deal with national disasters. Only a few months after her inauguration, a terrible accident occurred: the [passenger ferry] *Sewol* sank. Among 476 passengers, only 172 people were rescued; 304 people could not escape. The rescue and the sinking of the ship were televised. It was a national traumatic event. The following year saw the MERS epidemic. The outbreak of MERS, the Middle East Respiratory Syndrome, could have been rather easily contained if appropriate measures were immediately taken. Instead, the disease resulted in more than twelve thousand people quarantined and thirty-eight people dead. The next year, Park's third year in office, during a large street demonstration by farmers, one of the protestors was hit by a powerful blast of water from a fire engine's water hose. The man fell into a coma and was hospitalized for ten months, after which he died. The hospital issued a death certificate where the cause of death was identified not as "by an external shock," which was the obvious cause, but as "sickness." This was seen as clearly done due to pressure from the government.

There were more injustices. The government had a secret blacklist that cut funding for actors, actresses, and art productions that were critical toward the government. Scholars and professors who were critical had research funding cut as well. The government also created a white list and poured tax money to supportive groups and institutions. The government ran an operation [in which] internet commenters systematically wrote comments on news articles and in SNS messages in order to manipulate public opinion. It also ordered the Korean intelligence agency and military to do the same. They also created fake news [stories] and systematically spread them. The government made it policy to allow only one national history textbook, which glorified and idealized [Park's] father's achievements while ignoring his crimes.

When the incompetence and corruption reached its peak, people went out into the street and shouted, "Is this a country, really?" They also asked, "What is the spirit of the Constitution?" On the street, people posited that they themselves are the power holders, the proponents of the spirit of the Constitution, the source of constitutional power.

In her article "Civil Disobedience," Hannah Arendt identifies civil disobedience as "the violation of a law for the purpose of testing its constitutionality."[2] And she gives several qualifications for a collective action to be [deemed] civil disobedience. Now I will describe several characteristic features of the Candlelight Rallies of 2016–17 following Arendt's qualifications.

First, the Candlelight Rallies were grounded in people's collective political opinions. They performed actions in concert, [as] representatives of all the people.

Second, people performatively expressed that they are the subjects of power and that their actions were the expression of the most fundamental spirit of the Constitution.

Third, people believed that the government did not function properly and that it even went against the law and the Constitution. However, people could not find a legal way to request corrections or to bring about change.

Fourth, people did not use violence in their collective expressions of opinions.

These features clearly make the Candlelight Rallies an exemplary case of Arendt's civil disobedience. While these rallies went on, the National Assembly voted overwhelmingly in favor of impeaching the president. The Constitutional Court, which deals with judicial review, also decided to impeach the president. So she was fired.

One interesting question regarding the Candlelight Rallies is whether the campaign was really an action of disobedience. During and after the rallies, not one single person was arrested. Huge congregations campaigned in an orderly way, and they also stopped any deviation by participants. Police stayed behind the police line and did not provoke the protesters. Police asked people to keep the laws during the campaign, and they did. The representatives of the participants filed for permission from the courts to rally each time, and the courts issued the permits immediately. When they filed for permission to rally at the Blue House,[3] the court issued [a series of permits that allowed participants to get] gradually closer to it: 300 yards, 200 yards, 150 yards, and eventually only 100 yards from the Blue House. The mayor of Seoul recruited volunteers to keep the subway areas safe. He also asked nearby shops and buildings to open their restrooms to the public and install several portable toilets. He ordered the city water department to cut the water supply if the police tried to use fire engines to suppress the rallies.

How could people campaign so peacefully? It was because they learned from past experiences. People knew that any illegal or violent acts make participants turn their backs on the rallies. Thus, they showed great restraint despite their great anger. The result was a campaign that gradually felt like a cultural festival. They set up huge stages, speakers, and huge screens. All of the money came from donations from the people. Pop stars performed, and participants took turns giving speeches. Given this, we need to ask if the campaign was really an act of disobedience. The atmosphere was happy. There, people experienced what Hannah Arendt called "public happiness" in *On Revolution*.[4]

I still believe that the whole campaign was an action of disobedience although there was no illegal activity. It still was an act of disobedience to the current regime, to the current political environment, to the current political consciousness of the politicians, and even to the participants' old political consciousness. Thus, it can be an action of civil disobedience.

This point, however, has another interesting implication in regard to Arendt's conception of revolution. If the same thing happens in the States, it will mean the recovery of the constitutional spirit. The term "recovery" does not aptly describe the Korean situation because the spirit of the Korean Constitution has never before been substantially recognized, although the Constitution technically asserts a democracy. Korea was declared a democracy ever since the Constitution was written three years after the liberation from Japanese colonization, under U.S. martial [law]. It was democratic but in word only, not in reality. Now, during the rallies people experienced the identification of the Constitutional sprit and people's power. So I would say that through the rallies people became citizens, that Korea now has a civil society in its genuine sense, and I would like to say that the Korean political environment has experienced a paradigm shift—a quantum leap.

In this sense I believe that the Candlelight Rallies fit Arendt's idea of revolution. She says that the most important thing in a revolution is the existence of the spirit of revolution. Political freedom comes [into being] and is to be constitutionalized through revolution. In order words, a new secular order, *novum ordo seclorum*, is the essence of revolution.[5] Of course, Koreans did not create a new constitution, but real political freedom came into existence and legal institutions were reborn under the people's power. Korea thus saw a new political order that is grounded in people's awareness of their constitutional power.

In the heart of the spirit of the Candlelight Revolution, I believe, lies people's intentionality toward the peace between the two Koreas. This intentionality is clearly identified in people's rate of support for the Korean president's peace initiative. After his election, his approval rating did not fall below 70 percent until strong disagreement with his domestic economic policy and real estate policy emerged. During this controversy, the approval rate rapidly dropped down to 50 percent—still a high number. After his visit to Pyongyang, where he met the North Korean leader, Kim Jung-Un, his approval rating went up to nearly 80 percent.

One remarkable fact is that the approval rating of the opposition party, which once supported the impeached President Park, stayed near 15 percent even when the support rate for the president was at its lowest. I believe this means that South Korea will never go back to the situation before the Candlelight Rallies. And since Koreans have very strong intentions for peace in the Korean peninsula, they cannot let things go according to Trump's whim. For this is a matter of life or death for all Koreans.

---

1. Park's confidant Soon-sil Choi secretly involved herself in politics, cultural policy, and the hiring of government officials, and President Park followed her decisions closely. Choi even ordered a rewrite of Park's inauguration speech, and Park complied. Choi controlled Park and her administration from the shadows with more authority than Park's secretaries or her highest-ranking government officials.

2. Hannah Arendt, "Civil Disobedience," in *Crises of the Republic* (New York: Harvest/HBJ Books, 1972), 53.

3. The Blue House is the executive office and official residence of the South Korean head of state.

4. Hannah Arendt, *On Revolution* (New York: Viking Press, 1963), 122.

5. Richard J. Bernstein, *Why Read Hannah Arendt Now?* (Cambridge: Polity, 2018), 106.

Whistleblowing as Civil Disobedience: Leaks in the Era of Trump and the Deep State

Allison Stanger

I want to begin by introducing my interlocutor, Professor David Bromwich, who is not listed on your program. He is Sterling Professor at Yale University, a frequent contributor to the *New York Review of Books*, enormously intelligent, and erudite, and I feel fortunate to be sharing a stage with him.

I am keenly aware that I am standing between you and wine and cheese, and I am also following a fantastic panel of students. What I'd like to do is very quickly sketch an argument that will give you a taste of my forthcoming book on whistleblowing in America. My aim is to generate a good discussion, both with David and then with you. I will leave plenty of time for your questions.

My book *Whistleblowers: Honesty in America from Washington to Trump* will be published by Yale University Press in 2019. I'm happy to report that I finished final edits and sent it into production last night from Bard's Stevenson Library, so I'm feeling rather enthusiastic about the Bard community right now.

To start us off, it is helpful to define some terms. I will use the acronym IC as a stand-in for the Intelligence Community. The IC is part of the Deep State (the bureaucracy that stays in place as presidents come and go), which serves the government regardless of its partisan orientation.

Writing in the March–April 2018 issue of *Foreign Affairs*, the political philosopher Michael Walzer, whom some of you may know as the author of *Just and Unjust Wars*, identified several types of leaks and whistleblowing and explored their ethical implications. Walzer defined whistleblowing as conveying what a person "believes to be immoral or illegal conduct to bureaucratic superiors or to the public," and he implied that there was no way to make an objective judgment about intelligence community leaks in the Trump era. "All governments, all political parties, and all politicians keep secrets and tell lies," he writes. "Some lie more than others, and those differences are important." The article mentioned Donald Trump by name only twice. He concludes that whistleblowing has only "an unofficial role to play in the democratic political universe" and "one must recognize both its possible value and its possible dangers."[1]

Walzer wrote about secrets and lies yet avoided rendering a judgment on the Trump White House, in part because he rightly thinks that whistleblowing in America is ultimately defined by the perceptions of the American people. Yet at roughly the same time the piece appeared, the *Washington Post* on March 1st reported that Donald Trump had already made 2,436 false or misleading claims in a little over a year in the White House. So my argument with Michael Walzer, which I elaborate on in my book, is simply that we cannot ignore the elephant in the room without missing something of critical importance: the intelligence community is breaking the law to blow the whistle on Donald Trump for violating his oath to preserve, protect, and defend the Constitution of the United States.

That might sound to you at first pass like a partisan argument. I'm going to argue that it's not a partisan argument; it's an American argument that looks only all the more that way with the passage of time. Perhaps this point can tie in very nicely with some themes we heard coming out of the last panel about the desire for unity and understanding when fundamental American values are at stake.

So, what's my argument? Here is the nutshell version. Walzer's reasoning in early 2018 is thoughtful and nuanced and absolutely fine for politics as usual; but American politics today are highly unusual. I do not meant to suggest that there aren't all sorts of continuities to which we can point. Professor Skocpol brought some of those out so well in the first presentation this morning. Yet taken as a whole, American politics today are extraordinary with Donald Trump in the White House. We need to take that particular context into account, because it changes the moral calculus that Walzer presents for ordinary times. Because the current administration has launched an assault on the rule of law itself, as well as the norms and practices of American democracy, officials in a position to expose the full extent of that misconduct are justified in so doing. And I'll say a little bit more about that in a moment.

It's important to define my terms before proceeding, because I'm going to define whistleblowing slightly differently than Michael Walzer did. I am keeping morality out of the definition, because it renders the concept too malleable, although I ultimately want to make an argument about right and wrong in extraordinary times. For Hannah Arendt, Socratic morality becomes "politically relevant only in times of crisis. . . . When standards are no longer valid anyhow . . . nothing is left but the example of Socrates."[2]

What's a better definition? I define whistleblowing as the insider exposure of illegal or improper activity. We know something is illegal when it violates the law, as determined by a court. We know something is improper when the relevant community of which the whistleblower is an insider deems it to be so. Here it is important to know that whistleblowing has long been recognized as an important part of American political life. Whistleblowers were first given protection by the Second Continental Congress in 1778. My book provides an episodic history of whistleblowing in the United States from the founding to the Trump era.

Comparing this definition with partisan alternatives brings into fuller relief the vital role truth telling plays in sustaining civil discourse and American constitutional democracy. Whistleblowing is not a mere weapon for advancing

Citizenship and Civil Disobedience

partisan or personal interests in a fake-news world. It is not what denigrates others or vindicates our own political biases. The extreme left and right may view any revelation of secret information that serves their political ends as whistleblowing, but that is to blur important lines.

All whistleblowers are leakers, but not all leakers are whistleblowers. Leakers expose secrets, but secrets are not always a cover for misconduct, even if their revelation can often embarrass individuals and destroy careers. In contrast, whistleblowers expose lies and wrongdoing, which their perpetrators would like to keep secret.

Just as all leaking is not whistleblowing, all dissent is not whistleblowing. All whistleblowers are certainly dissenters in that they refuse to accept current circumstances, but all dissenters are not whistleblowers. Whistleblowers reveal truths that the powerful do not want to be made public, whereas dissenters simply disagree.

Defined in this fashion, whistleblowing is a cousin of civil disobedience, but they are not one and the same. In the United States, the term *civil disobedience* was first coined by Henry David Thoreau. John Rawls in *A Theory of Justice* defines it as the "public, non-violent and conscientious breach of law undertaken with the aim of bringing about a change in laws or government policies."[3] Whistleblowers expose secret misconduct, which may or may not involve breaking the law.

Whistleblowers differ from civil disobedients in that they appeal to the law or Constitution—to the American rule of law tradition—for justice, whereas civil disobedients challenge directly the legitimacy of particular laws. Both variants of dissent require political judgment.

Another way of thinking about the same thing is to point out that civil disobedients often aren't insiders; they're outsiders. In contrast, whistleblowers are always insiders. They are members of the elite who expose misconduct they see that may be illegal, that may even be unconstitutional.

Whistleblowing in the national security arena has always been the most controversial, because it conflicts with another professional obligation, namely, anybody in the national security community is supposed to guard classified information. National security employees are breaking the law by disclosing classified information without authorization.

For Hannah Arendt, "civil disobedience arises when a significant number of citizens have become convinced either that the normal channels of change no longer function . . . or that, on the contrary, the government is about to change and has embarked upon and persists in modes of action whose legality and constitutionality are open to grave doubt."[4] Civil disobedients break laws that they want to see changed. In this sense, just like whistleblowers, all civil disobedients are dissenters, but not all dissenters are civil disobedients.

Arendt saw civil disobedience as uniquely American. It was a manifestation of what Tocqueville deemed America's greatest strength, the vitality of its associations, more commonly known as civil society. "Civil disobedients," wrote Arendt, "are nothing but the latest form of voluntary association . . . , quite in tune with the oldest traditions of the country."[5] Civil disobedience is "primarily American in origin and substance. . . . No other country, and no other language has even a word for it. . . . To think of disobedient minorities as rebels and traitors," Arendt continues, "is against the letter and spirit of a Constitution whose framers were especially sensitive to the dangers of unbridled majority rule."[6]

The same could be said of whistleblowers—and I show this in my book—who often illuminate the gap between American ideals and a fact-based world, the real world, where ideals usually are not realized. Whistleblowing, like civil disobedience therefore, is distinctly American. It is ultimately an indirect call to renew the rule of law through new legislation defining corruption and the abuse of power; because whistleblowers are often very focused on corruption and the abuse of power, and there's plenty of it going on, I need not tell you, in Washington today.

Whistleblowing thus has a larger context. I'm focusing on public servants and the national security community, but obviously it's prevalent in the corporate world, where protection of whistleblowing has become increasingly formalized in legislation, such as the 1986 amendments to the False Claims Act, or Sarbanes-Oxley, or the Dodd-Frank reforms. But what's interesting here is that national security employees are explicitly excluded from the Whistleblower Protection Enhancement Act of 1989, and that exclusion was ratified when Congress updated the act in 2012. So whistleblowers in government have protection except in the national security realm.

Extending whistleblower protection to the national security realm is admittedly a complex challenge. In ordinary times, we don't want officials to have the right to decide for themselves whether classified information should be made public. My expertise is in American foreign policy, and I can elaborate on the reasons why classified information is important, if that's not immediately obvious to you. And even today, leaks such as the release of transcripts of the president's conversation with foreign leaders, where he sounds completely ignorant and simply not up to the challenge of leading the free world—those don't constitute whistleblowing, because the behavior revealed did not involve any gross violation of the rule of law. In such circumstances I would argue that Walzer's invocation of the ethical calculus of civil disobedience is valid. Those leaks shouldn't happen.

But when high officials in the executive branch who are sworn to uphold the Constitution openly flout and subvert it, and Congress fails to exercise its oversight responsibilities, then internal channels of dissent atrophy and a whistleblower's calculations change. That is, when the rule of law itself is threatened, whistleblowing can be necessary to defend liberal democracy as a whole. I would argue that illegal leaks that expose true betrayals of American democracy are neither partisan nor political; they are patriotic invocations of Socratic morality.

Which brings me to the elephant in the room: within days of taking office President Trump fired Acting Attorney General Sally Yates, and a few months later he fired FBI Director James Comey. Since then he has repeatedly tried to impede the investigation of Special Counsel Robert Mueller, attacked and slandered anybody who criticizes him or refuses to accept his claims of absolute authority, and has basically polluted public discourse with a stream of lies. "Our whole system falls apart," Sally Yates would later say, "when the citizens of our country lose confidence in the justice system and the Department of Justice." And Yates continued, "Almost from the very beginning of the Trump administration we've seen breaches of these rules and norms from the White House." Now, she was a dedicated public servant confronting the danger firsthand, and she came out in a different place than Michael Walzer. Her recommendation: "When you see something happening that you think is wrong, and that's different from something that you don't think will be effective, I encourage you to speak up."[7] That's the former acting attorney general.

I don't need to rehearse all the evidence for you here. I can if you're interested when we get to questions, but suffice it to say that Yates was not alone in believing these are exceptional times. I'm not making a radical argument. As you may have noticed, an unprecedented number of former senior officials from the intelligence and national security communities of both political parties, every CIA director back to the Ronald Reagan administration, have spoken out against what they consider a unique threat to American political culture and American institutions. And many of their counterparts inside the system agree and feel obliged to cry foul themselves—not from whim, not from partisanship, but because they believe they are honoring their own sworn oath to preserve, protect, and defend the Constitution of the United States.

In his memoir, *A Higher Loyalty*, James Comey repeatedly compares Trump to a Mafia boss. In *Making Democracy Work*, Robert D. Putnam delineates how Mafia justice fills the vacuum that is created when the people have lost faith in their legal institutions as enforcers of impartial justice. I mean, that's what some people would argue was at stake in the Kavanaugh nomination, the very idea of impartial justice. We could talk about that if you like in the question period as well.

I think what's interesting here, and Comey writes about this, is that Donald Trump's idea of governance mirrors the way in which a criminal corruption network advances its interests, which is obviously not how American democracy was designed to work. According to Masha Gessen writing in the *New Yorker*, the indictments in the Mueller investigation have exposed an attempt at state capture by an international crime syndicate.[8] The Trump team has subverted democratic norms in an unprecedented way. Trump has shamelessly used the presidency for personal enrichment. While the jury is still out, he very much appears to have obstructed justice. All of Trump's self-serving actions reflect faithlessness to the American legal order rather than partisanship. And for those who have dedicated their lives to public service, his abuse of power has been a call to arms.

So I'll just give you one example, and there are many more in my book: if you look at the FBI director, only Donald Trump thinks that is a partisan appointment. FBI directors serve ten-year terms, and they're supposed to be above politics, impartial, loyal to the Constitution rather than to a particular political party. When Barack Obama was thinking of naming James Comey FBI director, he only met with him twice, once to interview him for the job, and once to tell him he was going to be nominated. At their second private meeting, President Obama told James Comey it would be their last private meeting. Why? Because impartial justice requires an FBI director to be independent of the president.

Now contrast this with Donald Trump's behavior. You don't have to add it up; I'll add it up for you. In the short four months before Trump fired James Comey without informing him first on 9 May 2017, Trump met with his inherited FBI director without others present no fewer than four times and spoke with him four times by phone. Trump also sought out Comey to hug him publicly at a White House reception for the leaders of law enforcement agencies on 22 January 2017 (Comey dodged the hug but wound up instead appearing to get a public kiss).[9]

Now, I am sure that some of you might point to Obama's use of executive orders as subversive of the rule of law. I am not arguing that others are above criticism. We have all contributed to the mess we are in. Instead, I would simply like to focus attention on where we are right now, and what Americans should want to see happen from here.

In his classic *Just and Unjust Wars,* Michael Walzer discusses the case of Arthur Harris, the leader of Great Britain's Bomber Command during the Second World War. He's the man who was the architect of terror bombing raids on Germany that killed countless civilians. Walzer argued that in cases of supreme emergency, when the very existence of the state is at question, it might be possible to fight unjustly for a just cause.

Walzer warns us to beware of the community that does not take full heed of the moral implications of invoking supreme emergency. After all, Adolf Hitler declared a state of emergency and suspended the Weimar Republic's constitution through the 1933 Enabling Act, unleashing the Nazi revolution. In contrast, Walzer cites the British dishonoring of Arthur Harris under Prime Minister Winston Churchill as an example of leadership that fully acknowledged the supreme danger in using immoral means, taking symbolic steps to put the community back on track after the war was won and the threat to democracy had receded.

Who was Arthur Harris? Harris was the leader of Britain's Bomber Command and an advocate and administrator of terror bombing. After the war, Harris did not win a peerage, nor do the names of the fallen members of his bomber squadron appear on the plaque honoring the fallen in Westminster Abby. Churchill's dissociation from Harris after the war had been won, Walzer points out, was part of a national dissociation to restore the moral universe that Harris had violated. Churchill needed Harris to do dishonorable things during the war for a higher cause, but he also needed to condemn Harris thereafter to reaffirm the values that the British people had temporarily overthrown.[10]

Once these unique depredations of the Trump presidency end—and let's be clear, utopia will not be immediately forthcoming, as many problems we have discussed today will remain and require our vigilance—I would argue that the illegal leaking that is occurring in response to the Trump presidency will obviously need to end as well. At that point it will be possible to draw up the ethical balance sheets and assign everybody involved their proper penance as a means of restoring the moral universe that Trump endeavored to overturn.

But until the immediate danger has passed, it makes sense, regardless of your political affiliation, to focus on the shocking substance of the information being revealed rather than the questionable means by which that information is coming to light, and to do what we can to put the rule of law back on track. "The new always happens against the overwhelming odds of statistical laws and their probability," Arendt reminds us. "The new therefore always appears in the guise of a miracle."[11]

---

1. Michael Walzer, "Just and Unjust Leaks: When to Spill Secrets," *Foreign Affairs* (March/April 2018).

2. Hannah Arendt, *Responsibility and Judgment* (New York: Schocken Books, 2003), 104, 106.

3. John Rawls, *A Theory of Justice* (Cambridge: Harvard University Press, 2005), 364.

4. Hannah Arendt, "Civil Disobedience," in *Crises of the Republic* (New York: Harcourt Brace, 1970), 74.

5. Ibid., 96.

6. Ibid., 76.

7. Becky Beaupre Gillespie, "Saying No to the President: Schwarz Lecturer Sally Yates on Standing Up to Trump—And Why She Thinks the Rule of Law Is Under Siege," University of Chicago Law School, November 29, 2017. law.uchicago.edu/news/saying-no-president.

8. Masha Gessen, "The Trump-Russia Investigation and the Mafia State," *New Yorker*, 31 January 2019. newyorker.com/news/our-columnists/the-trump-russia-investigation-and-the-mafia-state.

9. On 6 January 2017 to inform him of the Steele Dossier; on 27 January 2017 for a private White House dinner; on 8 February 2017 after meeting with Chief of Staff Reince Priebus; and on 14 February 2017 in the Oval Office to discuss Michael Flynn. President Trump also spoke with Comey four times by phone (on 11 January 2017 after *BuzzFeed* published the Steele dossier; on 1 March 2017; on 30 March 2017; and on 11 April 2017). James Comey, *A Higher Loyalty: Truth, Lies, and Leadership* (New York: Flatiron Books, 2018), 223–27, 232–44, 247–55, 257–61, and 232 for the creepy hug/kiss.

10. Michael Walzer, *Just and Unjust Wars: A Moral Argument with Historical Illustrations*, 5th ed. (New York: Basic Books, 2015), 257, 260, 323–25.

11. Hannah Arendt, *The Human Condition* (Chicago: University of Chicago Press, 1998), 178.

Discussion: Violent and Nonviolent Protest

Mark Bray
David Bromwich

Mark Bray: I'm going to speak about violence and nonviolence today. My main purpose, though, is to really address all of the unaddressed assumptions and political perspectives that inform what we think of as violence and nonviolence, because all too often we have a conversation about what is or is not violent, what is or is not politically useful or ethical, without addressing the context in which these conversations happen.

So something I would throw out as a potential ground rule for consideration is to never or very rarely say that violence or nonviolence in the abstract, without context, is good, or bad, or indifferent; but try to situate it in a context, situate it in a politics, and really be very specific about what we're talking about. I think that might be useful, regardless of your perspective.

It's really interesting to discuss what is or is not violence. But personally, I'm less interested in that than I am in how society views what is or is not violent. For me it's about that definition, so I think it's important to understand these terms contextually, historically, and how popular receptions to different types of action have been changed over time and have been actively constructed by different historical actors, different political movements in time. We didn't just naturally end up where we are with the perspectives we have. The perspectives we have on what is called violence, on what is called nonviolence, have been very intentionally created by different political movements and actors over time.

We also need to understand these terms politically, and look at tactics and how people respond to them politically, and think about them in terms of what the goals of our different actions and our different campaigns are.

I'm also going to throw out a sort of unpopular, but I think thought provoking, perspective, which is that not all political actions or political movements need to gain majority approval in order to be successful. Now, I am very much committed to popular politics. I've been involved in several social movements. I think long-term transformation definitely needs mass support. But you can be successful with a lot of people thinking that you're not doing what you ought to be doing. There are a number of examples. For example, if you look at strikes: strikes can be successful even if society thinks the strikers' demands are illegitimate, if they can garner enough economic pressure on their boss to accede to their demands. For example, the *Washington Post* I think a year or two ago published interesting statistics from the civil rights movement, about how, in 1961, only 22 percent of the general public approved of the actions of the Freedom Riders; only 28 percent approved of the actions of the lunch counter sit-in activists; and only 15 percent of white people back in 1966 thought that civil rights demonstrations helped the situation of African Americans.

Moreover, I've been writing about antifascism, and I have a number of documented cases in my book *Antifa* where antifascists have been successful in stopping small-to-medium-scale neo-Nazi groups without the public ever hearing about what they did or necessarily approving of their tactics.[1]

Let's talk about protests a little. The default understanding of protest in society is that protest is a subset of politics, and that politics are about holding signs and voting. In our country most politics at a popular level are assumed to constitute voting or holding signs. Anything else is considered a "mob," as the Republicans have attempted to paint the anti-Kavanaugh protestors, and by extension the entire Left. So this norm, that change happens through the ballot box or it happens through hearts and minds in the abstract public sphere, is really it. Everything else is anathema. So that norm creates a powerful pole that pulls politics toward it. In the past I've called it "protest as election," where the success or failure of a protest is thought to have everything to do with the percentage of society that gives it kind of a metaphorical thumbs-up, rather than seeing it as a contestation over power. And this norm of protest as election, where protests are seen as essentially live-action opinion polls, allows politicians, pundits, and activists to argue that acquiescing to this standard will alienate fewer people, and therefore is the most effective way of doing politics. So, based on this perspective, the recipe for success is to get as close as possible to what people already think, and encourage people to behave politically in ways that they are already most receptive to.

The danger there, of course, is that the more you mirror the society you want to change, the more you become that society. For example, one iteration of that might be a critique of some of the anti-Kavanaugh protests, because they have fueled a certain section of the Republican base. So you could, based on this perspective, say, "You see, you shouldn't be so confrontational, you shouldn't be so upset, you should be *civil*."

I don't think that that one-dimensional recipe is actually how successful social movements work, but we can get into that later. Moreover, rarely in any successful or significant social movement is there only one way of doing politics, is there only one tactical formula, so any assessment of any group or any tactics needs to situate it within that wider context if you really want to understand what's going on. Not all politics is simply about changing the minds of one's opponents. You can win in a campaign without necessarily convincing those who disagree with you. We should think in terms of power, not just in terms of abstract opinion.

The assumption, of course, is that what we call nonviolent protest tactics are the best way to convince the people who disagree with you to join your protest and therefore gain as much popular participation as possible. But what do we think of as nonviolent protest tactics? That, to me, is not always self-evident. So I'm going to run through a few examples of things that might or might not be considered nonviolent protest tactics, and we can think about them.

So, how about breaking windows or damaging property where no living being is harmed? There have been a lot of debates in social movement circles about this tactic. It certainly was a successful tactic for British suffragettes, but I think most Americans would think of that as violent.

What about workplace sabotage, a hallmark of the labor movement, but not really what people think in terms of nonviolent action? What about blocking roadways, subways, entrances to banks? Blocking police stations, occupying ICE offices, squatting in abandoned property? Not exactly what people think of in terms of nonviolent action. What about kneeling or sitting during the national anthem? More people would support that, but many say it's not the right place or the right time, that one shouldn't politicize sports or disasters or tragedies, etc., etc. What about boycotts? Yes, people love boycotts. What about boycotting Israel as part of the BDS (Boycott, Divest, and Sanction) movement against the occupation of Palestine? Not as popular. What about interrupting racist speakers? What about yelling at politicians like Ted Cruz at restaurants, or refusing to serve them, like what happened with Sarah Huckabee Sanders? What about confronting Ivanka Trump on an airplane, making her feel uncomfortable during a vacation? What about doxing, where you publicize someone's personal information to make their life more difficult, as is often done with neo-Nazis? What about throwing fake blood, pieing, glitter bombing, flag burning, shoplifting, looting? These are all examples where you could make a case that these are nonviolent actions, but these are wildly unpopular for the most part.

Why? Because these things are often illegal and/or uncivil. Civility is the box into which nonviolent protest is expected to fit. And you can't talk about the efficacy or political ramifications of protests in terms of violence and nonviolence without addressing civility. Of course, the dimensions of this box were designed to limit the scope of resistance and reinforce the myth of national unity, or bipartisanship, or whatever you want to call it. And so, in that way, most forms of nonviolent resistance are actually super controversial. And when we talk about nonviolence we're really actually referring to a very small cross-section of what could be considered nonviolent, really a handful of things—holding signs, doing a sit-in.

So if you advocate for civility, that's fine. But I think you need to be willing to answer the question, when are things grave enough for you to agree with escalating tactically? Is it when fascists are marching in the streets? Is it when black and brown people are being systematically murdered and caged? Is it when we have a climate apocalypse a decade away? In the future, will they look back and say, "Sure, they let corporations and the military wreck the planet, but they sure were civil."

What about violence? What do we consider to be violence? Let's start with the most violent institution in human history. Which one is that? I think if I were to poll people about which is the most violent institution in human history, a lot of people really wouldn't get the right answer. The answer is, the state. Few people would offer it as an answer because the violence of the state is so normalized and taken for granted that it is made invisible. Few even utter the name of its organizational structure. I would offer that you cannot actually call yourself an enemy of violence or a pacifist if you do not offer your harshest criticism to the violence of the state.

Now we can argue that the state is legitimate violence, that it adequately represents the will of the people; but then we're actually taking a step away from violence or nonviolence in the abstract into a political argument, which is exactly my point. The irony is that self-proclaimed pacifist activists who assist the police in apprehending violent protestors are actually engaging in more violence than those that they condemn.

It is rather strange talking about antifascism in the public [sphere], where the media says that the violent ones are the antifascists who actually, as part of their political agenda, aim to abolish the police, military, and prisons; yet their occasional physical confrontations with the fascists are the relevant violence.

True for me as well with my critics. I've been involved in nonviolent social movements for nearly two decades, to a greater extent than most of the people who criticize me for being violent. I'm a pretty nonviolent guy. So I would actually argue that there—get ready for this one—I would actually argue that there is no nonviolent way to stop fascism. There is only that which trusts the violence of the state to do it, and that which does not, because fascism is inherently violent. It will inherently come for those people that it wants to destroy unless it is met with a superior force. That could be the police. If that's your perspective, that's fine; but that's violence. If you ever think that violence is okay, then again, you have to think about how your positionality influences when you think it's okay.

We're all familiar with the poem, "First they came for the socialists. I did not speak up because I was not a socialist." The assumption of that poem is that it's in everyone's interest to stand up or eventually they'll come for you. But if you read, for example, *What We Knew*, which is a book of oral histories of people who lived through Nazi Germany,[2] you'd find out that if you were a German in the 1930s and '40s who [was] not part of one of the demographics the Nazis wanted to exterminate, you did not have to worry that they would come for you. Actually "everyday Germans" lived relatively carefree lives under the Third Reich and could actually engage in a wide variety of illegality and criminality because they were not the "other." So the point being, if you're not one of the demographics that they are coming for, think about how that affects your perspective on self-defense.

I mean, I think about the experience of my Jewish ancestors who were exterminated in Poland in the 1940s, and to me that kind of experience informs my perspective on self-defense and nonviolence. If there is a time when self-defense is legitimate—and I would strongly argue that that would be such a time—the question is, how bad does it have to get? And we can disagree on the answer to that, but you have to have an answer, I believe.

But this panel focuses actually on the role of violence or nonviolence in protest. And most of the circumstances when most people would be most sympathetic to the use of violence in politics actually don't quite fall into what we traditionally think of as protests. Like, for example, resistance to the Nazis in Eastern Europe in the 1940s—not exactly what [comes] to mind when we think of protest. And so, in that way, since the most legitimate uses of political violence don't happen in what we think of as protest, it reinforces the notion that violent protest is bad or counterproductive.

We think of protest as the exceptional, as the corrective remedy to keep a system on track—the slogan Protest Is Patriotic, that protesting actually helps the status quo. But what about when protest is not patriotic? We're talking a lot about citizenship here, but I think we also need to recognize that, even if we do things as citizens, the history of citizenship is the history of exclusion. Citizenship means nothing if it does not mean excluding those who are noncitizens. Not to mention, of course, the omissions in history of the citizen being originally thought of as male, as white, and so forth.

So I'm much less interested in having conversations about what we can do as citizens than how we can build a world without borders, where no one is illegal. Any protest that does not in one way or another explicitly or implicitly aim to weaken the violence of the state ultimately serves to reinforce the violence of the state. We talk a lot about violence and nonviolence in protest in terms of tactics, but rarely in terms of political content. So we talk about nonviolent or violent protest; but what about protests for violence, like for tighter immigration controls that therefore forcibly detain and cage human beings? I would argue that's a protest for violence. In many cases, such "peaceful protests" end up producing more violence than those engaged in what could be called violent tactics.

What about protests for the jailing of a killer cop? It's a protest in favor of an act of violence, forcibly locking up a police officer in a cage, that aims to reduce the violence overall by getting a killer cop off the streets and disincentivizing police murder. It's a protest for an act of violence to cut down on acts of violence.

Now, this is all becoming kind of confusing and long-winded and difficult to follow. That's the point, because that's what happens if you look at it apolitically, simply in terms of acts for or against violence, without actually seeing it as part of a broader politics. So again, violence or nonviolence in the abstract to me doesn't make a whole lot of sense. Situating it does make sense.

I'm about to wrap up by listing my four—if I can break it down—four main points for your consideration from this talk: Number one, let's look at violence and nonviolence historically and contextually in a way that resists lumping wide ranges of tactical and strategic action into a singular, flat ahistorical category. Number two, let's look at violence and nonviolence politically and holistically without ever for an instant naturalizing the greatest violence of all, that of the state. Number three, this conversation is not primarily about violence. It's mainly about sovereignty and political legitimacy. How are the terms defined? Who gets included? Who gets excluded? How is it violence? Or how is it nonviolence when a sheriff evicts someone from their home but it's violence if they fight back to hold on to their house? When, where, and how can violence be deployed? Terms like "political violence" or even "terrorism" are rhetorical weapons in the service of sovereignty. Even if we look in Roger Berkowitz's very interesting talk yesterday, he quoted Hannah Arendt as defining violence, at least in that circumstance, as taking the law into one's own hands. Taking the law into one's own hands—that's a definition of violence that inherently privileges the violence of the state.

And finally, this debate will never be resolved. Sorry. Not today, not anytime soon. So, rather than assuming that we will ever be able to convince each other, I think we should recognize how the dichotomy of violence and nonviolence is a wedge that creates a way to split and demonize resistance. If you are not asking these questions with a commitment to resistance and building power, then you will probably come up with answers that reinforce the existing regime of violence, whether in the name of violence or nonviolence.

Thank you.

---

1. Mark Bray, *Antifa: The Anti-Fascist Handbook* (Brooklyn: Melville House, 2017).
2. Eric A. Johnson and Karl-Heinz Reuband, *What We Knew: Terror, Mass Murder, and Everyday Life in Nazi Germany* (New York: Basic Books, 2006).

David Bromwich: You have just heard Mark Bray deliver, as he told me he would be doing, a talk on the historical contexts for violence, with emphasis on the always prior condition of the overwhelming violence of the state. He speaks as an anarchist—a not necessarily pro-violence anarchist.

One assumption behind his talk, and it grew in intensity as the talk went on, is that the violence of the state is something we recognize as a permanent condition.

I would put it to you that the state is, rather, a construction—an artificial construction. It is a power that has the monopoly on the use of legitimate violence; but the state, to the extent that people can conceive of it at all, is not perpetually an instrumentality of violence in the lives of most people. Stop signs aren't experienced as an act of violence. Delivery of mail by the postal system is not experienced as an act of violence. So when you hear the sort of dichotomy on which Mark Bray ended, bear that in mind as part of your experience. Not only that the state is something we in a democracy have a part in creating and modifying, but that the state is a convenience—maybe a convenience that we overrate because we don't want to be disturbed by demands for justice, but nevertheless, something we don't all always experience as an insult or an imposition, or that we all *only* experience as that. Let's not say: the only reason we would not experience it as a constant assault on our freedom and dignity is that we are the privileged, we are the protected. There are a great many people whom it would be unfair to describe as *either* downtrodden *or* privileged, who just like the mail being delivered on time and, on the whole, prefer to live with stop signs rather than without them.

The same goes for the word "civility," which Mark Bray's talk made out to be pretty much an excuse, a pretext for violence by powers outside ourselves that we just don't perceive properly. Think about the role of civility, or the reverse of civility, in your own lives. It has to do with politeness; it has to do with a decent approach toward people. Yes, that decency can be just a veil, a covering to hide terrible injustices. But think of it within a family. If you want to think the family is a system of domination and injustice, be my guest; but there are ways of interacting with people that are assumed to be better than other ways, and civility is a poor name, but maybe still the best we have, for that. I myself have opposed the use of an idea of civility, particularly by education leaders, as a cover for suppressing free debate; but I'm a defender of the First Amendment, and I think the First Amendment allows for incivility so long as it does not enter into the realm of physical violence, disruption, or intolerant inhibition of somebody else's right to speak. So those are just some initial reservations.

I'll be talking not about the state, but about society and its relation to the individual, including the individual protester.

It has been said that "with or without right, a revolution will be the very last resource of the thinking and the good." The reason is, a revolution turns society upside down. It causes disruptions that are hard to repair, makes a society changed overall, in ways that are hard to get back. And anyone who has talked to a Russian who lived through or was born just after the Russian Revolution of 1917 will be aware of the grave reservations even supporters of that revolution had about its effects.

So here are four, I think, commonsense reasons for engaging in the overturn of society and, with it, the state. The object of the change, the institution involved, what you're looking at, must be great and consequential. The evil must also be great. The abuse or many abuses in question must show no sign of abating: you know that they're going to continue on their course or grow worse, unless something is done about them. And last: there's no other means of remedy at hand, no available means except revolution, nothing that will *not* create so vast a disturbance, disruption, violence, death.

If you look at American society today—even looking at it pessimistically, in the light suggested by President Botstein a few moments ago—well,

Citizenship and Civil Disobedience

remember, the object in view must be great. What do we wish for? Let's say: a peaceful and equitable society and a planet that remains habitable. We're not getting that under current conditions. That great object is not being supported. We are against (let's say) growing inequality and the unrepresentative character of our representative government. So, the object being great and the evil being great, I think, are conditions that do obtain now, that do justify the use of formerly unthinkable means to achieve a necessary end.

Does the abuse show no sign of abating? Do we know that it will continue to get worse? Has it been getting worse for a long time? I want to point out, just as a little reminder, that the first African American president of the United States was elected twice and served as president between 2009 and 2017. That could hardly have been thought of even twenty years before. But it happened. It didn't happen that long ago. Are the experiences of the last twenty-three months sufficient to create a doubt in our minds so great that we will now say the abuse shows no sign of abating? That it will continue to grow worse unless some violent impediment is introduced in its way?

And last: there must be no other means of remedy at hand. Well, during the two terms of Obama's presidency the Democrats lost upward of one thousand persons as representatives in the state legislatures. That was, I will put forward, in some part a fault of negligence by the National Democratic Party, whose leading figure was Barack Obama. One of his weaknesses was that he paid insufficient attention to that kind of detail. It is imaginable that an opposition party leadership will arise, in the not too distant future, that will attend to the state legislatures more closely. The individual states can conceivably be the means of reforms that are not violent, not "spontaneous action" kinds of reform. Gay marriage became legitimate within the last decade—unimaginable at any previous time in the century. That is not yet abolished. The prospect of its abolition doesn't seem very close. So, as for grave abuses that show no sign of abating—the "emergency" feeling—and the lack of any other means for introducing reform: I think those final two conditions are *not* met. And I am as apprehensive as Mark Bray and Leon Botstein about the dangers we face; but I would ask for a dry, sober look at the facts—just the very thing that our feverish and chaotic president is unable to do.

Mahatma Gandhi was very keen on distinguishing nonviolent resistance, as he called it, from passive disobedience. He wanted the word "nonviolent" to be the adjective, not the word "passive." There is a great difference between the two. I'm going to take a short excursus on Gandhi's thinking, and I would ask you to recall, or introduce you to the fact that Gandhi was a *thinker*. His published works run to a hundred volumes, and you can buy them, I'm told by a colleague of mine, so cheaply that the cost of postage from India is greater than the cost of the books themselves.

What is violence actually, violence in action? Gandhi taught his readers and the participants in his movement to examine the violence in themselves.

What is it? What does it mean when we grow angry—angry, or enraged—and want to act punitively toward the person or thing that has aroused us? What would it be to generalize that emotion? It takes some thinking, and it takes some thinking in the presence of the possibility of remorse in oneself, remorse for violence that one has done or contemplated doing.

War and imperial domination have been the rule of human interactions. You can put them all down to the state, but from what we know of the development of human nature, from the apes and the earliest versions of creatures walking on two legs like us, the patterns of domination set in before anyone invented the state. Many things that were once the rule are wrong. Could it be that violence is one of those things?

This was also part of the gospel of Christianity, as delivered by Jesus Christ, and it was the part that won over Martin Luther King Jr., who held religious beliefs not exactly coincident with those of Gandhi. But it was the study of the preaching—not of Paul, not of the Apostles, but of Jesus—that made Martin Luther King (studying Gandhi too, as he did) a preacher of nonviolence as a form of *action*, a form of action by which to achieve radical reform—in short, that made him the kind of figure that he was.

A revolution seeks to use violence in order to achieve the termination of violence. And here I would echo, but with a different meaning, something that Mark Bray said just a moment ago: *We don't want to mirror the society that we mean to change.* I'll repeat: revolutions use violence to achieve the termination of violence. The question that is hard to ask is, how will you have trained yourself for this end by the energy you employ as a means? Not "How bad is the object? How violent is the state?" Not "How ugly are some of the sayings of the Tea Party? How unthinkably crass and base are the utterances of the president who exerts so much power, in so many directions, on us right now?" Not that, and not "How great would it be to get rid of all these evils?" But rather: "What am I doing to myself? What is the work I'm performing on myself, as I get rid of them?" This question, "What am I doing to myself?" is omitted in almost all discussions of politics—and in the history of political theory as well as among the tacticians of political action. And it is a question that Mark Bray does not bring up in the thoughts he asked you to consider.

Gandhi did seek to coax from his followers thoughts about this very matter: What are *we* doing? What do *we* represent? Who are *we*, not how bad are *they*. He asked those questions constantly, and he did it through the doctrine of *ahimsa*, nonviolence, in the belief that thinking is rare but desirable to achieve; that we are surrounded by violence in the world outside us and in ourselves, and it only clears away as clouds may clear on a day that becomes serene. It's only by trying to effect such a change in ourselves that we are able to think about our actions in the world. That's *ahimsa*—nonviolence. And it goes with the other famous word Gandhi has introduced even into the English-speaking vocabulary: *satyagraha*—truth and the idea of living with truth. This doesn't come to us all that naturally. It doesn't come, in society, to those in power; it doesn't come, in society, to those who are in dire straits or who become dissidents. Living with truth is something worth achieving, and it's worth achieving for the reform of society, too.

So, you're not always asking, "Who are *they?* Why are they so wrong? What must I do to crush the wrong they are bringing to us?" But also—*also*—"Who are we? What are we doing to ourselves?" And I will put it to you from personal experience, from introspection—I don't pretend to have it be true for everyone in the audience, but it seems to me from observation that it's true of quite a large number of people in the world, perhaps men a little more than women—violence is exciting. It means going out of your head. Sometimes it can be done with discipline, or it can begin with discipline but it goes to other places. Paramilitary groups of the Left and Right know this experience. It can be interesting to be a soldier in a platoon. Forcing another person or group of people to bow to your will can be interesting and exciting. We, if we're old enough, witnessed this mood in America in the years 2002–4. The reaction against the bombing of the World Trade Center; the extreme, brutal, violent defensiveness that arose as a national mood in this country; the talk about torture and legitimating torture, which led to the practice of it, unheard of before, unheard of as a legitimate thing; and finally the bombing, invasion, occupation of Iraq on false pretenses. Violent thoughts led to all that, and we're still not out of that mood, as a nation.

This is getting longer than I thought it should be, so I'm going to close with two passages from Thoreau's essay on civil disobedience[1]—both of them familiar, I think, but they work together in ways that bear some reflection.

He is talking about the injustice of paying taxes for the war with Mexico, which was also a war to extend slavery, and Thoreau sees no just cause why he should in any way continue to support slavery in the United States. It is not clear at every point in this essay whether he therefore considers the United States government of his time to be thoroughly corrupt and insupportable; but it's clear that the thoughts of the paragraph I'm about to read bear on both a particular action and the potential for generalizing that action. And he says:

> If the injustice is part of the necessary friction of the machine of government, let it go, let it go: perchance it will wear smooth, — certainly the machine will wear out. If the injustice has a spring, or a pulley, or a rope, or a crank exclusively for itself, then perhaps you may consider whether the remedy will not be worse than the evil.

Thoreau means to ask: are there existing checks, balances, counteractions built into the system? For example, right now, think of the lower courts and the extent to which they have provided friction against the worst suggested policies of this president on immigration. Thoreau continues: "but if it is such a nature that it requires you to be the agent of the injustice"—if the state is forcing you constantly to do things that are against your understanding of right and wrong; for example, forcing you to give up somebody who's been your neighbor for twenty years because he or she is now hunted by the immigration authorities—"then, I say, break the law. Let your life [he means your way of life, as well as your physical being] be a counter-friction to stop the machine. What I have to do is to see, at any rate, that I do not lend myself to the wrong which I condemn." Notice the defense of the self-involved here is the same as I was mentioning in Gandhi, who was, of course, a reader of Thoreau. "Civil Disobedience" was one of the texts that made him think hard about political action.

Then we come to Thoreau's vision of society, from spending a night in prison. "It was like traveling into a far country," he says,

> such as I had never expected to behold, to lie there for one night. It seemed to me that I never had heard the town-clock strike before, nor the evening sounds of the village; for we slept with the windows open, which were inside the grating. It was to see my native village in the light of the Middle Ages, and our Concord was turned into a Rhine stream, and visions of knights and castles passed before me. They were the voices of old burghers that I heard in the streets. I was an involuntary spectator and auditor of whatever was done and said in the kitchen of the adjacent village-inn, — a wholly new and rare experience to me. It was a closer view of my native town. I was fairly inside of it. I never had seen its institutions before. This is one of its peculiar institutions, for it is a shire town [he's talking about the *jail* as a peculiar institution]. I began to comprehend what its inhabitants were about.

That is a not unfriendly view of the neighbors he disagrees with and whose law-abidingness he is dissenting from; and it's this sort of mingling with people, even against whom one may be working politically and socially, that seems to me an important lesson of Thoreau and Gandhi and Martin Luther King. And it seems to me that Thoreau's emphasis on being alone—being alone with myself, seeing what it is that constitutes my motive, my reason for dissent—is also essential to the idea of what protest can be if it's minded to act on behalf of right, to care about what one is doing to oneself as well as to provide a counterfriction to an utterly visible, transparent wrong.

---

1. Henry David Thoreau, "Civil Disobedience," in *Yankee in Canada, with Anti-Slavery and Reform Papers* (Boston: Ticknor and Fields, 1866). Originally published as "Resistance to Civil Government" in 1849.

Citizenship and Civil Disobedience

Q&A: Violent and Nonviolent Protest

Mark Bray and David Bromwich

Kevin Duong: Thanks for those two presentations. I have some questions myself, but maybe I'll save them for later. Why don't we go ahead and open the floor for questions from the audience, and then I'll maybe weave my questions in later. I'm sure we have lots of hands.

Q: Thank you for calling on me. My name's Michael White, and I want to ask a question of Mark Bray. First, I want to say thank you. I think it is obviously very difficult to argue the position of violence, because we do live in a situation where most people want to defend nonviolence. And I think at the same time it's obviously clear that we do need people to argue a vigorous defense of violence, because if violence is necessary we need to know that—we need to know that information.

But I want you to go deeper, okay, because I think that it's clear that obviously there is a distinction between revolutionary violence and nonrevolutionary violence. And to me, I think my biggest critique of the Antifa is that it still feels like it's nonrevolutionary violence in the sense that they are not doing what you reference, which is trying to attain and hold sovereignty. So I guess what I'm saying is, give us a self-aware critique of Antifa that shows how violence can and should be used to attain sovereignty going forward.

MB: I think that's a good question in the sense of understanding militant antifascism—Antifa—as what one German antifascist that I interviewed described as a firefighting operation. It's a politics intended to stop what is perceived as an immediate threat. I think the most accurate way of understanding it within the broader radical Left is sort of one tool on a kind of Swiss Army knife of revolutionary politics. The goal of militant antifascist groups in most cases at most times is to respond to far-right organizing; but it's important to see it as part of the broader whole, where most of the people that are part of these groups are also union organizers and environmentalists and community organizers who, in a sort of positive, constructive politics sense, are doing that under a different umbrella heading. So in most cases, most Antifa groups . . . do not see that vehicle as the vehicle for creating a new world so much as stopping a descent into a much worse world, and do the kind of politics you're referring to under other headings at other times.

And one of the kind of most ironic things about the conversations around it is that many of the people who create the harshest critiques of antifascism are really actively supporting the very same people when they do different things without wearing masks, without knowing it; because the antifascists that I interviewed, many of them have been active in Occupy Wall Street, in Black Lives Matter, were at Standing Rock. So this is basically just a cross-section of the American radical Left.

I just wanted to quickly address a couple of the other interesting points that David made. I think we should distinguish between civility as a dictionary definition and its political usage. I'm not arguing for being a jerk; I'm just arguing that people who support separating migrant families shouldn't have a moment of peace on Earth, that's all. And also, stop signs are not obviously violent, but if you run through one and you get a ticket, and you don't pay the ticket, and then a collection agency comes and you refuse to pay that ticket, you will find state violence eventually. So that was sort of my broader analysis, but point taken that stop signs are really useful. Just talking about violence.
. . .

DB: I'm aware the last question was not addressed to me, and I'll be brief, but there is a history of resistance to fascism which is itself complex. There were street fights in pre-Nazi Germany between the Communists and the Nazi Brownshirts. That was a part of the organized enthusiasm of Germany preceding January 1933, when Hitler became chancellor.

There was a doctrine then current among the Communist Party of Germany, called the theory of social fascism, which said that the moderates of the time, the socialists, those who were not revolutionary communists but merely what we would now call social democrats, were "objectively" on the side of the Nazis, and therefore it was important utterly to disdain and reject their help and to fight them as hard as one fought against the uniformed Nazis already in the street. This was so disastrous a miscalculation that it prompted Trotsky, who wrote some very good pamphlets about those street battles, to say that the theory of social fascism seemed to have been invented by Stalin for the mere purpose of gumming up our brains.

I'm no friend of the establishment of the Democratic Party at this moment, but to suppose that every officeholder is someone you should fight against, and every governor who's trying to maintain the rule of law is somebody you should fight against, just as intensely as you do against the right-wing crowd—that's a dangerous argument, and tactically it's going to lead to unhappy results. Street fights will lead to a police crackdown; and if you think the result of a police crackdown is going to be greater strength for the insurgency, you might want to look at the kind of popular support that exists on the other side, too. So I want say: there is a prehistory to the theory of spontaneous action against actual fascists, and the prehistory is not altogether encouraging.

KD: I think in public discourse we hear the terms "radical" and "radicalism" thrown around a lot. My favorite definition is from Angela Davis, which is that radical simply means grasping things at the root. How would each of you define radical or radicalism, and how or when do you think radicalism is useful?

MB: I like that definition. Yes: "at the root." So what you consider to be radical has everything to do with what you think the root of an issue is. In terms of how it's used in the left spectrum, a radical left would be in some way or another anticapitalist for starters. Others would just say that's sort of a precondition for actually left, in a meaningful sense. But again, these are kind of ongoing debates. For me, though, I love that definition of being at the roots, so I think that's a good point of departure; and then everyone can kind of take it where it takes them.

DB: I gave the floor to Mark just now because I'm not quick to identify a single radical*ism*. There can be radicalism of so many kinds and in so many areas that I would first want to have a sharp definition. I would say of myself that in some sense I am "radical," but it is not a political conviction that names any present tendency. It comes under another heading.

I am radical against arbitrary power, which means unchecked power; and I'm radical against impeding the telling of truth, which I think is one of the most difficult things human beings do. I won't go so far as "the truth shall make you free," but without truth nothing that I could call freedom will ever come about. So those are two thoughts—I prefer the adjective to the noun: radical opposition to arbitrary power, radical support for the freedom to tell the truth. And: I think that we don't have any better protections than (in the case of freedom) the Fifth Amendment in the Bill of Rights and (in the case of truth) the First Amendment in the Bill of Rights. If anybody asks, I have it in my pocket, and I'll be glad to read you the wonderful words.

KD: Maybe if we have time.

Q: I just wanted to make a comment that I'd like you to comment back, because I don't know exactly how to phrase this as a question. But movements that we tend to think of as nonviolent in a way have been sanitized after they've been successful. So the liberation of South Africa did not come entirely as a result of nonviolence. There were mass demonstrations, there were boycotts, and there was also an armed wing that committed what would today be called terrorist acts. The civil rights movement, led by Martin Luther King Jr., was not nonviolent in the sense that we would define it today, that is, as the common parlance would define it today. In the civil rights movement, people who worked in the South armed themselves. They had self-defense units because people knew that they would be attacked. And I can tell you from knowing civil rights workers who worked in the South that at night they were attacked, and they shot back. They didn't wait, and they were not murdered by the Klan.

So I think the more interesting question might be to look at how nonviolence gets redefined by the hagiography of successful movements, and how the mix of a popular movement, supported as it may be by violent means, differs from the way in which a popular movement that arises solely by violence works.

Just one last example I would like to give, which is the way in which the generally nonviolent demonstrations of tens of thousands of people at the Gaza border now has been redefined by the Israelis—who, by the way, are killing them by the hundreds—as a violent movement.

So I'd just love your comments on that.

MB: Yeah, right on. So that's why I concluded by saying maybe a point of focus can be questions of solidarity, because, despite a lot of these disagreements about philosophy and tactics that people pursuing justice have, there are a lot in terms of what we want that's actually overlapping. And how can we avoid having wedges driven within our movements that make us turn and attack each other verbally, rather than working together?

And the issue of this wedge doesn't exclusively pertain to questions of violence and nonviolence. We can already see it in terms of the efforts by the Republicans to turn anti-Kavanaugh protestors into a mob simply for shouting at politicians. There is an example where, even if you disagree with the actions of some of these protestors, by all means we can have informed, interesting conversations and debates about it; but I think looking instead at how we can stand in solidarity and build a broad movement that can weather the fact that we're going to have a very interesting, complex, difficult array of tactical perspectives. I'm not encouraging violent movements; I'm just saying there are some times when self-defense politically makes sense, and recognizing that historically violence has coexisted with most liberatory social movements.

But I think that that point of departure is useful, and it's useful to get beyond the kind of apples-or-oranges debate that this often boils down to.

DB: Now I'll be the one who speaks of context—briefly. Israel, in its response to the protesters in Gaza and on the West Bank—a long-lasting response—has been much more oppressive than the British in India were in the 1940s or than the U.S. government was when the civil rights movement came forward in force in the 1950s. And if you're dealing with a state that has no respect for a mass nonviolent movement by something approaching a majority, you are in a very different situation from what either Gandhi or Martin Luther King confronted. I want to agree with that, without pretending to know what, if I were a Palestinian in Israel now, I would say should be done.

South Africa in the '70s and '80s, when the movement against apartheid arose, was a black majority country. That's a very important fact. Just think about what that means in relation to the acceptance or rejection of certain tactics. But it is an error, and a very common one I'm afraid, to ascribe to Gandhi or Martin Luther King the view that nonviolent resistance was merely tactical for them. It was a *principle* for them. They followed it, practiced it, in both cases at the cost of their lives, and preached it steadily to their followers.

Now, the arming of themselves by some civil rights workers in the South not under the direction of Martin Luther King (because it was a wide movement)—that is a different thing, and their self-defense is defensible. But don't amalgamate those two phenomena and say Martin Luther King told people to shoot back. That is simply false.

Gandhi addressed this particular question, the difference between individual self-defense and the principle by which a mass movement should be guided, in a very interesting passage of an essay called "The Doctrine of the Sword," from August 1920. I'm going to read it just because it's so interesting, and because I said he was a thinker, and this will prove it to you. "Such being the hold that the doctrine of the sword has on the majority of mankind"—he means violence—"and as success of noncooperation depends principally on absence of violence during its pendency and as my views in this matter affect the conduct of a large number of people, I am anxious to state them as clearly as possible. I do believe that where there is only a choice between cowardice and violence I would advise violence."

Now, I'm reading all of a passage that is often quoted with distortion in part, so take it slow:

> Thus when my eldest son asked me what he should have done, had he been present when I was almost fatally assaulted in 1908, whether he should have run away and seen me killed or whether he should have used his physical force which he could and wanted to use, and defended me, I told him that it was his duty to defend me even by using violence. Hence it was that I took part in the Boer War, the so-called Zulu Rebellion, and the late War.

He served on the English side, by the way. "Hence also do I advocate training in arms for those who believe in the method of violence." *For those who believe in the method of violence*—with whom he disagrees. And Gandhi continues:

> I would rather have India resort to arms in order to defend her honor than that she should in a cowardly manner become or remain a helpless witness to her own dishonor.
>
> But I believe that nonviolence is infinitely superior to violence, forgiveness is more manly than punishment. *Kshama virasya*

bhushanam. "Forgiveness adorns a soldier." But abstinence is forgiveness only when there is the power to punish; it is meaningless when it pretends to proceed from a helpless creature. A mouse hardly forgives a cat when it allows itself to be torn to pieces by her. I, therefore, appreciate the sentiment of those who cry out for the condign punishment of General Dyer and his ilk. They would tear him to pieces if they could. But I do not believe India to be helpless. I do not believe myself to be a helpless creature. Only I want to use India's and my strength for a better purpose.

Let me not be misunderstood. Strength does not come from physical capacity. It comes from an indomitable will.

It is a very complex thought.

Q: My name's David. I'm actually a public official. I'm a town manager. And I hear this conversation visited in my communities: civility, suppression, civil disobedience—all the things you talked about—violence, nonviolence. And my question is, when we heard the comments about "when we envision this society, this is the society we become," we have these conversations about the justification. Do either of you see how this is not just working on a national level but how this is working on a community level; that the way we treat each other locally, and the issues that we choose locally, and the violence with words and shunning and behavior, how this is starting to become part of American society at the local level—are you guys seeing that, or is this only a national academic conversation about global issues . . . ?

DB: I'll be the fast one this time, first and fast.

I would associate myself with President Botstein's remarks a few minutes ago about the importance of physical conversation, of the public space being used for public discussion. I don't like the word "conversation"; I probably react against the word "conversation" as strongly as Mark Bray does against the word "civility." Discussion can be occasionally impolite, though there are bounds it shouldn't cross. But when we're talking to people, the idea usually is: we're going to keep on talking, and that some good—getting to know each other's views, and maybe improving each other's views—comes out of that.

I think that social media are the enemy of democracy as we have known it. I think that's true on all sides. They're a very good means of rapid organization, and at the time of the hopeful feelings about the Arab Spring in Tahrir Square and elsewhere, there was a sense—at least Americans were made to believe it—that social media could be a means for good: unprecedented good, unique in human history. But I think they are also a means for harm to political discussion because they close off conversation between neighbors. In colleges, this hardly becomes an issue. At a place like Yale, where I teach, and

I imagine Bard too, the opinion runs so far in excess of 99 percent against the current government that there's no reason for argument—and yet, even so, within the kinds of divisions and shades of political views that we have, there is almost no freewheeling conversation because students walk out of class wearing earbuds and looking at their gizmos. That situation has to be improved if there's going to be discussion at the social level that leads to political change, to rational reform.

MB: I might add that you can follow this conference on Twitter through a hashtag.

Quick responses to the relationship sort of in my workplace and everyday life: Yes, it has affected me quite a bit on a local level. I was denounced by the president of Dartmouth College. Fortunately, more than 120 faculty supported my academic freedom, and this kind of campus organizing generated the faculty to form an AAUP [American Association of University Professors] chapter at Dartmouth to address a variety of other grievances, and actually in the long run was, I think, a pretty productive thing to happen. I received a number of threats for my work, etc., etc. So yes, it has affected me personally, immediately, and locally.

I think it is interesting that you use the phrase "violence with words." Not that that's wrong. We can very well make an argument that words can be violent. . . . I'm not saying that you're wrong; I'm just saying it's interesting, that that's one way to look at violence that we should take into account when we look at the whole conversation as to what is or is not violent. The notion, though, that when people are being very heated verbally in political spaces in a way that's contentious and perhaps uncivil, that that is the most problematic aspect of American politics, I think—not that you're saying that it is, but some people portray it as if it is—that that is a concern; that if in your community you have a prison, or you have a detention center, these are things that people should get heated about addressing, and if they're not, that's kind of violence as well. . . .

Q: Yesterday there was a panel on activism, and they talked about how students went to the Kavanaugh protest, and they were kind of systematically told, "Here's where you're going to get arrested, and here is your bail, and this is what we want you to do." Now, I'm just wondering what the panel's thoughts are, if this is still considered a form of protest and what you think—if there is a point to this sort of systematic way that we protest now.

MB: There's a lot of debate in Left circles over the kind of stage-managing of civil disobedience and resistance. I think there're legitimate arguments on both sides of it. But I think that the critique that maybe you're hinting at, that I am very sympathetic to, is that there comes a point when, like if you negotiate with the police for arrests in advance and you stage where people are going to be, the level of resistance and conflict that is potentially in an active nonviolent resistance dissipates. So I think it is problematic when you have NGOs or political parties or organizations dictating how everyone should resist. I think that is a problem. That having been said, though, I think there is something to be said for people who show up to a protest respecting the work of people who have made the protest happen all along. So I think it's not black-and-white, but I do think there is a concern at times when we stage-manage to such a degree that it kind of loses its force.

Q: My question is for all three of you, and it's about civility. President Botstein brought up this idea of physical space versus social media; David, you just reiterated it. And this idea of the physical public sphere is an idea that's very important to Arendt, as you know. My question is, do you think that we have an ethical political responsibility today to ensure that all people feel safe to go into the public sphere and voice their opinions and engage in political conversation and protest actions?

DB: Gee, so much hangs on the word "safe" there, and in the campus context, that's a word I have suspicions about. You should be free to invite whom you want and to remove or rather exclude whom you want from the room you live in. But, you know, public spaces on campus I don't think should be designated "safe" on the basis of some group's desire to have it be just to themselves for a certain occasion which has not been planned in advance.

I suppose what you're getting at also is the feeling of impotence that a great many people without experience of public speaking or of public interactions on political issues may now have. And to use a word that has come up occasionally in these days: I think the remedy for that, to improve that state of things, is *education*, which gives you (in a setting like Bard or Yale) some serious practice at speaking, at hearing other people speak, at replying to points with evidence and argument. A lot of people don't have that kind of practice. They don't get it in the shouting matches at Thanksgiving in their families, or at Passover where one faction, usually younger, disagrees about Israel with the other faction, usually older. And it would be good for education, including adult education, to develop an increasing confidence about the good of free speech among citizens.

On the other hand, I'll go back to my anti–social media point: the belief that you're engaging in public discourse by writing 140-character-long messages seems to me such an abject defection of responsibility that, to me, it beggars belief that any intelligent person would do it. And yet we know we have colleagues in these places, in universities, who do it. We have public officials who do it. Bad an example as Trump may be, there are a great many public officials who are copying him and doing as badly as they can, even if they're on the other side. So we need more exemplary public speech of the sort that Arendt had a very high-minded notion of. But how to make it exemplary is the problem.

KD: I'll just say very quickly, I think it may be better to speak of multiple public spheres, and I think we on the Left should view them tactically. So we should be committed to creating welcoming, inclusive public spheres for those who have less power, and we should be prepared to say that there should be no safe public sphere for white supremacists. The public spheres should be seen as weapons and resources, and those are just as subject to political and tactical considerations as anything else.

Q: My name's Austin Dilly. I'm a sophomore at Bard. I've been taking, or just finished up, a summer class at the Hannah Arendt Center with Micah White, and we've been talking a lot about a theory of activism, this idea that we can teach how to be an activist, teach how to create social change. And I've been struggling with this question myself: is it possible to dilute three thousand years of revolution and social movement into something that works at any time and place? I'm wondering what your thoughts are on this idea.

MB: Well, my first comment would be that I think there are practical skills that can be taught that are useful for political action, that are vaguely transferable across various different contexts; but that my political focus is less on activism per se than organizing that empowers people to pursue their material and social interests. And you don't have to be an activist to be involved in a movement that pursues that or to work with people in similar circumstances to [learn their approach to political action], though of course those skills help.

There are interesting debates within the Left on what is called activism versus what is called organizing. I think it gets unnecessarily polarized, and there are benefits to what is called both, and there's a lot of gray area. So I'm not trying to make a larger point, but that I think that there's a tendency toward a notion of professionalization of activism which I think is really problematic and counterproductive [in terms of] people feeling like they can build a better world without having to step outside of who they are.

DB: Almost all my protest that could have registered in the public eye has been in the form of writing, not marching and getting arrested. And most of it has been since the year 2001, when I think my country drove off a cliff and we haven't recovered from it yet. Therefore the objects of my protest have been America's wars (we're now in six, including Yemen) and in support of civil liberties. It is a source of regret to me that in campus discussions particularly, the Left can't be assumed to be friendly to civil liberties.

I only want to make one point—not even a point, a reminder—about the potential cooperation, always, between a protest movement and a political party. So in the late 1850s you have the founding of a new political party, the Republican Party—Abraham Lincoln close to the roots of that—whose policy on slavery was "No extension of slavery." No extension of slavery, period. They saw themselves as constitutional moderates on the pattern of the Whig Party, not at all identical with Abolitionists. One of the leaders of the abolitionist movement was Frederick Douglass. In his great speech at the unveiling of the Freedman's Monument—in 1876, in Washington, D.C.—Douglass spoke this sentence about Lincoln, and it's about the relation between a radical protester and—what shall we say?—a wise and courageous leader working within a political system. Douglass said (I'm paraphrasing), "Viewed from the genuine abolition ground, Mr. Lincoln was tardy, cold, dull, and indifferent. But considering of the sentiments of his countrymen, which he was bound as a statesman to consult, he was swift, zealous, radical, and determined."

You have to live with that complex thought, I think, if you want to look ahead in some way to the cooperation at times between a political power or an established large organization and the smaller protest movements that are seeking to be an impetus to a different kind of change.

KD: We've just about three minutes left, so I think what we'll do is, we'll collect several questions, and then we'll give final comments to our guests, and we'll wrap it up there. So maybe three questions . . .

Q: I just wanted to sort of ask about the implicit violence in nonviolent protest—specifically, you brought up Gandhi a lot and Martin Luther King, for example. Some of the most powerful images that come out of the civil rights movement are of the police violently assaulting protestors. Gandhi's tactics involved a lot of sort of creating an object of violence to be presented in a public sphere. And then I wonder, what is a public gathering, or this enormous mass of people, in the example of Gandhi or Martin Luther King? Is it a public opinion poll, as Mark Bray put it, or is there some sort of implicit threat of violence in large public gatherings? And I was wondering—the question is, is the power consolidated in public protest and public gathering based in violence, in implicit violence, in the threat of a large group of people, or is it something else?

Q: Yesterday, from the discussion from Rise Up Kingston, there was a mention of capitalism. And when you asked the question "What is violence?" so far I've heard no discussion of the market, the coercion of work, and if you can't work, you starve. So the state is not simply a creature of its own. It's related to the market, it enforces the market. And I was wondering if anticapitalism is an important part of protest movements today.

Q: I was interested in hearing each of you speak on the Second Amendment and the original context for which it was drafted—not what some of my neighbors in my small town think of as the right to go deer hunting—and its applicability, if any, as a tool of protest for today's issues, because I know there are groups on the Right that think that, and I'm just wondering your thoughts.

KD: Short, final responses.

DB: I'll jump into all of them.

On the matter of the violence that has resulted from mass nonviolent disobedience, where policemen directed hoses and brought dogs to attack King's protestors in the American South, or the British ordered their soldiers to fire on Gandhi's protesters in Amritsar—I'm not sure quite what (maybe metaphysical) point was being made. The protest in both cases was nonviolent; the response of public authority was violent. In both cases, in the very long run it led to the abolition of the oppressive system in question. The nonviolence one is speaking of refers to a principle of conduct followed by the protesters. It is not doubted that the state is a source of violence; and perhaps mass gatherings as such, or perhaps the very scene of disorder as such, causes friction, causes—what to say—neurotic abreactions in people who see that authorities are going to clamp down, and so those people conclude that nonviolence is the cause of violence. But I think that's an oversubtle point. The principle of nonviolent action is not itself violent.

I won't comment on capitalism, just that we have a rich vocabulary for talking about these things: misery, oppression. "Violence" tends to be a word that we use for something more immediate, physical, and causing physical pain. So I'm not going to get into that.

For the Bill of Rights: the Second Amendment—which I'll read the text of—you're quite right, has been very much abused in interpretation. "A well-regulated militia being necessary to the security of a free state, the right of the people to keep and bear arms shall not be infringed." That's one sentence with one grammar. If you have any Latin, the grammar is ablative absolute and the key phrase is "being necessary to the security of a free state." The militia is the hook on which the right to bear arms hangs. These people were readers of Machiavelli and of *Cato's Letters* and Locke. They believed that a standing army was an undesirable thing. We've now had a standing army in the U.S. since 1945, completely against the principles of the Constitution.

In view of the danger posed by state power, smaller groups of people, if they were well regulated—that is, drilled, trained, etc.—were allowed to bear arms. Something like the National Guard is there contemplated, but a national guard that is not controlled by the central state. Whatever you think of the Second Amendment, it doesn't mean everybody can buy a bazooka or any of the other automatic machine gun–like weapons that are now available. I think the greatest danger is from a merging of the Second Amendment with the First Amendment. As I am a defender of free speech and assembly, the idea of weapons being carried to assemblies by some people attending them seems to me antithetical to free speech. It impinges on free speech.

MB: Yes, anticapitalism's important. Yes, capitalism is violent; it's a violent social relation. I would have gotten into it more, but I focused more on examples of violence that I thought would be more popularly self-evident; but you're right that that is a good example.

The issue of the kind of potential spectacle of popular resistance I think is an interesting point, but I would make two follow-up points: one is that most instances of nonviolent protest that are brutally repressed by the police do not generate popular support, unfortunately. Attached to that is the point that many nonviolent protests, when they get attacked by the police, are labeled as violent in the media. I've been in plenty of protests where the police started the violence, and it gets reported as conflicts or scuffles or what have you, which points to the fact that, as much as in theory you may want to have a nonviolent protest, it may not be reported that way.

Also, there are times in the past when violent protests have been brutally repressed and still generated support. One example that comes to mind would be May '68 in France. The brutal suppression of students on the barricades, brutal suppression by the police, generated a lot of popular support. So it's important to look at it contextually, politically: what do people think as different kinds of legitimate action?

As far as the Second Amendment per se, I'm much less knowledgeable about the intricacies of the Constitution; but the way it is interpreted, whether or not it should be, is that many forms of firearms are legally available. There are some groups on the Left, both in the past and in the present, that take up arms—Red Neck Revolt, for example; Trigger Warning, which is a queer and trans gun club; Huey P. Newton Gun Club—there are a number of examples like this. I understand why that would be a decision that people who feel like they're under threat of attack would take, but it's not the kind of politics I do.

Organizing from the Ground

Sarah Jaffe

We're here to talk about organizing on the ground. I actually wrote a book about that subject, which I'm going to plug shamelessly.[1] I could talk about many, many different examples of organizing and how that builds and sustains social movements; I'm sure we'll get into many more of them in the Q&A, and I'm happy to answer questions about anyone that you can think of.

I wanted to talk today about teacher strikes, because it's my favorite subject and because we're in the middle of a massive teacher strike wave. That provides me a great opportunity to talk about organizing and history and how all of these things are used to build and sustain the movements that we see and that we often assume are spontaneous.

Last year teachers in West Virginia began to walk out of the classroom, in February. That led to strikes, statewide strikes, across West Virginia, Oklahoma, Arizona, strikes in Colorado, North Carolina, and Kentucky. This year, the school year started with strikes across the state of Washington; a strike in East Strasburg, Pennsylvania, that I went and visited recently; and strike votes in Seattle and Los Angeles. Seattle has settled; Los Angeles is in mediation, meaning we could soon see teachers on strike in the second-largest school district in the country, the largest being New York City, where it is illegal for teachers to strike, for all public employees to strike in fact. I will get back to those laws at some point, I am sure.

But I want to start out by talking about what a strike is, because a strike is not a protest. A strike is something very specific. It is the withdrawal of your labor in order to stop the functioning of your workplace or a system. It is a very specific way to disrupt the functioning of an institution, to demonstrate your power. In the case of teachers, it is to demonstrate the fact that, if teachers stop going to work, the entire school system shuts down. It screws up a lot of people's lives because their kids are now not at school. It throws a wrench into everybody's day-to-day functioning, and, it turns out, when you can organize that across an entire state, you can effectively force a hostile governor and a hostile state legislature to do what you want—i.e., vote a 5 percent raise for every public employee in the State of West Virginia.

I write about labor. This is my favorite thing to do. It was not a very popular thing to try to be a labor journalist about ten years ago. And then people started going on strike, and suddenly people are calling me, going, "Hey, can you write a thing that explains this to people?" Because strikes were out of fashion in this country. Strikes had dropped off since the 1980s, when, famously, Ronald Reagan broke the air traffic controller strike. And if you pull up a strike frequency chart it drops right off in about 1982. So the revival of the strike among teachers, among public school teachers and particularly among public school teachers in what we think of now as red states, is significant for a lot of reasons. One is that we're seeing strikes at all. Two is that teachers in particular are challenging the narrative of austerity that we have been fed for a while, but particularly since the 2008 financial crisis; they are challenging the idea that it is overpaid public employees who caused the crisis, and not an out-of-control financial industry.

Teachers in these particular states that got a lot of attention last year are in states without strong unions, in some cases without any legal protections for their unions, without any right to collective bargaining at all, and they still managed to organize statewide strikes. We heard a lot already this morning about how social media is bad for you. I will just counter that with saying that the West Virginia strike started in a Facebook group; the Arizona strike started in a Facebook group. And what we've seen with social movements, again in the era of social media, is that they spread like things do on the internet; they go viral, they get replicated, and this is true of a lot of different movements. What happened with these strikes is that they did indeed go viral, and people replicated the way that they were done. They made Facebook groups; they started having walkouts, protests, built up to getting every county in their state to go on strike.

These are strikes across multiple unions in many cases. These are strikes of largely workers who are not members of unions. In most of these states a majority of the teachers were not members of unions; but nevertheless they all managed to go on strike, demonstrating the thing that I call the Newsies Rule. You've seen the musical *Newsies,* or the Disney movie, where the lead characters says, "If we strike, then we're a union."

These strikes seemed spontaneous, they seemed quick; they were organized in a Facebook group. But there were two things at the roots of these particular strikes, and this started in West Virginia: the counties that went out on strike first in West Virginia were the mining counties. It was Mingo County, Wyoming County. These were the places where the mine wars were fought. We heard a lot about violence in the previous panel, and I could talk a lot more about the violent history of how labor unions were formed in this country. People died, a lot of them in some cases. There were actual shootouts. There's a wonderful movie called *Matewan* that you can watch if you're interested in the history of the mine wars, because what happened, sometimes you had state violence, sometimes you had private security violence—some folks called the Pinkertons shot a lot of miners back in the day.

This history is not that old. This goes back to before the 1935 National Labor Relations Act, which governs labor relations in this country; although at this point the legal regime behind it has basically been dismantled. And again, these were violent, violent struggles against capital. When you're talking to teachers in West Virginia, you have teachers who have parents and grandparents who were in the mines, people who remember this. They don't just remember it because they saw a movie; they remember it because it happened to their grandfather, and that is deep in this memory, that this is how you have power: you go on strike and you stop the workings of the machine until you get some sort of fair treatment from the boss.

The other, more recent history that led up to these strikes starts in 2011, and it starts in Wisconsin, and it starts with, number one, austerity—blaming teachers and public workers for the state of the economy after the financial crisis. When Scott Walker was elected governor of Wisconsin, he pushed forward a law that took collective bargaining rights away from public sector employees, and he thought that he wasn't going to get much pushback. And then suddenly—well, first it started out with the graduate students. Since I'm at a university I've got to give a shout-out to the Teaching Assistants Association at the University of Wisconsin–Madison who started the protests. And then more people came, and then more people came, and suddenly there were twenty thousand, thirty thousand people camping out in the Wisconsin state capitol. There are wonderful videos you can find on YouTube, pictures you can see of people wearing red with the State of Wisconsin on their shirts, flooding the capitol. And when you saw the pictures from West Virginia, Oklahoma. One of the things that the movement was called among teachers this year was Red for Ed. Everybody wore red and showed up at the state capitol. And you look at this, and you go, *Ohhh, I've seen this before.*

The other thing specifically among teachers' unions was the Chicago Teachers Union strike in 2012. What happened successfully first in Chicago was that a group of teachers within their union decided that the union was not doing its job very well, and they organized a caucus, and they took power in the union, and they managed to clear a very high threshold for a strike vote, and they went on strike, and they brought, in this case, a hostile Democratic administration to the bargaining table—and won.

Since Chicago there have been reform caucuses like this all over the country. Some have succeeded in taking power; some have just succeeded in challenging the leadership to become more militant, to make demands, to take strike votes, to be willing to go on strike—in places like Los Angeles, which you might see on strike very soon; in Massachusetts; there's a caucus here in New York; there is the St. Paul Federation of Teachers, Seattle; many others.

This is all what's been feeding into the thing that we see and experience in the pages of major publications as a spontaneous eruption of teacher militancy across the country. This is also under the broader context of, again, austerity narratives, of both parties being willing to say that it's teachers' fault that public schools are "failing," the push for charter schools, etc., etc. And so: strikes. Strikes are dramatic, strikes get headlines, strikes win.

But after the strike you have to go back to the subject of this talk, which is organizing from the ground. In so many of these states they're out of the headlines, but they're organizing, adding members, changing how they think about making and taking power, wielding power. All of these things are still in the works, and so we don't know exactly where the next eruption is going to be; but I can tell you that there's going to be one.

---

1. Sarah Jaffe, *Necessary Trouble: Americans in Revolt* (New York: Nation Books, 2016).

On Constitutional Disobedience

Christopher Schmidt

In this essay I consider how reform activists use the United States Constitution as a tool of social movement mobilization. I focus in particular on situations in which activists advance a claim on the meaning of the Constitution that diverges from what the courts—and especially the court at the top of the American judicial hierarchy, the U.S. Supreme Court—say the Constitution means. In these situations, we have, on the one hand, an official reading of the Constitution. This reading is defined by judges, people trained in the law who are expected to follow recognized methods of legal interpretation and to explain their reasoning in written opinions, and is generally accepted as authoritative by government actors and the legal profession. And we have, on the other hand, an alternative, insurgent reading of the Constitution. Defined not by judges but by activists and iconoclasts, this reading is recognized as authoritative only by other activists and iconoclasts. Its power lies in its ability to motivate, guide, and legitimate a social movement.

What I'm describing is utterly commonplace. Judges are paid to tell us what the law is, and people generally listen to them. At the same time, people other than judges often declare their own beliefs about what the Constitution means. These alternative, unofficial constitutional claims, while commonplace, raise important and challenging questions about the role of the Constitution in the American reform tradition. We live in a constitutional democracy in which the people have largely accepted the Supreme Court as the authoritative interpreter of their Constitution.[1] The Supreme Court has even gone so far as to declare that its interpretation of the Constitution should be treated by everyone else as the same as the text of the Constitution itself; and that therefore the oath government officials take to "support and defend" the Constitution requires obedience to the Court's reading of the Constitution.[2]

The existence of unofficial, alternative, insurgent readings of the Constitution therefore can be seen as a kind of *constitutional disobedience*. As I show in this essay, constitutional disobedience can be a powerful tool for social movement mobilization. But it also presents distinctive obstacles and pitfalls for movement activists.

I illustrate the idea of constitutional disobedience as a tool of social movement mobilization through two case studies. One is the student lunch counter sit-in movement of 1960.[3] The other is the Tea Party movement.[4]

The Sit-Ins

The sit-in movement—the student protest campaign against so-called whites-only lunch counters—swept across the American South in the winter and spring of 1960. The event that sparked the movement happened on 1 February 1960, in Greensboro, North Carolina, when four African American men, all first-year students at the local black college, sat down at the downtown Woolworth store lunch counter and, upon being denied service, refused to leave. These young men, soon known to history as the Greensboro Four, came back the next day, this time with more classmates, and the group sat once again in defiance of the store's refusal to serve black patrons at the lunch counter. Day by day, the Greensboro sit-in protest grew. Students in other North Carolina cities started their own protests. Soon students in other states joined what had suddenly become a mass movement. By the end of February, sit-in protests had taken place in thirty cities in seven different states. A month later, the movement had spread to forty-eight cities in eleven states. In all, an estimated fifty thousand people eventually took part in the sit-in movement of 1960. Students sat-in, marched, picketed, and boycotted discriminating businesses. They faced verbal abuse; some were assaulted by gangs of white thugs. Thousands were arrested, charged with disorderly conduct, breach of the peace, or trespassing on private property.

The sit-in movement was a watershed event. It energized and transformed the struggle for racial equality, moving the leading edge of the movement from the courtrooms and legislative halls to the streets and putting a new, younger generation of activists on the frontlines. It gave birth to the Student Nonviolent Coordinating Committee, one of the most important activist groups of the 1960s. The sit-ins elevated the issue of racial nondiscrimination in public accommodations to a central issue of the civil rights struggle, alongside the right to vote and educational equality. The protest campaign set in motion a chain of events that would culminate in the Civil Rights Act of 1964, which banned racial discrimination in public accommodations across the nation.

Although the student protesters were key participants in what would become a revolution in American civil rights law, they had an ambivalent relationship with lawyers and courts. For many who took part in the sit-ins, direct action protest was as an alternative to litigation and lobbying—pathways to racial justice that these young men and women had seen promise much but deliver little. They saw the courts as something to be avoided—not because they might lose in court, but because even if they won, they were skeptical that real change would follow. This was the lesson of *Brown v. Board of Education*. The 1954 Supreme Court decision striking down state-mandated segregation raised hopes but produced little actual school desegregation in the South. Most of the African American students who took part in the sit-ins attended segregated schools, even after the *Brown* ruling came down. *Brown* made clear that racial change required more than proclamations from distant courts. The students admired Thurgood Marshall, the head of the litigation arm of the National Association for the Advancement of Colored People (NAACP), and his team of civil rights lawyers, but they were also wary of lawyers, particularly their tendency to steer issues into the formal legal processes. Skepticism toward lawyers was in part a way for the students to maintain control over their protest movement.

This skepticism was mutual. The civil rights lawyers admired the courage of the students, and they would eventually provide much-needed representation when the students faced criminal prosecution for their protest activities. Initially, however, many established civil rights lawyers were skeptical about the protests. Some were critical about the tactic the students had chosen, fearing the sit-ins would get headlines without securing real change, which required changing laws. And they believed the students lacked a strong legal basis for their actions. Prevailing judicial doctrine did not align with what the students, by virtue of their actions, demanded.

The lawyers' legal skepticism traced to an area of constitutional law known as the "state action" doctrine. In its most straightforward terms, this doctrine holds that the constraints of the Fourteenth Amendment only apply to government officials or "state actors." The amendment's equal protection clause thus clearly applies to, say, a public school, but it would not apply to a members-only social club. With regard to the lunch counter sit-in movement, the relevant constitutional question was where on the public-private spectrum to place a privately owned and operated business operation that served the general public and received a government license to do so. Even if one assumed that a privately operated public accommodation, such as a Woolworth lunch counter, did not itself meet the criteria of a state actor for Fourteenth Amendment purposes, the constitutional question was still not resolved. During the sit-ins, many store owners called on the police to arrest unwanted patrons on trespassing charges. At this point, the state clearly was involved in enforcing the store owners' racial discrimination policy. These doctrinal complexities made many civil rights lawyers wary of the viability of the sit-ins as a vehicle for constitutional reform. When the sit-ins occurred, the NAACP lawyers were having enough difficulty getting the courts to enforce school desegregation, where after *Brown* the law was clearly on their side. They did not think it wise to launch a new round of constitutional challenges in a situation where private property rights and the Fourteenth Amendment's state action limitation posed significant obstacles to success in the courts.

The students were not necessarily aware of these doctrinal complexities. These were the legalisms that occupied lawyers versed in the nuances of constitutional law, not passionate young men and women, some of whom were still in high school. Yet it would be wrong to say that the students were not concerned with the Constitution. From the earliest lunch counter sit-ins of the 1960 movement, participants and observers described the fundamental issue at stake—the right to racially nondiscriminatory service in public accommodations—as a matter not only of right and wrong, not only of dollars and cents, but also of constitutional principle. The students often spoke of their protest as a refutation of the idea of "second-class citizenship." And although they did not necessarily see themselves as following in the footsteps of the lawyers who won *Brown*, they did see themselves as following the example of those brave black students at Little Rock and elsewhere who risked their lives and endured unimaginable abuse to exercise their constitutional right to attend desegregated schools.

Lawyers and legal scholars recognized that as a matter of constitutional law a substantial doctrinal leap was necessary to get from *Brown*, dealing with schools, which were unquestionable state actors, to a constitutional holding prohibiting discrimination in privately owned public accommodations. But in the popular discourse surrounding the sit-ins, the belief was common-place that the public accommodation problem could be resolved by the same constitutional principle as the school segregation problem. When Martin Luther King Jr. spoke to the student participants in the sit-in movement, he described the challenge they faced as the logical extension of the school segregation struggle. "Separate facilities, whether in eating places or public schools, are inherently unequal," he told the students, echoing the famous words of the *Brown* opinion.[5] The six-year experience with school integration as a constitutional issue allowed for this sort of intuitive transformation of the sit-ins into a constitutional issue to which the logic of *Brown*'s desegregation principle seemed to apply. "It seems clear that this 'lunch counter movement' will become a historic milestone in the American Negro's efforts to win the rights of citizenship which are guaranteed him by the Constitution," declared *Commonweal* magazine.[6]

As a claim pressed upon national opinion and the political branches of government, the students' actions offered, in effect, an effort to reinterpret the scope of the equal protection of the law. The protesters were making a case to the larger society that the principle of equal protection entailed a government responsibility to stand on the side of those combating the most egregious, dignity-sapping manifestations of Jim Crow, regardless of whether existing constitutional doctrine delineated these acts as "private" or not.

Thurgood Marshall and the other NAACP lawyers overcame their initial skepticism toward the students' constitutional claim, and by the spring of 1960, they were announcing that they would represent the students and, if necessary, appeal any criminal convictions of sit-in protesters all the way to the Supreme Court. They got their cases before the Court, but they were never able to win a great *Brown*-like victory. Between 1961 and 1964, the jus-tices heard case after case in which NAACP lawyers urged them to recognize a constitutional right to nondiscriminatory service in public accommodations. But they never did so. The justices found ways to overturn the protester con-victions on narrow, technical grounds, but a majority never embraced the students' constitutional claim. The state action doctrine held fast.[7]

The students' legal claim ultimately prevailed, but this happened not in the courts but in Congress. Pressured by the growing strength of direct action protests, and particularly the Birmingham campaign in the spring of 1963, Congress passed the Civil Rights Act of 1964, which included a provision prohibiting racial discrimination in hotels, restaurants, and other kinds of public accommodations across the nation.

The sit-in movement put on display a plea to the nation for an alternative vision of American race relations, one in which African American women and men could walk into a Southern store, sit down at the lunch counter, and be treated like any other paying customer. Thoreau called such a display "the performance of right."[8] This was a vision that, from the perspective of most Americans, flowed from the same constitutional principle that animated the *Brown* decision, the Montgomery bus boycott, and the school desegregation battles in Little Rock and elsewhere.

From the perspective of the courts and lawyers, however, the sit-ins raised distinct constitutional issues. The students' claimed constitutional right was at best an aspirational claim for the courts to rethink the limitations of constitutional doctrine. But to many—including a contingent of the Supreme Court—it was simply wrong as a matter of constitutional law. From this perspective, the sit-is were not only bold acts of defiance against Southern race relations, they were also acts of constitutional disobedience.

The Tea Party
Another episode of constitutional disobedience, this one involving protagonists pursuing a very different agenda under very different historical circumstances, was the Tea Party movement, which gained momentum in 2009 and 2010. Among the many distinctive and notable aspects of the Tea Party movement was the fact that its adherents placed the Constitution at the center of the movement's identity and used the Constitution, quite self-consciously, as part of its mobilizing strategy.

Tea Party constitutionalism revolved around several fundamental assumptions. One was that the solutions to the problems facing the United States today could be found in the words of the Constitution and the insights of its framers. The founding period was a special moment, never to be replicated. Tea Party advocates relied on texts that even argued that the founders were divinely inspired.

Another of its tenets was that the meaning of the Constitution and the lessons of history are readily accessible to American citizens who take the time to educate themselves. Tea Party constitutionalism was explicitly premised on a commitment to citizen empowerment—on the idea that individual citizens should read the document for themselves, come to conclusions about constitutional meaning based on this reading, and act upon those convictions. All Americans, not just lawyers and judges, have a responsibility to understand the Constitution and to act faithfully toward it. The Constitution is accessible. As Dick Armey, the former House majority leader who went on to be head of a major Tea Party group, told audiences: "If you don't understand the Constitution, I'll buy you a dictionary."[9] A popular Tea Party bumper sticker read: "I have this crazy idea that the Constitution *actually means something*."[10]

Yet another defining characteristics of Tea Party constitutionalism was its enthusiastic embrace of originalism as the appropriate method of constitutional interpretation. This was constitutional interpretation energized by a generous dose of founder worship. "In order to restore our country," said right-wing provocateur and Tea Party ringleader Glenn Beck, "we have to restore the men who founded it on certain principles to the rightful place in our national psyche." He called on his followers to organize groups to study the founders. "When you read these guys, it's alive," Beck once said on his television show. "It's like, you know, reading the scriptures. It's like reading the Bible. It is alive today. And it only comes alive when you need it."[11]

That the founders and the Constitution they drafted is "alive today" was central to Tea Party ideology.[12] For the Tea Party, the past was anything but a foreign country. Tea Party events featured the founders' portraits and words and even their modern avatars (in the form of historical reenactors). The founders were usually portrayed as comfortable companions—admirable, likable, and invariably in agreement with Tea Party dogma. The constitutional history Tea Partiers embraced was tendentious at best, and often it was simply wrong, but it worked. It served its intended purpose, which was the creation of a popular historical consciousness, of collective memory, all in the service of mobilizing people in the here and now.

Notably, Tea Party constitutionalism said relatively little about the courts, and what it did say was often dismissive. Although the rapid, and to most constitutional scholars surprising, emergence of a viable constitutional litigation challenge to the Affordable Care Act moderated this antijudicial sentiment for a time, during the Tea Party's formative period, the courts were not its preferred battleground for its project of constitutional reconstruction. Tea Party supporters generally felt that the Supreme Court was not on their side.[13] The Tea Party instead focused its efforts on constitutional agitation outside the courts.

As to the substance of the Tea Party's constitutional claims, they were controversial, and often quite extreme, but they were not particularly new. Its foundational constitutional claim was that the primary role of the Constitution is to limit the powers of the federal government. Several corollaries flowed from this master assumption. One is that the text of the Constitution and the history of its framing and ratification clearly define these limits. Another is that liberty and power are in inherent tension, and therefore the surest path for protecting individual liberty is to limit the scope of government authority. For the most part, the Tea Party's constitutional agenda was a standard libertarian menu of proposals, although with its own distinctive a populist and history-infused spin. The achievement of the Tea Party as a campaign for constitutional reconstruction was not in the novelty or creativity of their constitutional claims. Rather, it was in the movement's ability to locate effective mechanisms for promulgating these claims and making them compelling to a significant portion of the American people and their elected representatives. These mechanisms of constitutional practice, such as educational outreach efforts, state-level mobilization, and national electoral politics, provided the engine of the Tea Party as a constitutional movement.

Organizing a constitutional study group, holding public readings of the Constitution, working to elect a candidate who shares Tea Party constitutional commitments, convincing a state legislature to pass a resolution denouncing federal overreach, lobbying Congress to simply do *less* (because much of what it had been doing was beyond its constitutional authority)—while none of these acts were especially consequential individually, and while much of this can be dismissed as symbolic politics, they were, when viewed through the lens of popular constitutional mobilization, all achievements of Tea Party constitutionalism. Taken together, they add up to a significant achievement for a grassroots movement in an era supposedly dominated by popular deference to judicial supremacy on matters of constitutional interpretation. Tea Party activists located pathways to making claims and to having those claims recognized in meaningful ways without turning to the courts.

Three Lessons

I conclude with some lessons drawn from these historical episodes of constitutional disobedience as a tool of social mobilization. The most obvious lesson is that the Constitution can be a powerful mobilization tool for American social movements. A critical challenge for any movement that seeks to rally some contingent of the American people to participate in a campaign to displace prevailing social or political norms is to identify a stable foundation to promulgate and legitimate the movement's insurgent vision. In the United States, the Constitution often serves this role. It is a document that inspires unique reverence in modern American society. Even as Americans are increasingly disillusioned with their governing institutions, the document itself remains sacrosanct. Whereas invoking religious beliefs or moral sensibilities offers precious little common ground, most all Americans accept the Constitution as a legitimate foundation for forming our shared commitments.[14] People generally assume that the Constitution is relatively determinate in its content, that even if it doesn't contain all the answers about the proper balance between governing authority and individual rights, it contains many of them. Framing a bold call for change in terms of foundational principles that most accept as authoritative has often been a powerful move for reform campaigns.

But once we recognize that the Constitution is, to a degree, determinate— that it has meaning, which can be discerned by generally accepted modes of interpretation—then a new complication arises, namely that the constitutional claims a movement embraces may be deemed *wrong*. On the American scene, the risks and rewards of constitutional determinacy are magnified by the existence of the U.S. Supreme Court, an institution that Americans have widely accepted as the preeminent interpretator of our Constitution. So movements that want to rally around a constitutional claim have to take into account not only the viability of the claim as a matter of extrajudicial constitutional culture but also whether the Supreme Court has weighed in on the particular constitutional question and, if so, whether or not the movement's constitutional claim aligns with the Court's.

Movements often find strength in rallying around the Supreme Court's interpretation of the Constitution—in launching campaigns of constitutional obedience. Civil rights activists did so after *Brown*, the pro-choice movement has done so in the decades since *Roe v. Wade*, as has the gun rights movement in the wake of the Court's 2008 ruling in *District of Columbia v. Heller*. Aligning social protest efforts with authoritative interpretations of the Constitution not only provides opportunities for parallel litigation campaigns by movement-allied lawyers but also places the legitimating authority of the Supreme Court behind the movement.

But constitutional obedience also has costs for mobilization efforts. Rallying around a Supreme Court ruling can be less energizing for a protest campaign than attacking the Court. *Brown*, at least in its immediate aftermath, did more to inspire white segregationist backlash than pro–civil rights forces.[15] The decade following *Roe* saw the antiabortion movement make remarkable gains, which *Roe*'s defenders struggled to match.[16] Movements that align with prevailing judicial interpretations of the Constitution also run a higher risk of being coopted by lawyers. When constitutional litigation is a viable pathway, lawyers will often want to get involved, and it can be difficult to maintain robust movement activism when too much attention is turned to courtroom showdowns.[17]

From the perspective of movement mobilization, challenging the prevailing judicial reading of the Constitution—constitutional disobedience—has its own risks and rewards. One obvious risk is that the movement's claim will be dismissed as fringe, irresponsible, or just plain wrong. Many believe the Tea Party's constitutional claims fell into one of these categories. It's hard to take seriously, for example, a common Tea Party tenet that the modern administrative state violates the Constitution—in large part because that claim runs against almost a century of well-established constitutional case law. Lawyers versed in the state action doctrine often chastised the student sit-in activists and their supporters as naive and wrongheaded when they claimed the Constitution supported their claim to nondiscriminatory service at lunch counters. In modern American constitutionalism we have what one scholar has called the problem of "judicial overhang," which is a tendency to be excessively deferential to judicial interpretations of the Constitution, a tendency that often manifests in the expectation that even when the Court has not spoken on an issue, its word should be awaited as the determinative resolution to any given constitutional dispute.[18]

As I have sought to emphasize, under the right circumstances constitutional disobedience also has unique rewards. Challenging or dismissing the Court as out of touch or captured by some powerful special interests resonates with the populism and anti-elitism that often animates social movements. The student sit-in protests developed a unifying movement identity by framing their actions in opposition to the work of lawyers and judges. The Tea Party effectively stoked populist sentiments by lashing out against elites, a group that included lawyers and judges. Constitutional disobedience also can encourage valuable social movement creativity, for it channels constitutional claim making into nonjudicial pathways that can provide powerful reform agendas for reform activism. The sit-in protests located a tactic that advanced their demand for dignity and equality but did not require them to rely on lawyers to win cases in the courts. The mechanisms by which the Tea Party sought to promulgate their constitutional claims and to make them compelling to the people and their elected representatives were strikingly effective.

The challenge for movement activists who want to exploit the possibilities of constitutional disobedience is to locate tactics of constitutional claim making that function largely outside the realm of the courts, that retain some sense of constitutional reasoning as distinct from raw politics, and that energize and mobilize significant numbers of people.

1. See, for example, Keith E. Whittington, *Political Foundations of Judicial Supremacy: The Presidency, the Supreme Court, and Constitutional Leadership in U.S. History* (Princeton: Princeton University Press, 2007).

2. *Cooper v. Aaron*, 358 U.S. 1, 18 (1958).

3. This is the subject of my recently published book. Christopher W. Schmidt, *The Sit-Ins: Protest and Legal Change in the Civil Rights Era* (Chicago: University of Chicago Press, 2018).

4. I have also written on this subject. See Christopher W. Schmidt, "The Tea Party and the Constitution," *Hastings Constitutional Law Quarterly* 39 (2011): 193–252; and "Popular Constitutionalism on the Right: Lessons from the Tea Party," *Denver University Law Review* 88 (2011): 523–57.

5. Martin Luther King Jr., "A Creative Protest" (16 February 1960), in *The Papers of Martin Luther King, Jr.*, vol. 5, ed. Clayborne Carson (Berkeley: University of California Press, 1992), 368.

6. Editorial, "Negro Protests," *Commonweal* 72 (1 April 1960): 4.

7. I offer a detailed analysis of the Supreme Court's struggles with the sit-in cases in *The Sit-Ins*, chap. 5; and "The Sit-In Cases: Explaining the Great Aberration of the Warren Court," *Journal of Supreme Court History* 43 (2018): 294–320.

8. Henry David Thoreau, "Resistance to Civil Government" (1849), reprinted in *Thoreau: Political Writings*, ed. Nancy L. Rosenblum (Cambridge: Cambridge University Press, 1996), 8.

9. Kate Zernike, *Boiling Mad: Inside Tea Party America* (New York: Henry Holt, 2010), 67.

10. Schmidt, "The Tea Party and the Constitution," 207.

11. Jill Lepore, *The Whites of Their Eyes: The Tea Party's Revolution and the Battle over American History* (Princeton: Princeton University Press, 2010), 156–57.

12. See generally, Lepore, *The Whites of Their Eyes*.

13. See, for example, Angelo M. Codevilla, *The Ruling Class: How They Corrupted America and What We Can Do about It* (New York: Beaufort, 2010), 42–43.

14. See generally, Michael Kammen, *A Machine That Would Go of Itself: The Constitution in American Culture* (New York: Knopf, 1986).

15. See Michael J. Klarman, *From Jim Crow to Civil Rights* (New York: Oxford University Press, 2004).

16. See Mary Ziegler, *After Roe: The Lost History of the Abortion Debate* (Cambridge: Harvard University Press, 2015).

17. See, for example, Gordon Silverstein, *Law's Allure: How Law Shapes, Constrains, Saves, and Kills Politics* (New York: Cambridge University Press, 2009).

18. Mark Tushnet, *Taking the Constitution Away from the Courts* (Princeton: Princeton University Press, 1999).

Discussion: MLK and the Legacy of Civil Disobedience in America

Kenyon Victor Adams
Amy Schiller
Thomas Chatterton Williams

Kenyon Victor Adams

> "Perhaps more than any other people Americans have been locked in a deadly struggle with time, with history . . . and a great part of our optimism, like our progress, has been bought at the cost of ignoring the process through which we've arrived at any given moment in our national existence. "—Ralph Ellison

Since we are here concerned with citizenship, I want to preface my brief remarks by signaling the relationship between citizenship and national memory, and how the concept of race, as we see in various historical examples, necessarily replaces that of citizenship. Race, with its weird science and capacious imaginative scope, once assigned and proliferated, features the negation of historical and genealogical identity, but also, arguably, the national identity—of all subjects within its range of address.

The potential fruition, even beauty, of citizenship can perhaps be experienced only by a people who have access to recall or ingest the story of a nation's becoming, and their own place within that narrative. So the concept of race, and particularly of whiteness as it has been developed since the seventeenth century, imminently threatens the virtue of American citizenship, democracy, and the future of the national community. It was this insight, imbued by particular theological claims and critiques, that was Martin Luther King Jr.'s central concern, and it is there we must locate possible outcomes of his work—or apparent disparities in his legacy.

Before critiquing or even assessing King's legacy, we must ask ourselves, "How do I know what I know about King?" And I want to suggest that there is something distinctly inherent to American life that makes fragile our national memory and troubles any certainties about formal readings of King, and the freedom movements with which we identify his legacy of contemplation and action. So let me begin with King's own words, and an invocation of what I believe is his most rigorous and efficacious contribution to the American project—and to what may be its most ephemeral and essential expression: citizenship.

> If America does not respond creatively to the challenge to banish racism, some future historian will have to say that a great

civilization died because it lacked the soul and commitment to make justice a reality for all.

And, again:

The ultimate logic of racism is genocide.

I want to propose a reading of the Freedom Movement as a nascent antiracist movement that aspired toward an intersectional and pan-African identity, and that, despite its limitations, enacted a foray into various embodied discourses and discourses of the body. King's identification of racial hierarchy, and its predicate, whiteness, as a critical threat to American democracy must also remain central as we reflect on King's mission and strategies. Any identifiable fissures in his public activism will reveal a corresponding pressure from this immense site of social harm.

King's methodology of nonviolent, direct action relies on two basic elements that have proven artificial or unsustainable:

(1) the delusional character of American democracy; and
(2) the inherent and inextricable Christianness of white-identifying citizens.

Both of these assumptions can perhaps be attributed to a kind of spiritual naivete in King regarding the violent nature of whiteness, a sentiment nurtured within King himself as an article of personal faith, and also as a theological and political figure. King's tactic was to move the proverbial needle on white moral capacity, trusting that so-called "white America's" rendition of Christianity would serve as the ultimate arbiter—rather than the justifying agent—of America's liminal democracy. I'll offer three points on this, and an observation.

Elements of King's strategy that have proven artificial or unsustainable:

(1) That there is an equivalence between white identity and black identity, between black beingness and whiteness. This may have resulted from a failure to consider a historical and ontological account of whiteness.

(2) The idea that white-identifying Americans are fundamentally God-fearing people and will capitulate to the moral demands of historical Christianity.

(3) The problem of the "exceptional Negro": the idea that if black people can perform and depict such a high standard of moral,

intellectual, and physical rectitude, they will inevitably overcome white prejudice and therefore transcend racial hierarchy, by achieving through exertion the standards of superiority and entitlement upon which whiteness is based, placing the responsibility of eradicating systemic injustices on the citizens most negatively affected by those systems.

The first two assumptions are misguided in that they fail to identify that the most critical paradox separating blackness and whiteness is not contrasting heritages, but a dialectic of construction and erasure. Whiteness is fundamentally an erasure and therefore a violence, not only for the subject it makes white but also to those whose lives and narratives must be erased in order to preserve, sustain, and expand the preeminence—and indeed, the righteousness and innocence—of whiteness and its subjects. In King's terms, *it gives a false sense of superiority to the segregator, and a false sense of inferiority to the segregated*.

Whiteness at once assumes a givenness in relation to subjectivity, divinity, agency, and fruition, while it paradoxically erases family lineage, resists oral histories, rejects biological and theological claims of identity (as King argues in "Letter from Birmingham Jail"), and declares a self-pronunciation as origin. That is, whiteness names itself historically and persists in self-naming even as it paints over genealogies and other histories of the body.

While the concept of whiteness is rooted in erasure and forgetting—a way of making genealogy at once irrelevant and ultimate—blackness depends upon memory, not only embodied memory but also national memory. Blackness has emerged as the energy and vitality of pan-African peoples living in diaspora to claim and profess humanity, selfhood, citizenship, even divine adoption in the face of radical threats to their subjectivity, human dignity, and rights as citizens. Blackness as a construct of identity is a creative action, yielding robust and lasting contributions both within its subject and far beyond the bodies of those it seeks to liberate and imbue. King situated his own work inside of this expansive global energy.

Blackness can be and has been shared widely, often appropriated from its segregated contexts to be consumed by other peoples who relate to the context of violence in which blackness was engendered; but blackness also, as James Baldwin points out, has become one of the primary ways that white-identifying peoples seek to reconstruct or remedy the vacancy and disintegration that whiteness creates morally, relationally, historically, and cathartically.

Regarding black exceptionalism strategies: the exceptional Negro, in the case of King, offers moral license for the white-identifying person who accepts King to then be violent toward those who seem, by comparison, unexceptional. The *gospel of exceptionalism* has historically produced a backfire effect, by which white-identifying peoples and spaces accept the exceptional person of color on terms of proximity related to their own perceived superiority, and proceed to demonstrate deeper violence toward what they perceive to be standard or ordinary examples.

In Closing: An Observation

There has been at work a harmful misreading of the King legacy, which projects and sustains a patriarchal and individualist construal of the Freedom Movement, beginning with the idea that the Montgomery bus boycott was led and executed by a single man. This calculated fantasy has expanded to depict a contemporary, twenty-first-century Freedom Movement devoid of such leadership, and therefore bereft of critical, even moral, agency: quotidian lamentations claiming, "We don't have any leaders like that anymore." Yet various people remember the Freedom Movement differently, not only African Americans versus those who believe themselves to be white. And the ways in which we remember these things have become crucial to the prospect of progress.

The antiracist activist not only detracts from the legitimacy of whiteness but also seeks to construct an expansive pan-African humanism. Such as the kind we see in King. What might seem a weakness in King's antiracism, may actually be a failure of American memory to identify and contextualize the mission, character, and trajectory of King's work and thinking. And this breakdown of memory can be attributed, at least in part, to the effect of segregation on American identity, education, and the comprehensive, epistemological implications of racial hierarchy for human and social formation.

It is the antiracist position, and antiracist movements—including the work of Angela Davis, Black Lives Matter, various campus movements, the newly founded Antiracist Research and Policy Center, the Racial Imaginary Institute, and many others—that have carried on the deepest work of King, along with black liberationist, womanist, and queer theologies that are continually championing, and possibly recovering, the irrevocably compromised missiology, liturgies, and ideologies of Christianity in the United States.

If, in remembering King and seeking his legacy, we imagine a mythologized, patriarchal figurehead whose most significant contribution was the March on Washington, then we do not remember King accurately or well. Remembering King as an antiracist criminalized by his government, a strident opposer of white supremacy, a representative of the total activities of a resistance ignited in segregated communities across the United States, we will see the legacy still alive, and under threat.

Finally, we'd be remiss in this discussion not to mention directly the philosophy underlying King's work, which was the centrality of love. King's conviction that love possesses and demands centrality in every endeavor of liberation is echoed in the Black Lives Matter movement, which is predicated by the initiative to self-love and established as a "love letter to black people." Baldwin too begins and ends *The Fire Next Time* with a similar appeal to the agency and necessity of love. I have been encouraged by the ways in which queer theorists and theologians have advanced all liberation efforts by diversifying and expanding the normative ways of being embodied people, which inevitably expands perceptions and conceptions of love and loving.

Amy Schiller: I teach about race, along with sexuality and gender and politics, while my research independently has involved a lot of Arendt's conceptual frameworks. When a panel on Martin Luther King Jr., civil disobedience, and Arendt was proposed to me, I saw an opportunity to address one of the questions that has occupied my classrooms. My students and I have grappled with the lasting impact of the civil rights movement, which is where I think a framework from Arendt might be particularly salient.

Arendt presents two options for members of marginalized and excluded populations in relationship to mainstream culture. She is referring in her work to a context of Jews in Europe and the position of Jews in Europe; and the two options she identifies are the parvenu and the pariah. She illustrates this polarity of the parvenu and the pariah in studies of figures like Heinrich Heine and Rahel Varnhagen. For her, the parvenu is one who comes from this marginalized and excluded group yet is able to achieve through assimilation a certain status, a certain respectability among the dominant culture. This can happen through wealth, this can happen through social connections; but it always happens as a part of a striving on their part—for example, in her portrait of Rahel Varnhagen. This is a wealthy German-Jewish woman who took great pride in running a highly regarded intellectual salon. Varnhagen was a woman who did everything she could to assimilate, including changing her name and becoming baptized, to seek respectability and status that was untainted by her Jewishness.

The parvenu yearns for acceptance attainable only through social climbing toward the rewards of mainstream society. By contrast, the pariah uses her detachment from mainstream society to see it more clearly, to speak against oppression that is rendered visible by the conditions of her own life. The conscious pariah resists oppression through embracing her marginality. She becomes a champion of oppressed people, and she's able to analyze the circumstances by which they become so. Elisabeth Young-Bruehl notes that the pariah's task includes this one critical component, "to avoid sacrificing the outsider's perspective for the parvenu's comforts."[1] I'll say that again: "to avoid sacrificing the outsider's perspective for the parvenu's comforts." That covers that polarity of the parvenu and the pariah and their relationship to each other.

Now, to me, Reverend Dr. Martin Luther King Jr. was a conscious pariah par excellence. The anniversary of his assassination this year has included much revisiting of King's political breadth, which goes far beyond the mainstream narrative that refers to him wanting all children to be judged by the content of their character, not the color of their skin. The actions of the early 1960s and the 1950s civil rights movement were far more controversial than our historical narratives will acknowledge at present. However, even more so, the King of the later 1960s who spoke against the Vietnam War at Riverside Church, who connected militarism, poverty, and racism, sometimes materialism, as his triple evils—that King leaned even further into the position of the pariah, someone able to diagnose and willing to speak against the most fundamental levers of oppression. He acknowledged that loss of social status, which was the parvenu's greatest fear, would inevitably accompany the struggle he envisioned of a multiracial, anticapitalist, and anti-imperialist movement. He said the first twelve years of the civil rights movement were a struggle for decency, a struggle to end the humiliation of explicit legal segregation; but the victories of those first twelve years "didn't cost the nation anything," meaning, to integrate lunch counters didn't cost the nation anything really in material terms. Ending poverty, providing quality education, dismantling the military-industrial complex—these would be an entirely different story. And, of course, King was not alone in these ideas; these certainly come from Bayard Rustin as well as the Black Panthers, a whole multiplicity of leaders of the civil rights movement and other, even more sort of radical wings of it.

I could elaborate even further on this case for King as a conscious pariah in the Arendtian model, but at an initial glance I can see a rather seamless application. However, I want to return to the other side of Arendt's binary, because it is there where I'm interested in what may potentially be a more generative conversation. I'm interested in juxtaposing King's conscious pariah-hood with the opportunities that black political figures had in the decades following his death to choose some of the benefits of incorporation into existing political structures, to be, in other words, a very modified kind of parvenu. I will note that even the most successful black parvenu in the United States will very likely remain a pariah figure to many, and that the sedimented forms of racism at the institutional and individual level would make it very difficult for black Americans to ever really feel themselves or believe themselves assimilated. This is a potential limitation of this thesis that I'm willing to debate another time.

However, the "betrayal by parvenu" thesis within sort of contemporary black political history is drawn heavily from Manning Marable, who locates the shortcomings of post–civil rights black politics in the class divisions within the black community, with opportunities for advancement available mainly to the black middle class and elite. Marable, along with Adolph Reed, Frederick Harris, and others, has been providing this analysis for decades; but perhaps it wasn't until the later years of the Obama administration and its end that the gap between black elite advancement and black emancipatory politics came into a shared, clear view.

Given the evolution of black politics following King's assassination and in the decades that followed the civil rights movement, we might wonder how King would have evolved when presented with opportunities that emerged, however brief and fragmented, for political incorporation following the civil rights movement. The 1970s saw twenty black mayors elected in cities like Atlanta and Los Angeles, where Maynard Jackson and Tom Bradley pursued to varying degrees economic development programs that benefited white and black elites, growing the ranks of the latter without engaging in mass redistribution.

The 1970s also saw the advent of neoliberalism writ large, an ideology of reducing the welfare state and turning to the market as an instrument of empowerment. Within this larger milieu President Nixon proposed the idea of "black capitalism," where there would be government agencies—surprisingly unfunded, as it turned out—who would promote and contract with black-owned businesses. This turned out to be mostly a cosmetic effort to coopt demands for economic equity and to provide some reassuring vision for white voters on how racial protests would be pacified.

We don't know how King would have changed or navigated any of these shifts; but we can see that the temptations of the parvenu's comfort through assimilation and incorporation crept into black politics very soon after King's death, creating a form of politics which was by no means the only form. This is not an attempt to erase more radical approaches; it's only to say that this possibility only came into existence at the time to create a black politics that bore little resemblance to King's radical critique of the totality of American power.

As a Jewish person I can draw from the example of my own community to say that Jewish members of the Trump administration, like Stephen Miller and Jared and Ivanka Trump, have thrown into sharp relief the sacrifice of conscience that the parvenu makes, and the never-ending mandate of a pariah to remain critical of the rationales for power structures.

If we recall the mandate of the pariah to avoid sacrificing his perspective for material comforts, we can at the very least mourn what we hope would have been the steadfast consciousness of Dr. King had he lived a longer life. We might also wonder whether the loss of his lived example and guidance caused a potential cross-class, cross-race coalition to fracture, and whether that fracturing made the commitment to the pariah's discomfort less appealing and the rewards of embracing some components of American power more possible. This could have been through the complicity in the carceral state evidenced by Kamala Harris's record of increasing felony conviction rates by 15 percent and drug conviction rates by nearly 20 percent while serving as San Francisco's district attorney, or by President Obama's embrace of capitalism in his deference to the heads of major banks as the height of the 2008 financial crisis, or even more recently, Michelle Obama's pronouncement of George Bush as her friend, someone she "loves to death," someone whose company that she enjoys because they sit next to each other at formal events.

So the question that these bring up for me is not, was Martin Luther King a model of civil disobedience; it's how can we rediscover the courage to be the kind of conscious pariah that he was.

Thank you.

---

1. Elisabeth Young-Bruehl, "From the Pariah's Point of View," in *Hannah Arendt: The Recovery of the Public World*, ed. Melvyn A. Hill (New York: St. Martin's Press, 1979), 5.

Thomas Chatterton Williams: In recent years I've found myself thinking about Aristotle's distinction between the good man and the good citizen, and the political conditions that allow that latter identity to come to fruition.

This is a distinction that Hannah Arendt draws on in her essay "Reflections on Civil Disobedience," and which Leo Strauss elucidates as follows:

> The practical meaning of the notion of the best regime appears most clearly when one considers the ambiguity of the term "good citizen." Aristotle suggests two entirely different definitions of the good citizen. In his more popular *Constitution of Athens* he suggests that the good citizen is a man who serves his country well, without any regard to the difference of regimes—who serves his country well in fundamental indifference to the change of regimes. The good citizen, in a word, is the patriotic citizen, the man whose loyalty belongs first and last to his fatherland. In his less popular *Politics*, Aristotle says that there is not *the* good citizen without qualification. For what it means to be a good citizen depends entirely on the regime. A good citizen in Hitler's Germany would be a bad citizen elsewhere. But whereas good citizen is relative to the regime, good man does not have such a relativity. The meaning of good man is always and everywhere the same. The good man is identical with the good citizen only in one case—in the case of the best regime. For only in the best regime is the good of the regime and the good of the man identical, that goal being virtue. This amounts to saying that in his *Politics* Aristotle questions the proposition that patriotism is enough. From the point of view of the patriot, the Fatherland is more important than any difference of regimes. From the point of view of the patriot, he who prefers any regime to the Fatherland is a partisan, if not a

traitor. Aristotle says in effect that the partisan sees deeper than the patriot but that only one kind of partisan is superior; this is the partisan of virtue. One can express Aristotle's thought as follows: patriotism is not enough for the same reason that the most doting mother is happier if her child is good than if he is bad. A mother loves her child because he is her own; she loves what is her own. But she also loves the good. All human love is subject to the law that it be both love of one's own and love of the good, and there is necessarily a tension between one's own and the good, a tension which may well lead to a break, be it only the breaking of a heart.[1]

In Donald Trump's America this distinction between partisan and patriot, good man and good citizen, seems more salient than it has at any other point in my life. What, after all, does it mean to be a good citizen in America at the moment when children, and even babies, are torn from their parents and isolated in desert cages; when so many unarmed men and women, often but not always black, are shot to death with no repercussion; when children are slaughtered in our nation's schoolrooms because our laws ensure that the most violent of weapons remain readily accessible and our lawmakers pantomime regret while enthusiastically sacrificing a percentage of our boys and girls to the gun lobby on the altar of commerce; when avowed racists march through our streets and the president condones them. "There are fine people on both sides," he tells us. At what point are we to conclude that blind patriotism to such a regime is incompatible with the dictates of good citizenship?

Though the realities are starkly different, the tension between these two kinds of good also makes me think of the powerful 2006 film *The Lives of Others*, which many of you probably have seen. Set in 1984 in East Germany, a Stasi agent is ordered to spy on a playwright who has thus far escaped state scrutiny due to his pro-communist views and international recognition. The agent and his team bug the writer's apartment, set up surveillance equipment, and begin reporting his activities. But eventually the agent comes to find out that the playwright has been put under surveillance at the request of a man who covets his girlfriend. It dawns on him that he cannot serve his state and not participate in a terrible wrong—here rendered in miniature, of course, but it is not hard to extrapolate from this personal wrong a much greater society-wide wrong any citizen serving such a regime would necessarily be complicit in. And so at great personal cost this agent, who reveals himself to be a good man, subverts and disobeys the demands put upon him.

We're now living in a time where a great many Americans in an enormous variety of nonviolent ways are deciding to disobey—in ways we may agree with and in ways that may repel us, too. We see in the country sanctuary cities, police officers and mayors unwilling to do the work of reporting and rounding up undocumented immigrants for ICE. We see men and women taking it upon themselves to rid their communities of monuments to slavery and diminution. And yet elsewhere we do see citizens refusing to adapt to our evolving understanding of gay rights. We see business owners refusing to serve same-sex clients, which is also a form of disobedience. In these instances, the disobedience is in contradiction to pressure that is considered legal. They are disobeying the law, whether or not we agree with it.

But there is also a more expansive understanding of civil disobedience which in some cases may even be harder, and this necessitates going against social norms, if not legal strictures, which is why Arendt distinguishes between disobedience of the law, both civil and criminal, and the defiance of religious, secular, political, and social authority. Is the football player Colin Kaepernick a bad citizen for kneeling during the spectacle of the national anthem and drawing the ire of the president and many self-professed patriots, losing his career in the process? "The law can indeed stabilize and legalize change once it has occurred," Arendt writes, "but the change itself is always the result of extralegal action."[2]

The case of Kaepernick and the national movement against police brutality, and the extraordinary backlash it has generated, particularly interest me in light of the themes we are here to consider. Like the agent in *The Lives of Others*, Kaepernick offers a prosaic glimpse of what can happen to a man trying to be good in a bad regime. Can civil disobedience help reunite majority opinion around a common truth? So far, I'm not at all certain. Is civil disobedience, however, an exemplary and courageous act of citizenship, a useful and necessary means, at the very minimum, of allowing the good man to continue looking himself in the mirror in an imperfect society, what Camus meant when he spoke of the individual's resistance to injustice as fundamental for the resisting individual's own health and welfare? Of all that I am positive.

It remains to be seen if what we are witnessing today can equal that which was harnessed during the civil rights movement of the 1960s, led by one of the finest citizens this country has ever produced in the figure of Martin Luther King Jr. But it is a start and a welcome divergence from the end-of-history complacency that mired us in previous eras. As others have remarked, the United States is a country in which an individual, through "one of the most serious oddities of our law . . . is encouraged or in some sense compelled to establish a significant legal right through a personal act of civil disobedience."[3] In some very real sense, then, loving America means knowing when and how to defy her, both legally and normatively. This is not partisanship; this is what genuine patriotism looks like if we insist on another definition of patriotism, of the patriot, one more expansive than that used by Aristotle.

I think of the two women who confronted Senator Jeff Flake in the elevator after the Kavanaugh testimony. I think of them holding open the door, demanding he not look away from them. And to my amazement I think of him actually, if fleetingly, listening to them and changing his vote. And for a moment I really do believe a new and better democratic American ideal can emerge. But to live up to the legacy of King and others, it may be the case that many more of us are going to be required to be courageous.

Thank you.

---

1. Leo Strauss, *What Is Political Philosophy? And Other Studies* (1959; repr. Chicago: University of Chicago Press, 1988), 35.
2. Hannah Arendt, "Civil Disobedience," in *Crises of the Republic* (New York: Harcourt Brace, 1970), 80.
3. Edward H. Levi, quoted in Robert Teigrob, *Living with War: Twentieth-Century Conflict in Canadian and American History* (Toronto: University of Toronto Press, 2016), 175.

Q&A: MLK and the Legacy of Civil Disobedience in America

Kenyon Adams, Amy Schiller, and Thomas Chatterton Williams

Ann Seaton: Thanks. Those were really three incredible pieces. Now we're going to turn the questions over to all of you. . . .

Q: First, thank you all for your presentations. Kenyon, I appreciate the connection you're bringing back to existence, an ontological question, so I was thinking about the connection that you were making between blackness as a space for creative action and the distinction Chatterton was making around the good man and the good citizen—the example of Kaepernick was what I was thinking of. Kenyon, would you say that that was creative action? And then, what is the relationship between creative action and being the good man?

KVA: That's a great question, thank you. Maybe we could split this, especially the bottom half. Is it a creative action? I think I was—for my purposes I was using the idea of what is constructive. I was trying to do a construction and erasure dialectic with blackness and whiteness to kind of demonstrate what I think drove King or really concerned him theologically. So creative action in terms of King—I think he would think that it requires, you know, a football player to contextualize direct action. The King that died before forty would probably—that person, that sort of anachronistic person would now have to say, okay, how are you going to contextualize direct action?

But the other part of creative action that I was trying to point to was that King was looking at the whole African diaspora, and looking at liberation movements not just for the African diaspora but for people all over, liberation movements all over the world. He saw that as creative energy, and he actually felt that the United States was a bit behind, and he thought it was pretty amazing that you're trying to do creative action to produce a cup of coffee—using constitutional law for a cup of coffee.

So I think contextually, yes, it's creative action, Kaepernick. My concern would be this kind of anachronistic, you know, assemblage. I think there are other places also to look and other ways that if you were to say, how does King's work now extrapolate itself and become contemporary, I think there are also other things to imagine.

TCW: Just about Kaepernick: I think about him a lot, and I'm confused about what he really means for the time and what he will mean in the future. And I think about, were King alive in a time like now, would he have a Nike contract or something like that? And is it possible to do something as noble as King did in a time like our own, which is—it's always going to devolve in some sense into something material and able to capitalize off of in a way that seems to devalue something that is there in the pristine images of the 1960s that are preserved for us.

So I think that Kaepernick is doing something very noble and very important, and I think that the reason that you can tell it's important is the extremity of the backlash that he generates. It means that he brought something new into the world that many people don't want to see brought there. But I'm not sure, maybe it is actually in fact frivolous on some level, and the Nike contract maybe makes it that way—I'm not sure.

KVA: We'll add to that: you made me think that the theater—King was interested in theater, and that was very conscious, to use your cue. It was very conscious, and if that's a modality, it is a modality, and I think Kap is involved with that modality.

Amy Schiller: I would just add that certainly Arendt, I think, would look at Kaepernick and the kneel as action, right? It's a political action that creates a new space and a new discourse and a new kind of chain of reactions that were previously sort of unthinkable or unanticipatable. So if we just want to refer back to her, certainly there's a way of seeing Kaepernick as a person of action, and political action—which for Arendt is inherently sort of creative and natal.

KVA: In no way to diminish Kap, I think like it's pretty powerful stuff, pretty amazing stuff.

Q: You mentioned, Kenyon, the concept of the exceptional Negro, and the patriarchal picture that was sometimes painted when we talk about Martin Luther King Jr., and it reminds me of the study I recently saw, actually, that says both white and black women equally look at natural hair, black natural hair, as being unprofessional, which shows this level of—I hate the word "colonizing," but I'm going to say it anyway—this colonized thought. . . .

I was shocked to find that it was equal: both black women and white women seem to think this in this study. And, you know, despite the intersectionality of the Black Lives Matter movement there is still this "exceptional Negro" concept, which then allows us to justify behavior that is bad behavior against others, and also this patriarchy where sometimes black men are trying to get freedom for black men, and not for . . . , you know, the trans community or women. So I guess my question is, how can we tackle our refusal to focus on a holistic liberation when survival is really what is on everyone's minds? I feel that we're not really focused on a holistic liberation of all within the black community.

KVA: Okay. A lot there. Let me just say the name Eboni Marshall Turman. In case you haven't engaged her, she can certainly speak and has spoken to this—also Howard Thurman. You know, we like to talk about King and Gandhi. I think that's another interesting memory we harbor or hold. Howard Thurman was the spiritual leader that likely mostly influenced King. If you listen to his eulogy of King, it's extraordinary. Thurman is a key to what you're asking at the end of your question.

I had a note, and I was saying I'd be remiss, and then I missed it. But I'd be remiss not to mention the underlying philosophy of King's work, which is the centrality of love. And I'm still learning about that; but his conviction about love, that it sort of possesses all this necessary centrality for every freedom and liberation endeavor, is, I think, rooted in self-love. So self-love, self-care, is something you're hearing a lot, and you've got to really recognize that Black Lives Matter put that out there as a whole new kind of infiltration of psyche and constructive beingness, a love letter to black people. So I think the holistic— If joy, according to Willy Jennings, is the goal of all this justice work, then love is the journey, is the engine, the driver, the power. But that has to be self-love, and Thurman is the really clear voice on this. So I think learning what King meant when he talked about love, and what Thurman means when he talks about love, and then applying critiques— You mentioned the patriarchal rendering. I think whiteness and straightness—these things are all connected, you know. Baldwin could have given that address. Rustin could have given that address. What would have happened if they had? So yes, it's important to not remember one man as being the Freedom Movement in the United States. That's important. That doesn't detract from King. As a matter of fact, he would tell you this, I'm confident.

Thomas Chatterton Williams: If I understood the question, you're juxtaposing the individual's kind of breaking apart from the oppression from the group left behind. I often think about this and wonder. I moved to Paris seven years ago, and I think a lot about some of the black—including James Baldwin—some of the great black writers who have done that, and I think a lot about what Richard Wright said, which seems on one level a little bit like betrayal but on a human level it makes a lot of sense to me too. He said he was so happy when he got to Paris, and he said, "Every hour that you're fighting for your freedom is an hour that you're not free." And he said, "I have more freedom in a square block of Paris than in the entire United States of America." It's a question taken up in *Paris Blues* with Sydney Poitier and Paul Newman, where Poitier kind of doesn't want to go home, but his visiting girlfriend prevails on him to go back because she says that's where the fight is. And he doesn't know why he's going back to the fight because if the fight is joy, the term you use, he already had joy.

There's a tension there that I don't know is fixable between the individual and the group. The individual is always subject to the *they*, and the only liberation from that is to separate from the they; and that feels like something wrong on a lot of levels as well. So there's always something being sacrificed.

Q: Hi. I really appreciate the opening comments. And the question and musing I'm posting, I am doing so acknowledged as a female person lacking color. But my concern and question really was prompted, Kenyon, by some of the things you said about ethnicity and pan-Africanism, and I'm kind of wondering about the position of maintaining racial identities over humanity as an identity. So it may be civil disobedience, but for most of my life, when given a questionnaire, if the question is race, I check "Other" and write in "Human." I have done so for I don't know how long. Both of our adult children have done so their whole lives. I will check ethnicity for demographic medical purposes. But I have gotten backlash from friends and acquaintances who are people of color that in doing so, a person lacking color, I am being racist in claiming that there are no races. And I claim that from a biological standpoint. I believe there are ethnicities, there are classes, there are cultures; I don't personally believe that race exists. I think there's humanity. So if you could address how that fits into or is against some of the struggles you represent, that would be great.

Seaton: Can we start with Amy, just because I feel she's getting a little left out—not to essentialize or anything.

Schiller: So, all right. So I'm also a white woman. Sorry: I am a white woman, not *also*. You obviously identify differently. I find it important— I can only speak to how I personally navigate this, and I think Kenyon may have a better theoretical couching for this. When I teach my classes, if I teach at Brooklyn College, they are almost entirely racial minority students. And if I'm teaching a class about race in American politics it is significant for me, on the one hand, to establish that the professor-student relationship remains intact, that my responsibilities to them and their responsibilities to the classroom and to me are all the same even in acknowledging the dynamics of race as an additional element of knowledge and power and knowledge production in that room. So I think it's important for me not only at the beginning of class but throughout the class to acknowledge that I will not have the same sort of personally informed experience, the lived experience, of race that other people in that room have, and that that informs my access to knowledge, that informs how my analysis and my instincts are shaped, and that is, I think, just a truth that I really believe about how people live in society. Because maybe races do or do not exist in an ontological sense, but many people are raced. I live in a world that treats me as a white person, that treats other people as people of color. The consequences of living in those two kinds of bodies are really different.

So I think it's really valuable, on the one hand, to be able to acknowledge the differences in lived experiences even while maintaining that, yes, the other roles that we have and the other relations we have to one another remain intact and respected. I don't know if that fully answers your question, but that's how I've handled it.

KVA: You can't have a democracy and maintain racial hierarchy. So it's not exactly about a subjective thing. Do you want to have apartheid, or do you want to have democracy? The two cannot coexist. What do we have?

I would check out some critical race theory. Read Nell Irvin Painter's *History of White People* as a start. There's a discourse that is historical. I think it's important to say no, there is no beingness to whiteness. No one can say I am white and that be true; yet, as she's describing, it's a false identity with real-world consequences; so it's one of those imaginary things that comes into reality in very strong ways. But that's because we have something that more resembles apartheid than democracy. So I think King was trying to take racial hierarchy down, he was trying to take apartheid down, and he tried to do that theologically, betting on the Christian character of the United States of America.

TCW: I want to thank you for that comment and for the question. It speaks directly to what I'm very focused on right now. I'm finishing a book about being the black father. I grew up under the rule of hypodescent and the idea of the one-drop rule. My father's black, my mother's white. I grew up not questioning the idea that I was white, and white people didn't really question it; black people are used to accepting people of all skin tones as part of the black community. It wasn't till I moved to France and had children who came out looking Swedish that the fiction of race kind of really presented itself to me. And I did a lot of thinking, and for four years I've been writing a book that's an adaptation of an essay I wrote about the shock of having a very white-looking daughter, and what does it mean if I'm a black man that can have a daughter like this, and what does it mean if my daughter is white and my father is black but they have the same smile and a lot of the same DNA.

Last spring I profiled a very brilliant woman named Adrian Piper who's an artist. She had a huge retrospective at MoMA recently. She lives in Berlin, she's a distinguished philosopher, and she publicly retired from blackness in 2012. We talked a lot about this, and there was some deep part of me that still, even as I was writing this book, was resisting. But I came out of these conversations with her thinking that the most radical act of civil disobedience that I can probably do and teach my children to do is to step out of this black-white binary that is a fiction that is forced on us and that produces a social inequality that I don't

Citizenship and Civil Disobedience

want to reproduce anymore. And I realize that's naive. Privileged black people can be really supportive of this position, or they can get really mad, saying that, "You live in Paris, you have light skin and a white wife, so that doesn't speak to me." That's possibly a compelling response to it, but I'm out of the game myself, and I'm really inspired by the little act of civil disobedience that you do every time you fill out a box, because those boxes are fake. So thank you.

KVA: If I can say one thing about the box: so we both have babies—I have a little daughter two years old now, and I could not get her out of the hospital. Listen, she was born two years ago. I couldn't get her out of the hospital, and I could not get a Social Security number—and I spent time—until I declared her according to a six-box half sheet of paper. This is the United States of America. If that's not apartheid, you're going to have to explain to me what it is.

The other thing I want to leave you with is this deep thing about they *made* us a race, we became a people: black people became a people. I am black, and that's a beautiful thing. It's one of the best things to be, especially now. But if you want to reject whiteness and white identity, who are you? You're going to have to creatively act that. Where's the creative action or constructive? Is there constructive whiteness that is not a violence?

TCW: This is a really interesting. If we can keep going with that question a little bit longer, I agree with you 100 percent that . . . it's not enough to just say, "Stepping out of race, race is over," and then it's business as usual. We actually have to do what Fanon was asking for, which is to create a new man. And I think that we could do that, because in human terms, in civilizational terms, white and black is not that old. It's like four hundred, five hundred years old. We have lived other ways, we could live other ways, if significant numbers of us wanted to, so desired to.

Last summer I spent time interviewing real white nationalists in Europe and Richard Spencer here in America, and one of the things that they think [that] is very dangerous is this kind of complacent idea of whiteness, where whiteness is neutral and everybody else is raced insofar as they deviate from white neutrality. They want to reawaken a white race consciousness, and they want white people to know that they're white. I certainly don't want white people to be reawakened to their racedness in the way that Spencer does; but I do want white people to step out of the idea that they have no race. I want them to rethink their social identity and collectively with other people of goodwill to think of ways that we can get past that and we can belong to a nation together as citizens, that we can be human together as you suggest.

It's really interesting that you say that about having kids in the States, because my kids were born in France, where they're about to strike the word "race" from the constitution.

KVA: We should specify between race and ethnicity or other notions. Race has its own space, and it really didn't exist as a robust space until 1620. So ethnicity—you are from somewhere and somebody, so that's good news. You're not white, but you are from somewhere and somebody. So you can claim that and then try— I think collectively the United States has to really—like I said, it's a laundry list. Taking racial hierarchy down may be at the top of that list, and then we can deal with other embodiments.

Seaton: Before I take a question, I'm forced to say something, which is that, as someone who wrote on race in the Enlightenment for my dissertation, and I teach about it as well, there is no human outside of race. So when the category of the human arose with Linnaeus's *Systema naturae*—I don't know if you're familiar with it. . . . He was the person who came up with the notion of the sort of scientific categories though which we describe the human species. Also a fellow named Immanuel Kant, a rather well-known philosopher. Both of them, when they describe the category of the human in the seventeenth and eighteenth centuries, respectively, [they] elaborately described it, and only described it, insofar as it related directly to race. So this fantasy fiction that there's some human category that anyone can step outside of—I mean, Adrian Piper knows this quite well; she's a Kantian philosopher herself. I think what she's doing isn't sort of saying that she doesn't want to be black; I think what she's saying is, she doesn't want to be violently racialized and segregated. I don't think those are the same thing.

TCW: She's actually saying both. She's saying that she wants to belong to a tradition and a culture, but she told me—we spoke about this, and she told me that. I said, "Well, do you believe in a black sensibility?" She said no. There's no Jewish sensibility, there's no black sensibility.

Seaton: Right, but I still think that's not quite the same thing as saying that there's this human category that exists outside of race. When she says there's no black sensibility, I think what she's saying is something much more complicated. I mean, I think that runs throughout her work; she's actually one of my teachers.

I'm not proposing that either of us can know for sure what she means—

TCW: I have a long profile in the *New York Times Magazine* on her where she's on record saying that she doesn't believe people are white or black, and she's not black.

Seaton: I've read that

TCW: She said it pretty clearly.

Seaton: Right, but I think that she's also— Well, anyway, I just don't think there's a human category that exists outside of race historically, philosophically, or intellectually.

TCW: Is it possible that we could imagine one going forward though?

Seaton: Well, right—yes. I mean, maybe Sun Ra would have to be the person to do that for us. Any other questions?

Q: I can't help but add as a medievalist [that] there was no conception of race the way we have it. The way they thought of a person was primarily as a soul, and the word for soul is feminine in Latin. And thinking of the Western European tradition in particular, but it's not unique to that, this was a tradition that was kind of shared in many ways by the Islamic and the Jewish traditions as well. So this soul was not the body—it had nothing to do with it. It was often envisioned as feminine vis-à-vis a kind of masculine god. So I think that there are kinds of notions, a way of talking, about a human being that are not racialized the way they've been since the seventeenth century, and they're interesting to consider.

Schiller: The thing that makes a soul into a human being is a body to some extent, right?

Q: That's a little complicated. Ultimately, Christianity would say that—I mean, that human beings are essentially body and soul. But the sense, when we would talk about the subject, for example, or the person, they would say the "soul." That's the word that they used.

Schiller: It's just a matter of how do we—I'm not convinced that we could subtract the body and remain, and somehow still be talking about human beings.

Q: Certainly in Christian theology that's absolutely true. . . . The major division was between the human being, the angel, and the beast—those were the three categories. And the human being is differently positioned. Also, it had to do with whatever court law you followed and whether the law was set in Christianity, Judaism, or paganism/Islam (considered to be the same thing). But if you converted to another religion you were considered fully 100 percent to be one of [that group] as opposed to the other, and there are plenty of examples of that. One of the first converts to Christianity was an Ethiopian in the Acts of the Apostles.

I'm not saying this is the answer to everything, but there are different ways of envisaging this.

KVA: King, you know, really proposed something that I think has been overlooked or ignored. His training was in his Western theological received traditions. He read all the medieval mystics, he quoted Aquinas, he constructed all these things. He was in the *Imago Dei*, and that was supposed to be something that was indefensible. People came to him and he said you basically can't be a Christian anymore and believe in the *Imago Dei* and then be a segregator—right? So that to me is his theological line in the sand.

The question is, does the theological tradition you're referring to matter to America? Because if you look at King's legacy, that's a question.

Q: I think that's very, very—especially in recent years, since 2016, we see the direction in which evangelical Christianity in particular, one has to say, has gone. Not all evangelical Christians: I want to make that very clear. There are certainly plenty of people who do identify with Christianity that cross all races, and of course other faith traditions and nonfaith traditions; but I think we can't hold on to theology.

KVA: But the racial imagination in the United States is wed to the Christian imagination through the lens of American Christianity, so this is, I think, still, still a debacle.

Q: In recent years I've heard a lot of people referred to as "people of color," or "I am a person of color," and this includes Arabs who are very light-skinned, some of them; it includes Asians. I don't know who else it includes. Is that a racial category?

TCW: That is a good question. I think that "people of color" is a term that doesn't mean much. It doesn't convey much. Arabs—that's an interesting category. They're technically Caucasian on the census, depending on which country they come from. But "people of color" doesn't make sense, especially when you get into the huge differences among Asian peoples. And where they fit on the whiteness scale is evolving still, and it's going to be very interesting to see how that plays out.

I never refer to myself in terms like that.

KVA: The term has been, I would say, claimed and howled and beloved by millennials—when I say millennials I probably look silly, but people I find to be younger than me.

Schiller: People of age?

KVA: No, I feel a lot of my students that I've had use the term, and with a lot of creativity and pride, and I think language, you know—we were talking a bit about language last night. I feel that certainly in the poetic realm where artists live and where poets live language is not this fixed thing that tells us what to be; we engage it in order to make meaning. And so I think in some very ingenious ways [they're] making meaning of all the sorts of things that come at them. So I think people of color—I think people keep trying to name *human*, so they'll keep doing that.

Q: I have a question about navigating identity. I've spent some time in Palestine over the summer, and I was really struck by, obviously, a million things but particularly about identity, the way in which identity is really constructed collectively, and that it was in stark comparison, especially on college campuses in the U.S., to the necessity and desire to identify so much with the individual, with all of your identifiers that cut all the lines of intersectionality. Without criticizing that form of identity, it was just interesting to see a different societal conception of collective identity around your heritage in direct relation to other people. So I guess my question is just if we are imagining that we can create a new, as you were talking about, a *human* category—if in the future we could engage with that, how do we navigate through the very different ways in which we collectively or individually identify?

TCW: May I? I think that it's important to [realize that] we're not all going to get on the same page at the same time, so I think that some people are going to navigate a broader understanding of common humanity than other people at the same time, and there will be spaces that are freer and others that are more traditional and restricted or even backwards. So I think that people can find each other who want to create that new man. But I'm not so naive or utopian to think that we will all do this, and maybe it won't happen in certain parts of the world ever; and the one that you refer to maybe is a place where group identities are so engrained that [they] would be very hard to get over.

Q: Mine kind of relates to what he was discussing about identity, because I identify as Latina, and that's an issue with certain people. I can never get on the same page with people who aren't Latina sometimes; they'll say that's not all right. And I understand where they're coming from, but living where I live and coming from where I come from, I'm not white enough for certain kids, and then I'm not ethnic enough for the black kids or other kids. Sometimes I fall right in that middle; I feel left out. When you address this, how do you address that, because I don't fall within either in this situation.

TCW: I think you should define yourself as yourself. I think that's hard, but it's the most meaningful definition you can come by. I understand that there's a lot of sustenance in belonging to a *they*; but you say you're Latina not because you choose to construct yourself that way, but because you don't get constructed into other binaries, right? But that seems to me inadequate to move through life as being defined. I think it's all of our work to define ourselves. Sometimes it's very easy just to slip on the cloak of communal identity because it doesn't demand as much; but you're young and you're here at a very [diverse] school, and maybe there's something else to you besides being given a social identity to the extent that you can.

Schiller: I will build on that and just say I think one of the things that interests me is what are the vectors by which we can find ways of connecting to one another and to other people? What are the shared interests? What are the solidarities? What are the goals? Do I necessarily need— I think everybody needs validation and everybody needs a certain amount of recognition and affirmation to feel solid in the world, and I really respect the need for that. I also think that finding one's social community and one's political community does not begin and end with that project, that it is bigger and more expansive than the project of identity affirmation. Identity affirmation can come through action, things that one does with others.

KVA: I only have one other thought, maybe with our powers combined. I mean, here's the thing: there's the subjective experience, and then there's the apartheid sort of resemblance of our society. The U.S. census, and I don't even know if the people who did this had master's degrees, but they created the term "Latin," right? This is a creative people who have done a lot with that sort of identity; so they're going to say the Cuban is the same thing as the Mexican is the same thing as . . . And that creates political power in voting. But the census made that. That's one reality. The 2020 census is coming up. How are you identified in that? You can claim identity, but at some point I will in this country be reminded that I am viewed on that paper a certain way, whether through violence or other situations.

And then there's the political aspect. So if you have an issue with the term "Latin," it has been made, so maybe you have an issue with the making. You can take that up.

Q: I was just wondering, going back to your previous discussion about people of color and there being kind of a spectrum of whiteness and not fitting into certain categories, whether you see those terms as being helpful or negative toward our country, and whether you see them changing in the future, and whether those terms should stay in [terms of] how we want to build our humanity or whether they might be degraded away in our future.

TCW: I would like to see the census— I would like to get rid of these categories, because in my own lifetime—I'll give you an example that the categories don't make sense. When I was younger, you could only mark one box on the census. Now you can mark multiple boxes. So I would have had to choose. I couldn't possibly reflect my actual heritage on the census until I was an adult. Now I can mark a number of things and it completely changes my official social identity. But nothing about me changed, nothing about my ancestry changed, nothing about my reality changed. What do these terms really mean? I mean, at one point Chinese were considered black, Mexicans were black. . . . It changed throughout the twentieth century. A term like "black" doesn't capture anything, and a term like "people of color" captures even less specificity. Whiteness is a category that has constantly evolved around the margins especially, and has expanded to include other groups, as other groups have always defined themselves against the lowest category on the social hierarchy, which has always been stuck at black. So whiteness didn't used to include Southern Europeans. These categories don't do anything. So in my own kind of naive, hopeful way, I hope we could get to a point where we don't use them.

This is actually possible. France is a society that has lots of flaws, but it doesn't recognize race officially; and the language, the word "race," if we really believe that there's no such thing as distinct racism in human beings, then why do we have these words inscribed in our legal documents? And so in France it's probably going to be struck. Language matters and precision matters, and these are moves that actually can have larger effects than just being nitpicky about how we describe ourselves.

Q: And in America do you see that happening in the future at any point?

TCW: I hope so. I mean, I think that there are a lot of people that feel that the way we organize ourselves right now is insufficient. I feel like the conversation could move that way, and there's always significant backlash, but I think it's possible certainly.

Schiller: I just want to add one more response to that. To me, race is such a lived reality, I think the disparity between median white household wealth and median black household wealth is so obscenely huge, I feel like the question of language must correspond with questions of justice. I think utopianism about moving beyond racial categories would have to be accompanied by a justice program exactly to resolve the material divides that have been wrought by the racial apartheid system.

TCW: But that gets into notions of class, not just color.

Schiller: Well, absolutely.

TCW: Class is something that's very difficult to talk about in this society, but that's actually where an important part of the conversation has to take place.

Seaton: I think we have time for at least one other question. And even though I'm supposed to be the moderator, I can't help saying that it's so easy for someone like you or me to question racial categories, or someone like Adrian Piper, because the racial categories of people who are racially ambiguous, racially indeterminate, who are much more likely to have descended from house slaves, free Negroes, masters, et cetera, people who constantly get asked, "What are you?"—it's very different for such people to question the idea of racial meaning than it is for someone who is always going to be inter-polated in a very quick kind of way.

TCW: Yes, but James Baldwin was one of the most eloquent questioners of these categories.

Seaton: I can't agree. What you're saying, a lot of it's actually reminding me a lot more of Jean Toomer than James Baldwin, and those things that Toomer said—

TCW: It's in Baldwin too, though.

Seaton: [Toomer's] *The Blue Meridien*—very differently. Anyway, we've got some-body back there.

Q: You said that you, in looking at this whole human race thing, that you see yourself as naive and hopeful. I do look at you as a bit naive, not that I don't respect you as a scholar—

TCW: No, I think we have to embrace naivete, so this is good.

Q: All right, this is great. So for me, being black, there's just so much that goes into it, whether it's being on this very white campus and going through the day and knowing that I have to operate in a specific way, I have to write in a specific way, I have to talk in a specific way or else people won't take me seriously. Being black, coming from a culture and being myself, yes, I could be myself, but also part of being myself is understanding my own identity, and I happen to use the word "black." I'm also Jamaican; I'm also a straight man. There are other ways to identify myself; but I feel like in terms of race I've never really had the choice because of the way that my race has affected me and, as she says, a lived reality. When I see you, I see someone who's a little bit out of touch, because I don't know if you come back to where I'm from—I don't know where you're from and I don't mean to judge you on that—

TCW: New Jersey

Citizenship and Civil Disobedience

Q: That's great. When I go back to where I'm from, I can't look at anybody and not tell them I'm black. They would look at me as a traitor. You know what I'm saying? I'm not saying I can't be myself because I've always been myself, and I'm also very proud of being black; but for you to try and strip that of my identity and then tell me it's not going to affect me and the way I live, I look at you as a fool. I'm sorry.

TCW: I thank you for your comments, and you're welcome to create yourself as you wish to. But you're basically saying that you're defined as black and so therefore you have to be defined as black. I don't find that a completely convincing argument. I think that there are other ways to imagine yourself.

Q: I want to reclarify. The law identifies black. It's like there are so many different kinds of black identity, and—

TCW: You're Jamaican, so that's already very different than the descendants of Southern slaves.

Q: So are you trying to tell me that I shouldn't identify as black, and I should identify as Jamaican? I'm not really sure—

TCW: I'm saying that there's a significant difference between coming from the West Indies and coming through the American South as a descendant of slaves.

Q: My parents immigrated to New York. I was born here. At the end of the day, when people see me, they're going to see my skin. They don't even— They would never assume my ethnic identity. They don't even assume that I'm Jamaican, which is fine. I have to find a way to promote that myself. But I'm telling you like the first thing that— On this campus, if I tell you what I've been through off this campus in this very rural community, which is also filled with a lot of white people, for you to tell me race is not a factor, I can't look at you and not see someone who's excelled and who has been privileged enough to sit with you all. And I respect your position, but I see you as someone who's really out of touch.

TCW: Well, thank you for your comments. There's always a negotiation between the self that you make and the way that institutions and other people regard you. You can't just walk out on the street and say you're white or Chinese, I understand that; but you can also have a much more critical view toward how your identity is socially constructed than you seem to profess right now. You're young, you're a college student; I don't mean to define your race for you. But I do hope that you might leave this conversation and question some of the ways that your blackness is constructed, and you might think about some of the ways with which your blackness differs from the blackness that my father had as a slave, as a descendant of slaves from Louisiana and Texas. It's extremely different. The thing that you think that unites you is extraordinarily abstract. You might question it more. You might not—that's fine.

Q: Do we leave history in the process when we try to take all these labels and revert to "the human race"?

TCW: I don't think you have to. I don't think that I ever said that what you should do is leave your history out in the process.

Q: Okay, thank you.

TCW: Thank you.

Seaton: Thanks, everyone.

The Shared World of Adversaries

Nikita Nelin

*We were raised to believe that by the time of our adulthood we would have
colonized the moon, be at war with China, and have jet packs, but instead
we are competing for part-time remote work with other invisible people.*
—The Voice of the Opt-Out Generation

Day 1

10:15 a.m. Citizenship and Civil Disobedience

"If history teaches anything about the causes of revolution . . . it is that a
disintegration of political systems precedes revolutions, that the telling symptom of disintegration is a progressive erosion of governmental authority, and
that this erosion is caused by the government's inability to function properly,
from which spring the citizens' doubts about its legitimacy. This is what the
Marxists used to call a 'revolutionary situation'—which, of course, more often
than not does not develop into a revolution."[1]

Thus, with this quote from Hannah Arendt, Roger Berkowitz opens the
Eleventh Annual Hannah Arendt Conference. He adds a caveat: Arendt's
caution against seeing too much wisdom in history as "the present is always
unprecedented and we must look upon it fresh." And yet, he admits, here
we are, at the foot of some crisis. Unquestionably, regardless of one's political
affiliation, it is this crisis that brings us here today—our one, tangible and
sense-worthy, common truth.

The four hundred–seat lecture hall is at capacity. It is filled with lifetime
academics, activists, artists, retirees seeking a revival of their fleeting ideals,
and high school and college students eager to understand the mechanism of
power and the feasibility of their generation achieving a grip upon its levers.

I am at the pastoral Hudson Valley campus of Bard College, at a conference hosted by the Hannah Arendt Center, of which a former teacher of mine,
Roger Berkowitz, is the director. This will be two days of lectures and panels
and conversations, mildly argumentative but ultimately civil, focused by the
topic of this year's conference, "Citizenship and Civil Disobedience." And in the
spirit of my immigrant conditioning I am asking myself: what am I doing here?

The conference breaks its topic into seven questions: Is civil disobedience
an exemplary act of citizenship? Why is citizen activism emerging across all
parts of the political spectrum? Can civil disobedience help reunite majority
opinion around common truths? Is civil disobedience usable by dissidents on
both the left and the right? Are we today in a revolutionary situation? Should
violence be used in civil disobedience? Does democracy require civility?

I have been asking similar questions for six years, and have added a set of my own: what is next? And, in this country I've come to call home, what really is possible? Maybe that's why I'm here: I want answers, and I retain the hope that this educated and thoughtful congress can offer me some.

No. I am here for the same reason I have done everything since 2012: I am looking for a vision, and though this conference will not offer me one, it may help to crystallize my own.

Roger started the conference in 2006 from a simple idea: "I want to get the twenty smartest people I know into the room and talk about the state of democracy." Back then this was merely a philosophical practice, to consider the range of tenacity in our governing system through the work of Arendt. But in our polarly drawn ideologue age, as the system nears breaking, it has become a tangible exercise.

"No ideologues," Roger said. This was one of the conditions. He wanted people who think. People who can have a conversation, capable of exercising Arendt's advice for "a civil discourse between rivals instead of enemies."

This has not grown without controversy. Last year's conference, under the title "Crises of Democracy: Thinking in Dark Times," received a lot of negative press when Roger invited Mark Jongen, a politician representing Alternative für Deutschland (AfD), a far right–leaning organization in Germany. In an open letter printed in the *Chronicle of Higher Education*, Roger was accused of knowingly providing a stage for an outspoken critic of marginalized communities. The letter was signed by a large contingent of professors and progressive thinkers, and though they agreed with him "that there is a need to engage with a wide range of political views, including illiberal and even neofascist ones,"[2] they ultimately condemned both Professor Berkowitz and the president of Bard, Leon Botstein, for not significantly denouncing Jongen and his views, to which Roger replied that the denouncement is clearly implied in the mission of the Hannah Arendt Center and the work and writing it has produced.

Roger says he lost many friends in the controversy, and yet he has also gotten to witness who of his contemporaries is fully committed to Arendt's mandate on civil discourse and to the possibility of politics within a public sphere, rising above the bubble-making of ideological encasement. Since then, the Hannah Arendt Center has become a sober source in contemporary political analysis and the defense of free speech. Their newsletter has replaced the *New York Times* as my Sunday reading, a source I trust to help me consider all the madness of American politics. So I wanted to witness nonpartisan dialogue in action. That too is why I'm here.

For those reading this who are not living in America, I have to state something that is at times challenging to explain without metaphysical considerations. We, here, have entered a time in which the political has become deeply personal, and vice versa. We are, quite frankly, losing our minds. Even my meditation app has a political package option. At times it can feel like even our psychic space is becoming partisan, blue or red to different degrees of intensity. Whatever one may think of President Trump, in his ugly and terrible way he has perfectly played his role, that of a trickster, revealing the most damning and unpleasant, but quite real and far too long ignored, tumors in our society. He is corporate hierarchy, as expressed by his sympathies with the Saudis: "I make a lot of money from them. . . . Am I supposed to dislike them? I like them very much." His loyalties lie with those who pay, he states clearly. If we define the genesis of fascism as the recognition of dignity by social hierarchy alone, and thus those with superior means are superior to those who do not, then Trump is merely the ultimate expression of this American way, one that has always trended toward recognizing humanity along hierarchical constructs. The Constitution and its Bill of Rights work to protect us from this construct, but the architecture of our society still functions along these lines. I am not claiming that hierarchy always ends in fascism; rather, that fascism is impossible without it, and we have always existed along its borders. Of course, it being rubbed in our face like this, so blatant and clear, agitates the most-tender insecurities of our personhood—that dignity is measured primarily by financial worth. To summarize: dignity is the product of class, class is the product of wealth, and wealth is the product of legacy and ownership. Trump has simply made clear what was once covered by the veneer of political decency, and thus made conscious a basic and unsavory tenet of our country. Contradiction, exposed. Now we deal with it.

And so, if at first it seemed like it was the political that was drawing me back to Bard, I must admit it was the personal too.

In truth, the conference is a return for me, the accidental completion of a journey I began in 2012. That summer I was living in Brooklyn, teaching at a CUNY college and bartending in the West Village to subsidize my adjunct pay. It was a reasonable life but one that left me with an irreconcilable longing. I had graduated into the recession and closely tracked Occupy and its dissipation. I sensed that something large was on the verge of our world, some incongruence bubbling to the surface, but I didn't know how to tap into it. I wanted a better view. I wanted to find a way to articulate what was coming, and for that I needed a dramatic shift of perspective. Through a few chance encounters I received the opportunity to work on a giant political art project at Burning Man titled "Burn Wall Street," and with the institutional cover of the Hannah Arendt Center I surrendered my jobs and my apartment, whittled my belongings down to two duffle bags and a computer, and went west to seek the future, hoping to report what I found.

My mission was to consider America at large from the fringe. The theory I sold to the Hannah Arendt Center then relied on abstracting the norm. I had considered how in many traditionalist cultures, when the dominant culture appeared to be on the verge of crisis it was necessary to journey to the fringe of the cultural landscape so as to attain a new perspective on what was broken and what could be next. I fancied myself an immersive journalist, connected both to academia and to the real world on the ground. I wanted to be a bridge. Roger Berkowitz agreed that this was a thread worth following and provided me with a platform.

A part of my plan was to return to the Hannah Arendt Center for its 2012 conference, the title of which was *Does the President Matter? A Conference on the American Age of Political Disrepair*, and to find a way to contribute my findings to the academic discourse.

But I didn't return. I kept going, for six years. In the interim, I have written about alternative communities, movements, ritual and ceremony in American life, Burning Man, sustainability practices in one's life and business, and the agreements of Standing Rock. This year, I finally made it back.

So again I ask, why am I here? And, six years later, who am I now?

I am here because I am one of a certain growing class in this America, educated and capable, seeking a purpose and caught between the old American Dream and its reimagining. I am here because life has disappointed me. I have chased neither the profiteer's nor the activist's dream. I have been in between them. I want to see what the panelists have to say to a person like me. Even today, after years of seeking stability, consolidating my student loans, upping my credit utilization, and buffering my FICO scores, as my girlfriend and I begin shopping around for a house in a small city that is only next to the city where we want to live, I feel some strange pang in my stomach. It is a sort of survivor's guilt, urging me to admit that something is not right even as my position in the hierarchy becomes more assured. Something's not right in the structure of things. Can I let go of that? I want to move on, build a house, a family, a community. I want to take vacations, but I feel like I am abandoning something, some struggle that still feels personal and far from complete.

I am an Eastern European immigrant. A naturalized American. I want to feel like what this country once vaguely promised still matters. And this promise was not solely individualistic. It was in the new structure of things, some allusion to equality in its founding charter.

I am a skeptic, seeking something that can move me to meaning, and once I admitted that I too am a part of this country, so too has the political become personal for me, and the rising decibel of rage all around me—a new voice taking a turn to scream out, seemingly every week, some other injustice of inequality—normalized day after day, will not let me disentangle the personal from the political again. But sometimes I just want to lay my head down on a soft surface and sleep.

Drawn out from the fringe into a room of thoughtful and institutionalized radicals, here I am. I want to know how these experts are faring in the confusion. If they sleep comfortably. If it is all still theory, or if we can be moved to act.

And so this essay is meant to examine a large void in America today, a void I witness on the ground every day. The conference simply helps to examine the void. This is a case study of the America in between, a consideration of the possibility of movement. If the conference asks whether we are in a revolutionary situation, where the legitimacy of the government is no longer trusted by the governed, I reply that we are in an existential situation, where the ideal of the American Dream no longer seems achievable, or more so, believable, as even many of those who achieve it do not feel content in the reality of their dream. Our suicide rates are up, as are our opioid abuse numbers. A whole generation now enters college having lived only against the backdrop of a vague war. The family unit has been driven further and further apart, and our state of aloneness is enhanced by the virtual tools that promised to unite us. Institutional mistrust is only rivaled by an escalating sense of competition, and we no longer even believe in facts. If an emaciated polar bear began making house calls, many Americans would still doubt global warming because Fox News told them so. We are seeking refuge across tribal lines, and no candidate but Trump has offered an inspiring alternative vision. And his vision is based on an assembly of lies to activate rage and fulfill his personal ambitions, and drive us farther away from nuance and toward our polar fronts. But we have bread. The saying goes that the people will only revolt when there is no bread. This is our unique situation, that we will always have bread. Something else has to move us to action. Another form of hunger maybe. In this lecture hall, I ask what.

* * *

I am not sure if this was intentionally done but the conference itself appears to have an arc and a structure. It begins with an examination of the resistance, comparing its mechanisms to that of the Tea Party, those who were "the resistance" nine years ago. It moves on to examine the role of art in politics; critical activism and if such a thing can be taught; and the patriotic duty of whistleblowing and leaks. It moves on to the more extreme considerations of movement: violence versus nonviolence; grassroots organizing and the legitimacy of the constitution; a consideration of citizenship in a postdemocracy world; and finally, Martin Luther King Jr. and the legacy of civil disobedience, which ends up, of course, more a conversation on the personal semantics of identity politics than civil disobedience. This structure closely mirrors the conversational arc of everyday American discourse. This arc, I sense, is alive and activated in everyone living in America today, and so of course a conference wishing to address this quagmire is going to reflect its arc. Like I said, even our psychic space is political. We need a vision out of this place.

Any good story needs tension, and again, straight from the pool of our most private thoughts, the conference reflects one: reform versus revolution.

Very few in our country are debating the need for change; rather, we are at odds about its form. You will see that the numbers confirm that the majority of our country believes that something has to change. We just lack agreement on how to go about this.

• • •

"It is fair to say," Berkowitz continues in his opening remarks, "that we are today in at least some version of a revolutionary situation, one in which large numbers of citizens reject the legitimacy of our established institutions." The irony is that this is a universal dissatisfaction, across seemingly diametrically opposed interest groups. Berkowitz sites recent poll numbers that state that "47 percent of Trump supporters feel like strangers in their own country. At the same time, 44 percent of those who disapprove of Trump report they feel like strangers in their own country. It is not simply that people disagree; an overwhelming majority of Americans—people in power and people out of power, persons of color and white people, women and men—all feel alienated, rootless, and powerless in their own country."

At times it can feel like it is only the diametrical opposition of our dissatisfaction that keeps up the illusion of balance and stability. Any individual organism would break under such tension. If we appear nuts from afar, it's because we are. Differing factions literally see different things and facts.

"We are," Berkowitz continues, "at one of those rare moments at which the country sits on a pivotal point amidst a conflict of fundamental values."

Thus we are asked to consider how we engender change without outward violence, as the history of violence is such that it breeds only more violence. I would suggest that the imbedding of our institutions is so deep that the prospect of an old-school revolution is now impossible. The numbers just don't add up, and, of course, we still have bread. And so we are left to reconsider the role of civil disobedience as a potential expression of citizenship itself.

The question animating this conference, Berkowitz states, is whether "civil disobedience is the kind of active citizenship that has, and might again, bring about revolutionary change without a civil war." For this we would need to learn how to share again, how to talk and how to listen. We need to reestablish the dominance of the public sphere, where disagreements can be aired. And in this duty, we are failing.

In an article published just prior to the conference, Berkowitz admits how Arendt would answer this question: "Hannah Arendt thinks it is possible to share a world with your adversary. And she saw the first step to such a shared world to be talking. . . . In talking with one another we create the kinds of shared experiences and common points of connections that might, over time, become the building blocks of a new shared world. In talking about the world, we also make judgments and decisions about the world. Those decisions,

Arendt admits, 'may one day prove wholly inadequate.' But even absent agreements on the nature of a crisis and how to solve it, the act of speaking with one another about the crises of our times will, she argues, 'eventually lay the groundwork for new agreements between ourselves as well as between the nations of the earth, which then might become customs, rules, [and] standards that again will be frozen into what is called morality.'"

This is the mandate that ushers us into a vital expression of theater as conference, where conversations among trained and thoughtful adversaries model for us the consideration of dialogue.

I can't help but wonder, though, can we be moved toward action or is this just another one of those academic exercises I fled six years back? I just don't know if dialogue is enough of an action for me now.

10:45 a.m. Saving America Once Again: Comparing the Anti-Trump Resistance to the Tea Party

The first to present is Theda Skocpol, a decorated political researcher out of Harvard. She has spent the last two years examining the tactics of Indivisible, a countermovement to Trump, launched right after the election by some of President Obama's staffers. The more popular moniker for this countermovement is Pantsuit Nation. It is a reaction to Clinton's defeat.

Professor Skocpol brings a careful study of the actions and makeup of the "other" imbedded political party, describing Indivisible as a guide for resistance that learns from and adopts the Tea Party's tactics, activated on the grassroots level and nationwide. As was the case for the Tea Party, the movement is led mostly by women (90 percent). Mostly white women in their fifties and sixties, heavily college educated. Men are mostly husbands or partners. But while the Tea Party was largely funded by the Heritage Foundation, Indivisible is built out primarily from individual donors.

As she describes the makeup of the "countermovement," I study the room. So many of them are here. Located just hours from New York City and Boston, and populated by liberal arts colleges every 30 miles, the Hudson Valley is an oasis for progressive retirees, many of whom bought summer homes here sometime in the 1980s and '90s, and later moved to the region to retire. The geographic makeup is almost a prototype of the rural liberal class. The election brought them out, away from brunch, as the vision of the America they supported, and which benefited their educated and merit-based vision of mobility, was endangered. I doubt that many of them risk anything more tangible than their ethical high ground. Sure, they have a soft spot for people like me, the immigrants, minorities, and service industry employees who their kids brought home for dinner. And they lend a hand where they can. But the struggle of my class, to which they are deeply sympathetic, is theoretical to them. Their sense of "rightness," a mostly nonreligious righteousness, is born out of their ideals. Their homes are paid for and their kids attend college courtesy of their parents' smart investments. Before Trump, they saw an America birthing into their egalitarian ideals, the symbols of which were the *New York Times*, brunch, and donkey blue. And then it happened. The enemy, the savages, won. Many of the Pantsuit Nation, though not all, believe that had Hillary taken office, everything would still be heading toward equality and prosperity. That's why their rallying call is "If Hillary had won we'd be at brunch." No wonder they elicit so much animosity, or, at the least, only lukewarm fellowship. They are, rightfully so, fighting against Trump, but like Clinton they fail to articulate a vision beyond protecting the gains of the Obama era and painting Washington blue again. I don't resent them, but I can't follow them. Skocpol states that they organize "as much out of fear and loathing, I would say, as out of hope." I already know loathing and fear. I knew it before Trump. As one who was once a second-class citizen in this country, I am not moved to panic by loathing and fear. I do need hope though.

Both sides, Skocpol states, the Tea Party and the resistance, began by "yell[ing] at the TV." And while the Tea Partiers were galvanized on Meetup.com by the threat of Obamacare and the contrived narrative of an immigrant invasion, the resistance organized on Facebook to save the status quo of the Obama era, which in truth was benefiting them more than those at the bottom of the ladder. That was both the gift and the issue with Obama. He gave us hope but, maybe compromised by the quagmire of Washington politics or his own donor base, the gains were small, more theory than practice. I believe in universal health care but I can't afford it as Obamacare, and I am challenged by the framing of the need to do so as a moral obligation.

I was in college, here at Bard, when Obama first won. I was surprised how emotional it was. I cried with the victory. We all here did. Something special was happening, and my emotional release that day was rivaled only by the tidal wave of anger at Trump's victory, ushered in by the memories of a totalitarian state I fled as a kid. And yet, I have to admit that though Obama was a pivotal cultural victory, he did not represent my issues. I wanted radical change—true universal health care, a restructuring of our education and loan systems, the divorce of money from politics. He, for whatever reasons, just played along in the old game, though doing so with a poet's dignity, which does align with my sensibilities. So when I see Pantsuit Nation courting my allyship, I balk. I think, "You are not enough."

This sentiment is echoed in the Q&A period by a hand in the crowd. Mark Bray, who on a later panel will represent Antifa, an antifascist group endorsing violence, challenges Skocpol. "This [is] a group of middle-class liberal white people who think they're the resistance," he accuses. He reiterates the brunch motto, calling to attention how this is a slight to minorities and the disenfranchised. His affect is contemptuous. He is here to instigate.

Like an old and practiced warrior, Skocpol takes this in stride. She sits easily in her chair after thirty minutes of standing at the podium, and responds confidently. She is ready for battle, convinced in her verdict. In the United States, she says commandingly, political power "has to be won by networks of organizations that have a presence" across the country. "The Left is too tied to biographical democracy in this country," she fires back at Bray. The Tea Partiers "were good citizens in the sense that they recognized that in America we have the right to organize, we have the right to say what we think." The result of our loss is "a cynical, privatized, increasingly unequal country that simply continues its decline"—*not civil war*. She nearly barks those last words as an admonishment. I can already see that Mark Bray wants war. He is satisfied with the tenor of the exchange. And, I can see that Skocpol is willing to wrestle for a return to the illusion of peace.

Skocpol's talk is followed by a roundtable on civil resistance, at which she is a moderator. Sitting with her are Callie Jayne, the director of Rise Up Kingston, a nonprofit across the river from Bard; Rebecca Saletan, an award-winning editor from Riverhead Books; and Judy Pepenella and Dennis Maloney, both Tea Partiers who have been brought in to play the role of the opposition. Everyone has their say. They are all passionate, and they care. I can see that this is their life—these conversations and issues define their sense of community. Maloney nervously reads a prepared manifesto on the concerns of the Tea Party, and Pepenella bubbles up with a message of neighbors and football, and the need to meet outside of politics. I like them. When I was here in college, living off campus and working a service job, these were exactly the sort of salt and mortar locals I gravitated toward when I was not studying. And now, here, I genuinely feel for them, even as I sense the show on the stage normalizing something that should evoke more outrage and passion. This feels, too much at times, like a game. And if so, then it is politics as usual, the thing we are all angry at. Later on I hear Saletan say something to the effect that getting politically involved creates community. I know what she means by that, but the statement throws me. I don't want my politics to rise up out of my desire for company. I want my politics to pass the test of my ethics, in company as well as alone.

Jayne's was the most educational exchange for me. Full of energy and enthusiasm, she, like me, picks her moments in this conference. A few times we shared cigarettes outside. We didn't really talk about Black Lives Matter, even though she is an active organizer. Instead we talked about inequality, the need to change the system, and the potential of creating communities across the country that can exchange skills and knowledge and foster mutual understanding. We talked about change. And strangely enough, for the first time I could see the universal potential that Black Lives Matters has. It is a first conversation, one that leads to others—on equality, justice, and the equal redistribution of dignity. In this nation of original wounds, someone had to lead us into admitting our hypocrisy. Only by admitting our fallacies can we heal. By grabbing the issue at its root, BLM has the potential to lead that charge.

And yet, with all these passionate individuals onstage, Skocpol still comes off as the leader. "This is not a revolution," she says. "This is political reform. Revolutions never turn out the way the revolutionaries expected."

She's right, as much of the wisdom of history tells us. And like a good social scientist, she does not describe a vision; rather, she describes what she sees. And I know it's not enough for me. But then again, I am an "other," and so I am rarely at peace with the status quo.

Who am I kidding? This isn't why I'm here. I came here to talk about revolution. I came here to meet Micah White.

• • •

About a year ago I came across an article in the *Guardian* written by a seasoned activist, the coorganizer of Occupy Wall Street and Rolling Jubilee. This writer addressed the tactical failure of contemporary protest, highlighting the absence of a larger vision. The article also noted the role of Russia as a sort of indicator species on the potential of coopting movements. The key quote I took away was this: "To protect against fake activism in America we must insist that every protest be globally oriented."[3] As an example, what this means to me is that Nike's support of Colin Kaepernick cannot be counted as a win because it takes for granted Nike's sweatshops in China. By marrying the message to an ethically compromised ally, Kaepernick's call for equality is depleted of its integrity.

The writer of the article was Micah White. I then read his book, *The End of Protest: A New Playbook for Revolutions*, where he examines the political emptiness of "clickism" and describes marching in the streets more as theater than a deliberate and ready act focused on the attainment of power. Additionally, he makes a case for four categories of activism: volunteerism, structuralism, subjectivism, and theorgism. You can do your own research on these. I highly recommend that you do. But the basic call of his theory is to consider effective activism as something larger than part-time contract work, as something that must be as agile in its tactics as is our approach to conducting our individual lives. Additionally, White makes a case for a new form of movement, involving a long view of politics and life, taking the message from the congested field of city streets to rural destinations. He and his wife attempted just such a thing when, after the "constructive failure" of Occupy, they moved to a small town in Oregon and White ran for mayor. He lost and left town, receiving a grant from the Roddenbery Foundation, and a fellowship from the Hannah Arendt Center, to build an Activist Graduate School. When I learned of this I reached out to Roger Berkowitz, who got me a seat at the conference and some access to its attendees, of whom Micah White was one.

"We have to stop targeting low-hanging fruit," White says to me as we sit at a windowed nook of the building where I did my undergraduate studies, "turning activism into culturally educational projects—myself included—starting a school. Or really low-hanging fruit like direct action against Whole Foods—so low on the spectrum of dreaming. I think we have to focus on global campaigns on the question of governance and power."

He is thoughtful and articulate; his responses to my questions come off as preconsidered and yet in the process of being reconsidered as well while speaking. He has an air of impatience—not with me, I don't think, but with the pace of our subject: real, political change. Similarly, he is frustrated with the compromised mentality of progressive activism, the "shifting the conversation" slogan that many of the attendees at the conference accept as a win. Additionally, his wife, Chiara Ricciardone, who is coteaching with him at the graduate school and copresenting at the conference, is pregnant and due to give birth any day. My fiction-writer self comes out when I listen to him. His mind has the scope of an epic, multigenerational novel, while the obvious circumstances of his life suggest a depth of character any writer would wish to explore. It makes me want to know how this human conceives the future, because if there is a visionary here, it is him. I don't have to fully accept his vision to see it.

"The reason I don't find the Right terrifying," White says soon after I refresh his quote from the *Guardian* article, "is that they hamstrung themselves because their ideology does not acknowledge global problems, therefore they can't put forward global solutions. But obviously there are global challenges, such as climate change, and so the movements that can actually say 'Look, there are global challenges and we need to have global solutions, and we are the movement that can do that" are the ones that can long-term win. The right wing will ultimately lose their populace."

We dig into what went wrong in Oregon, why he left and how it could have worked otherwise. "I think someone can pull it off," he says. "I think with more funding and I think with more people, yes. . . . It's easier to imagine building a revolutionary movement in rural communities than it is in someplace like NYC."

The root of the contest is sovereignty, he admits. That was the reason he moved to a small town. The question of power in America boils down to legislation, and legislation in America is, and always has been, about the power of ownership—the tactics of landownership. That resonates with me. After all, before it was "the pursuit of happiness," it was "the pursuit of property." I think about my recent attempts to buy a home. How until recently I couldn't even imagine such an act and thus forbade myself from considering its political and personal repercussions.

"Power in outcome" is what the Left is missing, White says in a sober analysis. "Not just powerful, but power in actual outcome. No one on the left has power in outcome. . . . You have to conquer the legislative. . . . I think you need a social movement that can take power. It's the only thing that matters right now."

White is imagining flipping the practice of gerrymandering on itself. He is working backward from outcome to battlefield tactics. But he also has the feel of someone exhausted with the negotiation of it all, tired of misbranding failures into moral victories. He has been fighting all his life, and he looks to me like a tired soldier, the one that retires to a walled-up garden by the ocean after the fighting is complete. His mind, in spite of its talent for essentializing and imagination, comes off decided in its core beliefs. "They are not your friends," he says to me, almost with pain, about his rural neighbors. "They are your opponents," he adds as he makes the case for a rural movement that is progressively minded.

I rephrase what he is suggesting: "Political gentrification?"

"Yeah. Because they have something that's extremely valuable. They have a small community that has sovereignty. But that's what we need. We need to go to a place and say, "Now that we own this place we can pass laws." That's what it means to have sovereignty, we can now pass local laws. The nice approach doesn't work."

I have the urge to counter this. I am less practiced than he is, and thus I may be less jaded. Then again, I may just wear the naivete of the uncommitted. I want to believe in the power of civil discourse and Arendt's vision for a shared public sphere. I want to believe that everyone has a seat at the table— that we are a reasonable, global tribe. I want to be neighbors, not enemies.

"I think people's minds are so polluted," White continues, "including myself, that I think this idea that we're going to educate and convince people is just not true. . . . Everyone is connected to the mental pollution. . . . I don't think I believe in changing people's minds," he admits, in a way that I see that maybe, once, he did.

And yet, when I circle around to his ideas on theorgism, after we've talked about Standing Rock, the mythology of the movement and the strange manifestation of individual dreams that brought people there, and my interpretation of that as having the potential of a linear and noncooptable movement, he replies with a piece of his own dream.

"I don't think you can explain Occupy from a secular interpretation," White admits. "There is some sort of spiritual interpretations of social movements. . . . There's some sort of a spiritual component to social movements," he says again.

I'm not sure we're talking about God, exactly. Neither one of us fits the mold. We're talking about connection. We're talking about mythmaking, or myth finding, really. We're talking about the support of life on earth, the one value that, at least theoretically, joins us all.

We are momentarily joined by Samantha Hill, a professor of politics at Bard and acting assistant director of the Hannah Arendt Center. They talk about the class White has been testing at Bard. It is the pilot for his school. Hill says she is looking forward to hearing what his students have to say.

"Bard students are really good," she says. "They're students who go above and beyond and are genuinely curious and interested." I remember my own experience here, in what felt to me a safe and theoretical field where one could experiment with their ideals.

"Yes, They're so full of . . . passion," White says. "Four of them went to the Kavanaugh protest and all four of them got arrested. I just think like, wow, this is so funny. It just reminds me of my college days." As he says this, I believe I sense some cynical scripting come back into his voice, as if here too he is tired of the theater of it all and hungers for real change, beyond the ivory tower illusions of safe practice.

Hill asks when his wife is due. "Tomorrow. She's at ten months now. . . . It's like a mystical process," White says, and I can see that he means it.

"It *is* a mystical process," Hill agrees, "and pregnancy is ten months, not nine. There is so much mythology about pregnancy [that] has nothing to do with pregnancy. It's amazing that we're there still," she says. And then we go our own ways.

I don't know exactly why it matters, this last part. I should cut it from the story. But in my gut, I know it does matter. In this conversation of reform versus revolution, sometimes it feels like this is the part that we are most removed from, married to the convictions of our political theory on a process so basic and at the center of it all: life, and the mystery that urges us on without ever revealing a fully detectable position of rightness. How do we encourage the world to go forward with less harm? How do we birth our political future into being?

• • •

My partner and I are both in our thirties. In some ways we are traditional. She is a socially fluid extrovert who can code switch with a savant's agility and wishes to evoke kindness in her every relation and social agreement. I like sports, am introverted everywhere but the page, and consider myself a closeted pragmatist. She has invited me into a life outside of theoretic contemplation, and I find ways to recontextualize things that may otherwise bore her into terms that may make them matterful to her—sports as a study in race and power negotiations, Russian literature as an experiment in the renegotiation of the human conditions. In other ways we are the new, modern generation, either sharing roles earlier divided by gender norms or switching entirely. Even now, as I edit this, she reads a book on effective business practices while I use an emersion blender to make soup.

We are both dreamers and hard workers, though she is slightly harder-working than I, while my love for her allows me to restructure my ethereal considerations into practical goals, and to work toward them.

Culture and its norms are being renegotiated around us all the time, and similarly, it occurs in our relationship as well. I guess, like any story, it is love that makes a thought real, the dream manifest through compromise and work. What we both know is that we want a family. We want to have kids and to give them everything that the circumstances of our families did not allow for us. And so, the political is personal here as well, as we encounter very real questions, shared by our generation: what kind of world would we be bringing kids into? What kind of world are we shaping for them?

If responsibility is the product of one's "responsiveness" and one's "ability," then to become actively responsible to these questions I have to strike a balance between the obeying of history and aggressive and real-time creation. I must remember, but if I want to change something, I must also be willing to instigate, to design an alternative and put it into play. I will address what White's students had to tell me, but the panel preceding that one directly tackles the tension I just described.

3:15 p.m. Activism through Art

Renata Stih and Frieder Schnock are German artists whose practice, they state, is devoted to "making history visible, tracing complex relationships between society, art and artifacts comprise [their] vision of institutional critique, shaped by studies about how memory functions in the social sphere and how it is reflected symbolically in the space of museums and the city."

It only makes sense that in Germany the focus of art is remembrance. One of their projects is titled *Bus Stop*. Designed to commemorate the anniversary of the liberation of Auschwitz, the project uses transit as "social sculpture" to "follow the traces of National Socialism in Germany and Europe." The project creates the sense of memorial as a map rather than a destination, a product of national narrative rather than a random episode.

Roger Berkowitz, mostly overseeing the conversation, moderates this panel along with Nelly Ben Hayoun, founder of the International Space Orchestra and the University of the Underground, a tuition-free postgraduate university based in underground urban spaces in London and Amsterdam and supporting unconventional research practices. Ben Hayoun defines herself as a designer of experiences, not as an artist. "I think through experiences and practice. I make things happen," she says. Art is part of her arsenal, but she defines the role of design as something that "reacts to social trends." Like art, it creates an experience, but unlike art the experience must always be directly experienced. Much of Stih and Schnock's practice orients us to the past, toying with memory, while Ben Hayoun's more often builds the immediate future. This match was meant to generate tension.

After giving a lengthy and rather dry presentation of their otherwise very thoughtful work, Stih and Schnock sat down for questioning. Immediately, Ben Hayoun launched into the question of biography, asking the duo how they contextualize themselves within the work. Stih brushes this off. In her view, the artist is absent from the art. She and Schnock create what is needed.

In this way they are craftsmen—keepers of history rather than visionaries. I would argue that for Ben Hayoun, the creation of experience and thinking requires personal perspective, as a reaction has no velocity without the designer's own perspective or style. Stih interprets this question as diverting the audience's attention from the art itself, and counters by highlighting America's obsession with identity and the overeager messaging of its art, a more common characteristic of marketing. She punctuates this by stating that the 9/11 memorial was created too soon, before reflection could take place. This argument accuses (and I am paraphrasing here) the memorial of being market art rather than art for history. Due to its eagerness, the memorial edits out the Iraq and Afghanistan wars. Already peeved at what she perceives in Ben Hayoun as instigation (it is important to note here that Ben Hayoun is French and not American), Stih looks to the audience and states loudly, "They're *your* refugees. Your war!"

In that moment I feel like the error of our entire foreign policy is exposed, by this less-than-graceful artist of history. It's not that she's right about art and the artist—that the artist only reflects the world rather than shapes it into being by the mere effect of making. But she's right about us. We don't reflect. Our symbols of remembrance serve us, not history itself. We don't know how to, or do not want to, talk about the trauma we cause. We much prefer to talk only about the trauma we feel. No wonder facts have become products of opinion. To have truth one must remember history, the building blocks that have brought us to our current state. But we, here, in part because of our power and in part because we have been so isolated for so long, have been divorced from this act of accounting, reflection, and remembrance. Of course the world is ticked off with us. We are arrogant, and our vision of history is self-serving and thus globally divorced, untrue. We fancied ourselves leaders, when really, we've become the perpetrators of a self-serving amnesia.

4:30 p.m. Where Do We Go from Here?
With this on my mind I watch Micah White and Chiara Ricciardone's students take the stage. The students have been enrolled in Micah's pilot course, How to Change the World: Theories and Practices. These kids are a perfect slice of America, representative across gender and race. Ricciardone and White oversee as the kids present their solutions for the world, a theoretic practice in activist campaigning. The repercussions of "campaigning" do not escape me here. Again I interpret this conversation on activism and the building of movements as a type of marketing. In his book, White argues for the power of memes as political warfare to be adopted by the Left. I see the tactical benefit of this but it rubs up against my basic beliefs, which may, in fact, be impossible to adhere to in the real world. Again it feels like a match between elite adversaries waging a war by marketing. I feel like I am being sold a vision, my idea of democracy and equality trapped again in the abstract battlefield

of designers. I wonder if these college kids sense this too, or have they been made more pragmatic than I?

The kids each take their turn at the podium and, at differing levels of excitement or public presence, articulate their campaigns. The campaigns are as follows: a call for the Twenty-eighth Amendment, to get money out of politics; a campaign to negate the practice of othering; lowering the voting age to sixteen; a guarantee to clean water access for all; education on power inequality; recycling and waste management; countering the pollutant effects of factory farming and red meat; an app to combat ICE; a campaign to tackle gender inequality.

I look for the passion Hill and White referenced earlier. If anyone is to have it, it's these Bard kids, still protected enough from the practice of disillusionment, still innocent enough to believe in change, its complexities theoretic and thus still fixable. But there is a sense of exhaustion even to them. In the Q&A period they talk about their experiences protesting the Kavanaugh hearings. Someone from the audience addresses the scripting of protest arrests, and the kids reply in agreement, exasperated by the theater of protest in a way that reminds me of White. He and Ricciardone, their guides, watch the kids tenderly, White offering them the stage, back-saddling his own disillusionment to the potential of these kids and their future. And Ricciardone, tender with them, proud of them as individuals, like a mother, placing the courage of their individual accomplishments above the logic of their campaigns.

I realize as I watch that most of these kids were barely conscious when we went to war. In his book, White stresses the moment the old ways of marching in the streets ceased working. On 15 February 2003, the George W. Bush administration and its conglomerate of allies prepared for war, and the world came out to protest in unprecedented numbers. That night, Bush went on television and declared, "I don't have to listen to these protests because I don't listen to focus groups." And just like that, the voice of the people was reduced to a social science experiment.

These kids have never known a world without war as a backdrop. And so too they may never have known a world with a true democracy, effective in practice. How can my generation, then, help them imagine that which they have never known?

A friend of mine says this of our generation—well, actually, he got this from another friend, who may have gotten it from another friend in turn: "We were raised to believe that by the time of our adulthood we would have colonized the moon, be at war with China, and have jet packs, but are instead competing for part-time remote work with other invisible people. Where are our jet packs?"

Of course we're opting out, be it with drugs, materialism, or the narcotic of simple cynicism. We are, at times, just too plain tired and disillusioned to imagine a future.

In my experience with activist movements, I have observed and interviewed some of those who went to Occupy and Standing Rock and have gotten involved in other time-intensive protests. I have seen many who have dropped their lives to go live for a cause. Though some of them were fully committed, others simply desired a purpose. The act of opting out was simple when the call came. In part, and ironically, this may be the greatest threat to the existing corporate institution—those who leave the infrastructure of the corporate bureaucracy state. There is a possibility, I sense, of a growing movement—an opt-out through disillusionment. It is a mass of negative potential that has yet to be tapped into and united by a collective vision. Once someone, be it an individual or a group, articulates that vision, the existentially disillusioned will move toward it. Maybe the zombie genre has tapped into this vision at its most primal state. Narrative aside, this may be the linear, and organic, generational revolution that comes next.

I talk to one of the kids outside. One who got arrested. "You planning to go to grad school? What's next?"

"No. I'm done," he says. "I want to travel America. I need to see."

What will he find waiting for him there? Further impossibility of change, or some pocket of spirited resistance that helps him, one day, to imagine democracy in practice?

• • •

Over my two days at the conference I talked to a number of attendees. At some point they became more interesting than the speakers.

After the student panel I talk to an older man who since retiring from public service has returned to school. He is attending classes at Brooklyn College, which happens to be the place I once taught. "In my day," he says, through a fixed and eager smile, "I took it to heart what the president said and I went into public service." He is speaking of President Kennedy's mandate to ask what you can do for your country. As he says this he looks around at the campus I have loved. "We used to protest war," he says, recollecting his first round in the institution of higher education. "Now the urge in the institutions is to blow it up."

"Like using the college campus as practice for revolution or war," I paraphrase, realizing I am more like him now than I am like the students, that a part of me would prefer to hold on to some nostalgia rather than build what comes next.

"Exactly."

A man who has been eavesdropping on our conversation about Vietnam chimes in: "Any world that uses a phallus for a compass needle is doomed to fail," the stranger says.

I am struck by this, and so is the retired civil servant. We both nod, him remembering the birth of his ideals in the '60s, and me, remembering their silencing in 2003, my thoughts between a rock and a hard place—the true reality of necessitating change, and the seeming impossibility of revolution. The structures, I think, are just too deep, and were they even to crash, the collateral—my Soviet emigrant self remembers—is just not worth it.

But then I remember something else, something another friend recently said of the world, quoting Joanna Macy: "Maybe the answer is building Gaian structures in the shell of the old." Maybe this comes off as too ethereal to resonate, but I think of one of the houses I recently saw for sale. The bones were solid but other things were failing. To restore it one would need to rebuild parts from within and then allow for the weathered and failed components of the structure to collapse. It's doable, I thought. Though my carpentry skills are not yet strong enough. But yes, it can be done. Though for that we would need a new breed of builders, those who have the guttural resolve to resist the mandate of an unforgiving market to put forward a compromised design, those willing to even expose the fault lines, so that when the time comes, we know where to direct the pressure. We need inspectors whose loyalty is to the *integrity* of a structure above all else.

5:30 p.m. Whistleblowing as Civil Disobedience: Leaks in the Era of Trump and the Deep State
The final panel for the day is headlined by Allison Stranger, a political scientist out of Middlebury College and author of *One Nation under Contract: The Outsourcing of American Power and the Future of Foreign Policy*, where she details the rise of outside contracting in American government and makes a case for less consolidation and more good governmental practices. In her lecture, Stranger builds from the premise that "all civil disobedients are dissenters, but not all dissenters are civil disobedients." She suggests that in a time of political crisis whistleblowers are those "who often illuminate the gap between American ideals and a fact-based world, the real world, where ideals usually are not realized." She notes that while whistleblowing has become accepted as a shadowy instrument within the checks and balances of a booming institutional complexity, the Whistleblower Protection Enhancement Act of 2012 specifically prohibits the practice in the area of national security. Yet, if we admit that extreme measures are necessary in a time of crisis, then we can accept the act as a necessary diversion from the mandate of governmental cohesion.

"When the rule of law itself is threatened, whistleblowing can be necessary to defend liberal democracy as a whole. I would argue," Stranger adds, "that illegal leaks that expose true betrayals of American democracy are neither partisan nor political; they are patriotic." And, "until the immediate danger has passed, it makes sense, regardless of your political affiliation, to focus on the shocking substance of the information being revealed rather than the questionable means by which that information is coming to light." So, in short: don't shoot the messenger, listen to the message.

David Bromwich, Sterling Professor of English at Yale University and the workhorse of the conference (he appeared on three separate panels), brings up two necessary points. First, that there is irony in the "left liberal side of the United States becoming so good-natured and trusting of the CIA, FBI, and NSA. . . . It ought to evoke a little suspicion, so let's call them spies and surveillance apparatchiks," he suggests, and not bestow upon them in these rare circumstances some level of moral objectivity they have not earned.

It strikes me here, the difference between these agencies and what in my first country was the KGB. While most members of the KGB were former soldiers, much of the American spy network is made up of lawyers. Thus, it makes perfect sense that their commitment is to the rule of law. Not rightness, or even justice, but law. And so, when an individual in power violates the legal structure, and Congress fails to act, of course these individual actors should move to expose the violation.

And here Bromwich sees the larger issue: "Is a generalized policy of leaks a legitimate method in defense of war against a chief magistrate in order to uphold a rule of law in the long-term against a chief magistrate who has declared war against the rule of law?" Basically, "Once you've lost it, can you get it back?" By "it" he means the equilibrium of institutional order—trust.

Stanger counters: "They are not blowing the whistle on the institution of the American presidency. They are blowing the whistle on one individual who is behaving unlike any past president." She argues that we should not make these people heroes. Rather, we should permit an indecent act for the better good.

Coming from a country that lost its soul under the banner of "the ends justify the means," I am naturally skeptical of such reasoning. And yet, I see the difference as well. While the Soviet Union suppressed individualism for the supposed fulfillment of the collective good, Stranger is arguing for the uncommon acts of individual dissent, in the Arendtian spirit of civil disobedience. And thus, such an act remains in accordance with America's founding ethos.

Hers is a powerful assertion, one that should stir the mind. Yet the feeling in the room is that we are already past all of that. The governmental disorder and institutional distrust now feel accepted as part of our daily lives. It seems that we are beyond structural arguments; rather, we are seeking an extreme proposal that can set the abstract whole again.

• • •

A wine and cheese reception follows, but I am too tired to engage in anything more than pleasantries. I consider whether I have an answer for what the future may hold. My friends back on the West Coast are hopeful that I will bring back some news of a coming transformation. But I have nothing, so far, beyond philosophical considerations, and after day one I have no illusions that this learned class will offer me any solutions. I fall asleep that night lucidly dreaming of having a family and a home.

• • •

I am standing outside a house, which we may or may not be preparing to buy. I am next to a dream. My credit has been raised, my debts mostly paid or consolidated, and my employment made steady in spite of my freelance ambitions. I am ready to buy. This position is in large part the product of my girlfriend's foresight and responsibility. She is American, tangibly aware and financially vigilant, understanding, in her body, what it takes to build a life here. She will make a great mother, in this modern age. On a very basic and primal field I know this. I want this dream. I want to cross into this dream with her. And yet something tugs at me as I make the calls to my bank and credit agency and student loan people, some sense that keeps me more connected to the realms of history and ideas than the tangible world of people and their systems, or the rules that govern them. Something akin to survivor's guilt. In my heart . . . no, not in my heart. In my heart I want to love, I want to marry and have a home and children, I want the promised American Dream. In some chamber very near my heart, maybe the liver—there, I want a revolution. I want something radical. That is what brings me to the conference. A subtly intoxicating mix of hope, curiosity, and guilt. I want the homeless me to embrace the homeowner. I want the radical and the thinker to join the father and husband-to-be. I want to be a citizen, and I don't want the polarity of my mind or my feelings—I want a nonpartisan life. I want for them to lead me, together.

• • •

Day two begins with an address by the president of Bard, Leon Botstein. Botstein notes the need for such a conference today and concurrently compliments Trump as one who "in his own way is gifted in manipulation of attention." In the argument that the revolution has already happened, this is actually key. Our greatest resource is our attention—literally, what we lend our time and psychic space to. What we think about is the ultimate currency, and what all other currencies seek to coopt. One who can galvanize this source leads the mob. Trump has done just that.

But how does a side that ultimately does not believe in hierarchical order do the same? How do we activate and organize ourselves, linearly? That is, how do we do so without becoming the thing we abhor?

9:15 a.m. Violent and Nonviolent Protest
In the following panel, Mark Bray finally gets the floor, and David Bromwich is back opposite him. Bray is a practiced agitator, a modern resistance fighter

whose experience has brought him to an A-to-B kind of logic, and he knows the arguments that are coming his way. "Civility," he says, "is the box into which nonviolent protest is expected to fit." Of course he argues that there are times when civility is just another mechanism of control by an illegitimate state. "There is no nonviolent way to stop fascism," he says.

I can't actually argue with that. As a former Jewish refugee, I am steeped in the stories of failed civility. I was brought up with the post-Holocaust slogan of "Never again," and while I disagree with many of Israel's positions, I recognize the quite real circumstances that brought the slogan into being. Then again, I also see Israel as a state that, by the quite real facts of its trauma, has become the carrier of the abuse it wished to protect itself from. A new issue arises when a victim assumes a position of power but still retains the impenetrable perspective of victimhood. A ruling philosophy of strength above all, and violence, seems to me like a dangerous virus we cannot allow ourselves to universally accept. But Bray is also arguing on the spectrum of privilege and legitimacy: Who has the right to be violent? Is it our government? Is it corporations? Why not the people? And he adds that this argument too often splits the resistance. That ultimately, Antifa is "one tool on a kind of Swiss Army knife of revolutionary politics."

Bromwich returns to the philosophical considerations. He outs himself as one whose practice of resistance and social action is his writing. He is not trying to break apart Bray's case. Rather, he asks us to consider each of the steps we are taking. I see this, in part, as an effort to map our path of agreements, so if and when needed we can find our way back. He states the four criteria we should monitor in our questioning of whether we should overthrow the state. The object of the change "must be great and consequential. The evil must also be great. The abuse or many abuses in question must show no sign of abating," says Bromwich. "And last: there's no other means of remedy at hand." In the world we wish to create, Bromwich asks, "how will you have trained yourself for this end by the energy you employ as a means?"

Here again I return to Micah White's call for a globally effective protest. The need to consider each of our steps in the context of the energetic effect they produce. Is the enemy of my enemy a friend, or is my allyship with him disrupting the basis of the beliefs from which I wish to rebuild the world? How rigid must one be to engineer an outcome? At what point does the rigid adherence to ideals extinguish the flame?

10:30 a.m. Organizing from the Ground
America's system of governance has always seemed like the greatest compromise of rule. It provides certain individual rights while still maintaining a large container for the whole of its potential populace. I am willing to accept that the founders of this country were not all good men. Obviously, they were not. Obviously, they were all men, all white. Yet they somehow delivered a uniquely

spirited document. That document is under assault now: at best, reinterpreted to fit special interests only; at worst, its basic tenets completely disregarded.

Christopher Schmidt, a constitutional lawyer joining the panel on grass-roots organization, states that, essentially, the Constitution is an antirevolution document. This can be read two ways: one, that it is just another lever of control masquerading as a pillar of humanitarian Law; or two, that its intent was to create a system of governance flexible enough to withstand generational changes in culture and government. The founders had likely been exhausted by years of tyranny and war. They wished, I want to believe, that we would never have to go there again. Of course, America still had to catch up, to remedy the aspects of its society that turned the document into hypocrisy, negating its logic of liberty. Thus we had the Civil War, to finally fulfill the promise of all men being created equal. And we have continued battling ever since, to make true the basic promises of our rights.

The Bill of Rights is a social agreement we enter into as individuals. When that agreement is not held up by the law, it appears to be our duty to disobey the law. Thus we become civil disobedients, and in Arendt's analysis, truly American. In that same panel, someone describes a radical as one who grabs a cause "at the root."

I am in a room of moderates and radicals, all in agreement that something is wrong but at differing points of orientation toward the root of the issue. This misalignment, between those who all agree that there is some collective error, some line of code gone haywire, but are unable to collectively fix their sights, energy, and intellect upon that line of code, reminds me of *The Matrix*, and it then reminds me of Jean Baudrillard's work in *Simulacra and Simulation* (the book upon which the movie was loosely based), where the French philosopher argues that we have entered some postmodern, postagreement, postreality age in which our collective abstraction is the product of the broken code.

This line of thought is brought to a crescendo for me in the next lecture.

2:00 p.m. A Politics of Radical Democratic Citizenship
Chantal Mouffe is a true political philosopher. She has been considering politics and the psychic space politics engenders for three decades. Hers is an effort to observe and describe, not just in the tangible world of Theda Skocpol but also in the theoretical space that governs our thoughts. She was also a key influence in the development of Roger Berkowitz's thinking; he in turn significantly influenced the way I think about politics and the world. And her statement blew my socks off.

"We live," Professor Mouffe states, "in a postdemocracy world." And the product of our state is a populist existence. Essentially, we have been globally connected, in spite of our disagreements, our economic and racial differences, into a single organism. One that is, at times and often, at odds with itself. This organism does not share set values; rather, it shares only the state of its interdependence, its collectivism. Her line of thought suggests that there is no going back, that any restructuring of its basic premise would only be made possible by an apocalyptic event, which no one really wants. And thus, we move forward, live and build, by the momentum of popular agreement rather than our ideals or principles. It is not equality that rages us on. It is popular opinion, which has its source in a myriad of earlier agreements. Thus, anyone talented enough to galvanize the public designs our reality. In this way, Mouffe propels social constructionism through the admission that we have lost our way, or the illusion thereof. She concedes, in a way, that materialism has won.

In a way, she also stands on the opposite bank of Micah White's thinking. While one wishes to imagine a true global revolution, the other admits global complexity as exactly the reason a revolution cannot be.

I think back to White and Ricciardone's students. That, if we are in a postdemocracy state, and have been there for some time, then we have a generation that cannot reference true democracy and thus will need to imagine it. If so, is it then not our job—us, those who have a however faint and fleeting sense of democracy—to concede the temporary loss, admit that maybe we were wrong about the effect of our citizenship, and thus create spaces that help encourage the imagination of the future? One that we ourselves lack the faith to imagine? Is it not up to us, then, to consider experimenting in the potential structures and technology that may ultimately help this next generation, or even the generation after them, to actualize what they imagine? Is it not a purpose worth living for, to basically prepare the ground for the revolution, and to let go of our own vision of the results?

I leave this panel with a darkness at the pit of my stomach. A sort of defeatism in the face of what appears to be a fact. This is no democracy. I can imagine a democracy in some alternate dimension but I cannot bring it into being. It runs parallel to this one but it remains an approximation only, a theory. This is not even conspiracy making, just an acknowledgment of some force that made us go, the gathered momentum of a wide and complex civilization. How do you change such a course? To do so, we would need to understand all of history, and to acknowledge all of the history that has been lies. And then we would need to remedy all those lies. We would need to become master weavers. Our truth is built upon a series of sometimes enlightened, sometimes corrupted agreements. It would take a supernatural effort to untangle this web, a miracle to inspire us toward the pursuit of integrity above all else.

• • •

I stand outside. The rain that has been coming in and out for the last two days has stopped. Students are rushing from one classroom to another. A few linger at benches, reading or in grave conversation. The sun hits the building in that way of hope and light.

"Life is worth defending," I think, in that way of subjectivism, as if that matters; just simply feeling it for a moment, because it does.

Maybe it does start in America, this disentanglement of lies. Simply because we, for better or worse, command the most attention. We don't deserve it, but we have it. To make America great would mean to make it a beacon of light, to enact a practice of democracy free of hypocrisy; but to do so, we must tackle the inconsistency of our agreements. America is built upon a tradition of slavery and land theft. Inequality, and the upholding thereof, is the structure our progress has depended upon. And though I balk at the prevalence of identity politics, I am considering how that conversation, in fact, is pulsing us toward the negotiation of a new design. This is not to say that we should be restructuring our world along tribal lines of belonging; that only spells further division and resentment. Rather, maybe we are being asked to reconsider the arising of a new value, above materialism, what Francis Fukuyama calls "the dignity of the soul." The innate need buried deep within each individual to be recognized, to be seen. What does this mean for me, then? Can I have both my personal joy and the peace of the soul that comes with global responsibility?

3:00 p.m. MLK and the Legacy of Civil Disobedience in America
The final panel evokes the name that brought civil disobedience into the American spotlight. The panel is led by four voices: Kenyon Victor Adams (little ray), artist in residence at Yale University, whose work aims to inspire empathy across diverse lines and whose play, *Prayers for the People*, will close the conference; Thomas Chatterton Williams, who authors work on multiethnicity; Amy Schiller, fellow at the Brooklyn Institute for Social Research; and moderator Ann Seaton, Bard visiting faculty, director of the Difference and Media Project, and director of multicultural affairs.

Adams kicks the panel off with a quote from King: "If America does not respond creatively to the challenge to banish racism, some future historian will have to say that a great civilization died because it lacked the soul and commitment to make justice a reality for all." Here, Adams places the struggle directly at the heart of the matter, the issue of institutionalized hierarchy, as what has been described as the struggle for America's soul. He adds King's analysis that "the ultimate logic of racism is genocide." Adams goes on to acknowledge a sad fact of King's optimism: "King's methodology of nonviolent, direct action relies on two basic elements that have proven artificial or unsustainable: one, the delusional character of American democracy; and two, the inherent and inextricable Christianness of white-identifying citizens." King believed that these facts would in the end move Americans to embrace true equality upon moral grounds. Sadly, we have seen the opposite happen, as a dark marriage occurred between Christianity, corporatism, and the GOP, and religion has become a gathering space for identity division rather than humanistic union.

This leads to these questions: what shall the movement toward equality look like today? Can there be a movement toward linear assimilation, or is disruption the last available method? Schiller speaks to this when she shares Arendt's observations on the Jews of Europe, a differentiation between those of the parvenu (one who comes from outside but is able to achieve through striving an assimilation) and the pariah:

> The parvenu yearns for acceptance attainable only through social climbing towards the rewards of mainstream society. By contrast, the pariah uses her detachment from mainstream society to see it more clearly, to speak against oppression that is rendered visible by the conditions of her own life. The conscious pariah resists oppression through embracing her marginality. She becomes a champion of oppressed people, and she's able to analyze the circumstances by which they become so. Elisabeth Young-Bruehl notes that the pariah's task includes this one critical component, "to avoid sacrificing the outsider's perspective for the parvenu's comfort."

Again, here I return to that sense of discomfort I feel as I prepare to buy a home. I feel, at times, almost entirely assimilated. That is, not like *them*—*them* as the *other* I once yearned to be (a starting point for my personal release comes from the knowledge that due to my history I can never be *them*)—but my difference has been made nearly invisible. And here the survivor's guilt returns. I acknowledge that this is a privilege available to one like me, someone, at least on the outside, who is capable of floating between outsider and insider cultures, but who, by the however subtle fact of their (my) outsiderness, immediately identifies with all the outsiders of the world. My *whatever* degree of otherness marries me to them. Something in me will not feel at rest until the potential of recognition for all is realized. And yet, I want *my* joy as well.

Williams addresses this in his own life. He is half black, half white, and now living in France. To a degree, he has found himself outside of the race conversation in America. In France, he admits, his race does not matter. In fact, France, in spite of its own like issues, is working toward taking all references to race out of its constitution. It's another experiment with the identity conversation. During the panel Q&A, Williams admits this is a sort of novel, and possibly enlightened, gesture toward complete equalization: "The most radical act of civil disobedience that I can probably do," he says, "is to step out of this black-white binary."

I remember the earlier quote about a radical being one who grasps an issue at its root. Clearly a thinker, and one desiring a long-view vision, Williams has moved to the great fringe of the race conversation. He is trying to admit the fact of race as a social construct, and to imagine a world that can accept such. By living in the theory of this postracial construct, he is attempting the practice of bringing it into being. Of course, while the fact of this construct may be true, in the practical world it does not work. Race, however it may have been a false invention once, has now been brought into factual being through the negative space of racism. What was once a social construct has been drawn by hate into a real condition.

Seaton, who also happens to be part black and part white, and Williams have a tense exchange where she nearly accuses him of cultural erasure and naivete. In the follow-up Q&A, a Bard student, also interpreting Williams's comments as an act denying him his own blackness and identity, calls Williams "a fool."

I watch this unfold on stage. Williams, who has clearly fought his own battles for inclusion, but maybe more so for the freedom to define his own self, sits quietly onstage. His voice falls in its authority but not in the spirit of its self-determination, as its tenderness becomes its power of delivery. He reiterates what Sidney Poitier said when he was asked why he hid in France while the race war raged on in his birth country. "If the fight is joy," Williams says, "he already had it." His own children, Williams adds with a laugh to underscore this thesis, look like they were born in Switzerland. He has found his freedom.

Adams jumps in with his own experience of becoming a father in America. He describes how when his daughter was born he was not allowed to name her until he'd checked off a box on a form indicating her racial identity. "This is the United States of America," says Adams. "If that's not apartheid, you're going to have to explain to me what it is." He's not arguing against Williams's thesis. Rather, he's stating the simple fact of a complex American construct.

If the dimensions of how one is defined depend upon an outside entity, be it government or culture, instead of the products of one's own choices, then how can we discover democracy again? If we have no personal reference point for such self-deliverance, then how can the world we build out together ever approximate freedom?

I have no answers. I ask you this only as I ask myself—not as a partisan or one convinced by the arguments of any special side but as both witness and participant in a massively complicated whole in which you and I, as individuals, however separate and distant, are still, by some mysterious butterfly effect, united. The end of my journey, ultimately, is not to bring you answers but to deliver from the fringe some questions on which we can, at the least, agree. Maybe you will find answers. Maybe I will, someday. But ultimately, it is faith that joins us in the possibility of creating a world more just than we have experienced it to be. Common faith, not supernatural at all, but nevertheless requiring a leap across a vastness that many will tell us is too dangerous. My faith, in you, that you will consider this from the uniqueness of your own individual kindness. Your faith, similarly placed in the global citizen in me. Or maybe our kids will find the answers together, better than we ever could.

• • •

I am outside the building again. The panels are complete. Only little ray's play remains, and then I will board a plane to return west, where my home is. A very old, very thin, very jolly-looking man stands next to me. We start talking. He is

Citizenship and Civil Disobedience

visiting from Queens. He is so excited by all the thoughts of the conference. His excitement feels like life itself. His name is Angel.

"Well," I ask Angel, "are you feeling optimistic?"

He giggles and smiles at me through his giant glasses. "Arendt talked about the need to live in the desert, politically," he says. "Some become utopian and optimistic, others bitter and hopeless. They build permanent structures in their thought." He pauses and smiles again, encouraged by the thought that makes him happy. "No, you must live in the desert," Angel says, as his cab shows up.

I remember the last time I left this place, to go work in the desert. Most markers of my identity had been lost or surrendered then. I had sold my car, the USPS had lost most of my books, and had I let go of my jobs and academia. And I was not yet what I would later become. In the desert I found peace. I found it at dawn. The vastness of the earth overcomes you in the morning, as the sun washes the sand clean of your dreams. You are not yet defined in such a place. You are the everything that is possible. It is almost bitter, almost euphoric, almost holy, were you to want to define such a moment, which in the moment you do not. You are, momentarily, free.

> From bitter searching of the heart,
> Quickened with passion and with pain
> We rise to play a greater part.
> This is the faith from which we start:
> Men shall know commonwealth again
> From bitter searching of the heart.
> We loved the easy and the smart,
> But now, with keener hand and brain,
> We rise to play a greater part.
> The lesser loyalties depart,
> And neither race nor creed remain
> From bitter searching of the heart.
> Not steering by the venal chart
> That tricked the mass for private gain,
> We rise to play a greater part.
> Reshaping narrow law and art
> Whose symbols are the millions slain,
> From bitter searching of the heart
> We rise to play a greater part.
> —Leonard Cohen, "Villanelle for Our Time"

1. Hannah Arendt, "Civil Disobedience," in *Crises of the Republic* (New York: Harvest/HBJ Books, 1969), 69–70.
2. "An Open Letter to the Hannah Arendt Center at Bard College," *Chronicle of Higher Education*, 23 October 2017, chronicle.com/article/An-Open-Letter-to-the-Hannah/241526.
3. Micah White, "I Started Occupy Wall Street. Russia Tried to Co-Opt Me," *Guardian*, 2 November 2017, theguardian.com/commentisfree/2017/nov/02/activist-russia-protest-occupy-black-lives-matter.

Heroic Politics on Screen

Heroic Politics on Screen

Libby Barringer

In early April 2019 the Hannah Arendt Center hosted an event that considered how superhero films speak to our contemporary political landscape, and whether they enable or undermine democratic practices. In recent years superheroes have dominated popular entertainment. The first DC and Marvel superhero films were released in the 1920s. Just counting Marvel and DC properties, about ninety films have been made since that time. Over seventy of these have been produced and released since 9/11.[1] The political backdrop of this broad cultural turn toward superheroes has thus been two decades of war, political instability, and crisis. Questions of the proper limits of sovereign authority, extralegal activity, and rising anxiety about the fates of representative, democratic institutions have defined a political world that, simultaneously, has become saturated with superheroic narratives.

For some time scholars have been interested in the ways narrative conventions of film and genre fiction engage the political expectations of their audiences, and vice versa. Theorists such as Lauren Berlant and Michael Rogin have shown how political desires and fears play out in popular, sentimental fiction.[2] John Lawrence and Robert Jewett have similarly argued that superheroes themselves draw from a long tradition of deeply conventional American storytelling, where "ritualized mythic plots . . . suggest important clues about the tensions, hopes, and despair concerning democracy within the current American consciousness."[3] In similar terms, Umberto Eco described superheroes as the products of an increasingly disempowered age, where "the positive hero must embody to an unthinkable degree the power demands that the average citizen nurtures but cannot satisfy."[4] By this view, superheroes stand as fantasies of the kind of individual strength that would be necessary to compete with the overwhelming power of contemporary global economic and political forces.

Yet more than simply operating as mirrors to public fears and desires, these stories shape political expectations in turn. Superheroes are easy to dismiss because of their outlandish premises: gamma rays, bat signals, infinity stones, and a questionable sartorial preference for spandex. But when viewing audiences see the same kind of story, over and over again, its emotional rhythms and conventions can begin to feel natural, and tend to bleed into political discourses.[5] As fantastic as they are, superhero films supply their own mythic organization of the world into moral and political cosmologies. They tell us who is heroic and who is villainous; who saves and who is rescued; and what kinds of violence, in what kinds of contexts, are legitimate or worthy of our admiration.

These mythic frameworks transfer perhaps *too* easily to public life. Faced with a world of shifting, complex global politics and a rising sense of popular disempowerment, retreating into emotionally satisfying worldviews where heroic actors redeem us, the innocent bystanders, from the actions of obvious villains is comforting, if dangerous. As Sheldon Wolin warns, speaking of the intensely mythological qualities of the notion of American "superpower," a concept that is itself drawn from comic books, "when myth begins to govern decision makers in a world where ambiguity and stubborn facts abound, the result is a disconnect between the actors and reality."[6]

If the stories we encounter on screen shape the expectations of viewing audiences in these subtle and powerful ways, it becomes a matter of pressing concern to examine their conventions. The introduction that follows and the talks that this special section collects take up this work. We ask what kind of stories these are, and what kinds of political life they imagine. Do superheroes speak only to democratic despair, a desire to escape conditions of powerlessness through redemptive fantasies of awesome strength? Or can we find resources in superhero films capable of fostering more open, empowering, and democratic ends? What can these films, and the ways they represent politics, teach us about our current moment?

Ordinary Politics and Emergency
Superheroes are generally distinguished from other kinds of heroes in three ways: to be a superhero an individual must have remarkable powers, a defined mission, and they must outwardly display or perform a deliberate identity.[7] Superhero stories also tend to follow specific conventions. They feature exceptional individuals who emerge in moments of crisis to protect average citizens from danger. Imbedded in the superhero narrative is thus an opposition where ordinary political life is reaffirmed through moments of emergency. As Richard Reynolds puts it, "Superhero narratives clearly give substance to certain ideological myths about the society they address. . . . Far from being as 'escapist' as is claimed, most superhero comics are intensely grounded in the normal and everyday."[8]

Reynolds focuses here on the ways that superheroic narratives can be deeply conservative: superheroes typically aim to preserve or restore order, not reinvent it.[9] This focus on the maintenance of ordinary life remains even in more critical films and comics, or those that take up explicitly progressive ends.[10] Films such as *Black Panther* (2018) and *Logan* (2017), for instance, which interrogate notions of what "ordinary political life" looks like, are nonetheless frequently modest in their revolutionary aims. It is supervillains who attempt to violently found new world orders, and superheroes who rise up to stop them. Even in their more critical modes, then, superhero films tend to depict ordinary life "from the vantage point of ongoing crisis."[11] They imagine a world that requires moral and political intervention, one facing exceptional disruption from within or cosmic threat from without. Superheroes thus engage a problem familiar to democratic theorists. They are *extraordinary* political actors.

In democratic political theory, "ordinary politics" typically refers to political life defined by the rule of law, everyday institutional practices, governance by elites, and the ongoing reproduction of the status quo. "Extraordinary politics," in contrast, refers to episodic moments of rupture, crisis, and intense change that transgress established, formal boundaries or result in the wholesale transformation of social and political norms.[12] Extraordinary politics, for these reasons, are often associated with moments of revolution and political founding where a decisive break opens the grounds for a people to constitute a new polity, or alter history. Alternatively, the *threat* of a decisive break, or the interruption of ordinary political life, can also yield extraordinary politics: a state of emergency, where sovereign power suspends ordinary practices in order to preserve itself against existential threat.

By far the simplest way to view superhero films is through the lens of emergency. Indeed, many features of typical superhero films parallel the narrative justifications of emergency state powers. Carl Schmitt, whose language features heavily in contemporary debates on the subject, defines the sovereign as the entity "who decides on the exception," meaning that sovereign power is proved by having (and enacting) the right to decide when the law applies and when it does not.[13] "Emergency situations" are those when typical rule of law must be suspended, and a "state of exception" instituted in the name of securing the whole.[14] It is a well-established trope that superheroes claim a similar prerogative for themselves. Like Schmittian sovereigns, superheroes spend most of their time operating within ordinary institutional or legal limits. Yet their secret, hidden powers—granted to them through extraordinary origins—enable them to act outside these boundaries when necessary, protecting ordinary political life by acting decisively above it.

Consider Marvel's 2012 movie *The Avengers*, directed by Joss Whedon.[15] In this film, a team of heroes is formed in response to an emergency of epic proportions. An alien invasion threatens earth, led by the villain Loki (Tom Hiddleston). Loki makes it quite clear that what is at stake in the film is nothing less than the freedom of the human world: "I bring you glad tidings of a world made free," he announces, "[. . . from] freedom." We watch as our disaffected heroes—led by Iron Man (Robert Downey Jr.) and Captain America (Chris Evans)—are coaxed out of their private lives to meet this threat. Initially they are called together by Nick Fury (Samuel L. Jackson), a spymaster who works for the covert government organization S.H.I.E.L.D. After a few false starts and disagreements, the Avengers finally assemble to protect the citizens of New York and save the day, before vanishing back into their respective private lives.

Importantly, when they ultimately emerge as a team to save the world, the Avengers do so under their own authority rather than at the behest of any governmental institution. The film narratively and emotionally ties the legitimacy of their actions to the suffering of ordinary people—a form of emotional appeal familiar to melodramatic narratives. Libby Anker describes this as "felt legitimacy," an "intensely affective state where legitimacy [of state action] is felt as righteous, true, and obligatory . . . , [working] in a contrary fashion to the formal procedures and collective practices of deliberation that define legitimacy in democratic and liberal political theory."[16] Indeed, the final emotional "push" that brings the Avengers together is not a formal order from Fury but a desire to "avenge" the death of everyman S.H.I.E.L.D. operative Phil Coulson (Clark Gregg).

In parallel ways, this same "avenging" dynamic plays out across the film, as civic vulnerability to outsize threat legitimates the Avengers' extralegal interventions. The initial shots of New York show us residents enjoying a sunny day, drinking coffee and chatting while commuters travel to work. These everyday routines are violently disrupted by hordes of alien invaders who crash into buildings, explode cars, and generally wreak havoc. The heroes respond in kind, battling to contain the invasion within several chaotic midtown Manhattan blocks. Whedon makes sure to track some of these civilian groups throughout the ensuing fight, focusing in particular on a waitress who appears three times in the final act, once in dire need of rescue, and again at the very end of the movie, where she is given one of the film's final lines: "[Is this disaster] somehow their fault? Captain America saved my life. Wherever he is, wherever any of them are, I would just want to say thank you."

Stories like this are politically comforting to the extent they connect great power with great responsibility. Yet this framing also reinforces the idea that the maintenance of freedom depends on exceptional, heroic agents (or exceptional, heroic states) to defend its conditions—above and beyond the powers of individuals to defend those conditions themselves. From this perspective, then, we might look at the popularity of superhero films as an expression of democratic anxiety. Many theorists have written of the difficulty, if not impossibility, of fostering democratic agency and citizenship in contemporary times.[17] In the widespread popularity of superhero films we might read a similar recognition of the difficulty of democratic action, and a parallel desire for governments or political elites who are morally trustworthy and deserve our gratitude; figures who redeem us and validate our suffering even as they wield tremendous, destructive powers in our name.

The film ends with footage of the team going their separate ways while the shadowy security council complains that Nick Fury has not properly bound the Avengers with any formal oversight. This sequence is cut in between a series of interviews with alternatively grateful and uneasy citizens who debate the recent heroic intervention, including the waitress's final speech mentioned above. "How do we know [the Avengers] will come back?" Maria Hill (Colby Smothers), another S.H.I.E.L.D. officer, asks Nick Fury as these interviews conclude. "Because we'll *need* them to," he reassures her. Needing heroes is a theme repeated across the Marvel and DC films, and in unsettled times it is comforting to believe that heroes we deserve will emerge in moments of crisis. But this, of course, creates a problem. If even on screen democracy and rule of law cannot be preserved through the concerted actions of ordinary citizens, what does this imply about the perceived sustainability, or even legitimacy, of democratic politics?

Rather than stories that affirm a basic need for heroic rescue and intervention, then, we might instead look for stories that remind ordinary persons of their capacities to act. If Schmittian emergency closes the political landscape into binaries of friend and enemy, sovereign and subject, actor and victim, a more democratic narrative would remind audiences of the limits of sovereign decision, the potential for creative action, and the irreducible complexity of the political world they inhabit. Can superhero films provide these resources? Must these extraordinary actors be read as antidemocratic figures of emergency?

Extraordinary Action

While questions of emergency and extrajudicial state action have—for good reason—dominated public conversations since 9/11, the prevalence of these concerns makes it easy to overlook the more democratic, transformative potentials of extraordinary politics. Earlier I defined extraordinary politics as episodic moments of rupture or change that transgress established boundaries, sometimes transforming political norms wholesale. It is important that such changes, from the perspective of sovereign power, can *themselves* appear as existential threats. Yet what appears as an emergency to an established order might simply be a necessary moment of political opening, or the start of something new. As Bonnie Honig puts it, "A certain kind of sovereignty . . . —unitary and decisive, committed to its own invulnerability—is most vulnerable to experiencing the political, with its contingencies and uncertainties, as a crisis."[18] In other words, the sudden or partial transformation of ordinary political practices is not necessarily a *threat* to democratic politics; it may simply be what *democratic practice actually looks like.*

Certainly the most extreme examples of this kind of extraordinary democratic politics are moments of collective (re)founding, where a multitude jointly constitute themselves into a people, defining themselves through social norms and legal boundaries. Such moments are rife with paradox and uncertainty. The powers that allow a people to found a polity also allow them to dissolve it, and there is never any guarantee that a people will use their democratic powers to establish democratic ends. Yet, crucially, these powers do not simply vanish once a polity is established. If we accept that it is within the capacities of ordinary persons to constitute or dissolve a polity, we must also accept these capacities sit in vital tension with everyday political practice.[19] The people are, in this sense, *always* founding themselves, and always potentially a threat to the stability of the communities they constitute—not because of inherent evil or ignorance but because of their capacities to create new beginnings.

Few political theorists are as sensitive to this aspect of political life as Hannah Arendt. Arendt frequently insists on the "miraculous" powers of ordinary persons to initiate new processes and relationships that "force open all limitations and cut across all boundaries."[20] The condition of political freedom for Arendt is plurality: to be among—and above all, to act with—other distinct persons.[21] Above all, freedom is shaped by the innate capacity persons have to begin, just as they themselves are each new beginnings: "With the creation of man, the principle of beginning came into the world itself, which, of course, is only another way of saying that the principle of freedom was created."[22] Freedom is in this sense far more than a formal, legal status. It is a kind of experience one has in the company of others. "Men are free as long as they act," Arendt writes, "neither before nor after; for to be free and act are the same."[23]

This element of Arendt's thought is sometimes described as "heroic" for its emphasis on action as a virtuoso performance that discloses the individual to the world, potentially yielding glorious immortality.[24] Yet, viewed "as a human faculty that makes certain kinds of politics possible," Arendt's account of action is not restricted to the abilities of specific, extraordinarily heroic actors.[25] Rather, what is affirmed is the possibility for persons to alter and rearrange established orders, often in unexpected ways. Indeed, alongside her emphasis on heroic virtuosity and disclosure Arendt consistently critiques modern conflations of freedom with sovereign control.[26] She insists that human action is inescapably tragic, prone to setting off uncontrollable chains of events that actors could not have anticipated but must live with nonetheless. "Because the actor always moves among and in relation to other acting beings," she writes, "he is never merely a 'doer' but always and at the same time a sufferer."[27] There is no way to definitively control the consequences of our actions, or to avoid living with the actions of others.

In her later works, Arendt increasingly turns toward this more collaborative, creative, and destabilizing dimensions of action. If heroic individuals can disclose their natality to the world through remarkable deeds, individuals acting in concert display similarly "miraculous" capacities to call "something into being which did not exist before, which was not given."[28] Here, freedom is associated with groups of persons who constitute new political norms, spaces, institutions, and practices. The capacity of ordinary individuals to act thus throws into question the idea that existing political arrangements are ever incontestable or given— for good or ill. As Andreas Kalyvas puts it, for Arendt "freedom is defined as a spontaneous, extraordinary event that erupts in the midst of the ordinary and everyday . . . [which] like a miracle, shatters the preestablished instituted order of things and radically changes the expected course of history."[29]

This leads to a very different view of extraordinary politics. As Fred Lee has succinctly put it, where "extraordinary politics for Schmitt [means] a conservative closing against enemies, . . . extraordinary politics for Arendt is a creative opening between citizens."[30] For Arendt it would be remarkably dangerous for ordinary persons to forget they hold these capacities to bring about the unexpected with one another; or to confuse political freedom with decisive acts of sovereign control. Indeed, one of the perils of the modern age for Arendt is the popular tendency to view political life in terms of "automatic" historical processes or statistically determined behavior:[31]

> For today, more may depend on human freedom than ever before—on man's capacity to turn the scales which are heavily weighted in favor of disaster which always happens automatically and therefore always appears to be irresistible. No less than the continued existence of all mankind on earth may depend this time upon man's gift to perform miracles, that is, to bring about the infinitely improbable and establish it as a reality.[32]

Much of Arendt's work attempts to provide a reminder of our mutual vulnerability and extraordinary powers as creators of the political world we inhabit. Against the seemingly inescapable economic and political systems that define the modern world, her work insists that persons retain their essentially human faculties to set new and unanticipated processes into motion "against the overwhelming odds of statistical laws and their probability."[33] What is needed, then, are stories that remind their audiences of these capacities.

Can superhero films speak to this ambivalent, tragic, but potentially "miraculous" side of extraordinary politics?

Heroic Failures

Returning to *The Avengers*, the first thing we might notice is the dynamics of the Avengers team members themselves. It is a striking feature of the Avengers that many of the key heroes are treated with suspicion and unease by both civilians and state actors alike. Joss Whedon's take on these characters, in particular, emphasizes their heroism as equally a form of monstrosity. Above, I described how in the final lines of *The Avengers* Fury announces that the Avengers will return because "we will need them to." This announcement is presented against news footage of citizens, alternatively grateful or disturbed by their recent heroics. While Nick Fury's confident assessment that earth needs the Avengers closes the film, the conversation started between worried citizens continues across the consecutive Marvel films, as villains, citizens, state actors, and the Avengers themselves debate their appropriate role in public life and grapple with the unintended consequences of their interventions.

Individually, these films show us triumphant, heroic actors saving the day and defending ordinary life from extraordinary crises. Collectively, however, these films show us the Avengers facing a series of failures where their own actions generate political problems for ordinary citizens *and* states *and* the Avengers themselves. In *The Avengers*, for instance, a superpowered team establishes itself outside of legal oversight to respond to extraordinary threat. In *Avengers: Age of Ultron*, also directed by Whedon, Tony Stark attempts to extend this mission and preempt future threat by "putting a suit of armor around the whole world."[34] He creates the supervillain Ultron as a result, leading to the destruction of an entire city. This catastrophe sparks global calls for institutional restraints on superheroics in Marvel's *Captain America: Civil War*, imposed by institutions that, in *Captain America: Winter Soldier*, we have already learned can be compromised, and sometimes must be resisted—and so on.

What is consistent across these films is that attempts to impose control or to close down risk, either by the state *or* by superheroes themselves, set off uncontrollable or unpredictable processes that alter the world around them. Their world operates tragically. The Avengers are thus alternatively heroic or monstrous in the eyes of the world—a point also debated by the Avengers themselves. "Ultron thinks we're monsters," Captain America says, to the gathered Avengers. "He thinks we're what's wrong with the world. [This fight is] not just about beating him. It's about whether he's right." This is a big, heroic moment in the film, dramatically scored and shot. By one view, the speech establishes the redemptive stakes of the film's final fight: in defeating Ultron, the Avengers save the world and prove their heroism. But it simultaneously underscores the larger ambivalent status of heroic actors in general. Ultron is defeated, but the movie ends with scores dead, a displaced civilian population, and a city falling out of the sky.

This disjuncture between the immediate heroic actions of the heroes and the unspooling consequences of their actions provides a potentially more critical and, I argue, more productive perspective toward these superheroic narratives. Instead of revealing democratic passivity, we might instead view these films as exposing the limits of sovereign control while simultaneously demonstrating the ambivalent, if potentially transformative, powers of political action. These films ask us to sympathize with a group of individuals who, together, are capable of saving the world; but not without changing or even destroying it. Their power is thus a source of anxiety for both ordinary citizens and state actors alike, but also a source of longing, hope, and wonder. "They are doomed," Ultron (James Spader) says of the Avengers, and the human world they protect. "Yes," the cosmic hero Vision (Paul Bettany) agrees. "But, there is grace in their failings."

The twenty-two-episode run of Marvel's Avenger films recently culminated in the two-part movie extravaganza *Avengers: Infinity War* (2018) and *Avengers: Endgame* (2019), where our heroes sort through the consequences of their actions and ultimately must face the villain Thanos (Josh Brolin). These films reaffirm the idea that heroic action always happens against the odds, at risk of real failure, and in ways that cannot be fully controlled. ("I am inevitable," Thanos repeatedly announces to the heroes who struggle against him.) In this sense these stories remind us that action is possible, disruptive, and extraordinary; also uncertain and prone to tragedy. Because we act in a world shaped by the actions of others there is no possibility for a single person—however heroic or villainous—to definitively control the meaning or even the outcome of what is set into motion.

For this reason, from the perspective of settled political life the capacities we share with others to act can appear monstrous, the source of great danger and suffering. But simultaneously, our vulnerability *toward* others is also a reminder of our power to act *with* them. It is in this spirit that Arendt suggests that "the world, in gross and detail, is irrevocably delivered up to the ruin of time unless human beings are determined to intervene, to alter, to create something new."[35] The monstrous and heroic capacity of ordinary citizens to begin and to act against what appears inevitable is, for Arendt, "the miracle that saves the world."[36]

The talks collected in this special section ask how superheroes represent politics, on screen and in print, and whether superheroes provide resources for making us better citizens in a healthier democracy. Each of the talks included here reaches ambivalent conclusions. These talks consider the limits and potential payoffs of superheroic narratives, their reception, and the kinds of civic life they might enable.

In his talk, "White Racial Innocence and the Superheroes We Don't Deserve," Joshua Plencner takes Ryan Coogler's 2018 film *Black Panther* as an occasion to revisit an episode from the character's long comic book history. Plencner uses this episode to examine how "the biggest and blackest blockbuster of all time" nonetheless arrived in a moment of emboldened white nationalism and an ongoing wave of police violence targeting black people, which, together, destabilize comforting liberal myths of racial progress. With reference to James Baldwin's conceptualization of white racial innocence, Plencner offers a close reading of *Fantastic Four* No. 119, showing how white innocence emerges visually within the comic book narrative, and discursively through fan communications about the comic. His talk pushes us to ask how these dynamics of racial innocence and disavowal can illuminate the critical response to Coogler's film, and what Black Panther might mean for us today.

In the evening's keynote address, "Citizenship in an Age of Heroic Representation," Joshua Foa Dienstag asks what it is to be well represented, and what role representation should play in democratic life. Dienstag argues that we live in an age where our political representatives have never been better informed about the preferences, interests, and desires of their constituencies. And yet we also live in an age where large groups of people are more dissatisfied than ever with the political representation they receive. Turning toward modern Hollywood studios' dependence on superheroic narratives, Dienstag suggests that the experience of representing humans—and superhumans—on film can tell us something about why our representatives perpetually disappoint us. Through a pessimist reading of Spike Jonze's 2013 film *Her*, he concludes that this experience can also provide clues about what we can do about it.

Taken together, these talks may raise more questions than answers about the role of superheroic narratives in contemporary political life. Superheroic films may be appealing because of the mythological portraits of resilience, courage, and fantastic strength they present. Or, perhaps such films appeal because they offer audiences comforting stories of innocence defended, and a world set right. Such seductive narratives might flatter and soothe audiences rather than engaging and activating them. Yet, as these talks demonstrate, if there is anything that superhero films accomplish it is to hold these tensions between saving and failing, innocent and agentic, ordinary and extraordinary, open to sight.

1. On the comic book industry's reaction to 9/11, see Bradford W. Wright, *Comic Book Nation: The Transformation of Youth Culture in America* (Baltimore: Johns Hopkins University Press, 2001), 287–95. I have only included Marvel and DC properties in this count. This includes figures like Zorro and the Lone Ranger, who are considered precursors to the first "superheroes." For these lists, see en.wikipedia.org/wiki/List_of_films_based_on_DC_Comics and en.wikipedia.org/wiki/List_of_films_based_on_Marvel_Comics (accessed 13 August 2018).

2. See Lauren Berlant, *Cruel Optimism* (Durham: Duke University Press, 2011); and Michael Rogin, *Independence Day* (London: British Film Institute, 1998).

3. John Lawrence and Robert Jewett, *The Myth of the American Superhero* (Cambridge: Erdmans Publishing Company, 2002), 5.

4. Umberto Eco and Natalie Chilton, "The Myth of Superman: Review, *The Adventures of Superman*," *Diacritics* 2, no. 1 (Spring 1972): 14–22.

5. Elizabeth Anker, *Orgies of Feeling: Melodrama and the Politics of Freedom* (Durham: Duke University Press, 2014).

6. Sheldon Wolin, *Fugitive Democracy* (Princeton: Princeton University Press, 2016), 14.

7. Peter Coogan, "The Definition of the Superhero," in *A Comic Studies Reader*, ed. Jeet Heer and Kent Worcester (University Press of Mississippi, 2009), 77–93.

8. Richard Reynolds, *Super Heroes: A Modern Mythology* (Jackson: University Press of Mississippi, 1992), 74.

9. For a contrasting view of superhero narratives focused on comic books, see Neal Curtis, *Sovereignty and Superheroes* (Manchester: Manchester University Press, 2016).

10. Ibid., 5–6.

11. Berlant, *Cruel Optimism*, 9.

12. See Andreas Kalyvas, *Democracy and the Politics of the Ordinary* (Cambridge: Cambridge University Press, 2009), 6.

13. Carl Schmitt, *The Concept of the Political*, trans. George Schwab (Chicago: University of Chicago Press, 2007), 5.

14. Ibid; Giorgio Agamben, *State of Exception* (Chicago: University of Chicago Press, 2005).

15. *The Avengers*, directed and with a screenplay by Joss Whedon (Burbank: Marvel Studios, 2012).

16. Anker, *Orgies of Feeling*, 27.

17. See, for example, Sheldon Wolin, *Fugitive Democracy* (Princeton: Princeton University Press, 2016); and Wendy Brown, *Walled States, Waning Sovereignty*. New York: Zone Books, 2010).

18. Bonnie Honig, *Emergency Politics: Paradox, Law, Democracy* (Princeton: Princeton University Press, 2011), 3.

19. On this point, see especially Bonnie Honig, *Democracy and the Foreigner* (Princeton: Princeton University Press 2001); and William Connolly, *The Ethos of Pluralization* (Minneapolis: Minnesota Press, 1995).

20. Hannah Arendt, *The Human Condition* (Chicago: Chicago University Press, 1958), 190. Hereafter abbreviated *HC*.

21. Hannah Arendt, "Freedom and Politics: A Lecture" in *Thinking without a Banister: Essays in Understanding, 1953–1975*, ed. Jerome Kohn (New York: Schocken Books, 2018), 224. Hereafter abbreviated "FP."

22. *HC*, 177.

23. "FP," 225.

24. Often critically: see, for instance, Sheldon Wolin, "Hannah Arendt: Democracy and the Political," *Salmagundi*, no. 60, Special Section on Hannah Arendt (Spring/Summer 1983): 3–19.

25. Fred Lee, *Extraordinary Racial Politics: Four Events in the Constitution of the United States* (Philadelphia: Temple University Press, 2018), 15.

26. *HC*, 234–35.

27. Ibid., 190.

28. "FP," 224.

29. Kalyvas, *Democracy and the Politics of the Extraordinary*, 202.

30. Lee, *Extraordinary Racial Politics*, 14.

31. *HC*, 44–46, 320–25.

32. "FP," 244.

33. *HC*, 178.

34. *Avengers: Age of Ultron*, directed and with a screenplay by Joss Whedon (Burbank: Marvel Studios and Walt Disney Pictures, 2015).

35. Hannah Arendt, "The Crisis in Education," in *Between Past and Future* (New York: Viking Press, 1968), 192.

36. *HC*, 247.

White Racial Innocence and the Superheroes We Don't Deserve

Joshua Plencner

In his searing review of Marvel Studios' 2018 film *Black Panther*, philosopher Chris Lebron (2018) condemns director Ryan Coogler's epic turn on the silver screen superhero playground by declaring that the breathlessly anticipated and purportedly black empowerment narrative is "not the movie we deserve." Lebron argues that Marvel's attempt to "diversify cinematic white superheroics" rests on a narrative foundation of disturbing anti-blackness. Indeed, despite *Black Panther* being "unique for its black star power and its many thoughtful portrayals of strong black women," its figuring of Eric Killmonger as the ultimate villain (as well as his final dismissal at the climax of the movie) "depends on a shocking devaluation of black American men." Why "should I accept the idea of black disposability," Lebron asks, amidst an increasingly open white supremacist American political context where "my president already despises me"—especially when that message is delivered by King T'Challa, the Black Panther, "a man in a suit, whose name is synonymous with radical uplift but whose actions question the very notion that black lives matter?"

While Lebron's critique is self-consciously provocative, I think it reveals an important point roiling beneath the shimmering surface of multimedia American superhero culture: if "we deserve" better movies, it follows that popular culture can fail not only our social expectations but also our political needs. Indeed, it assumes that popular culture can do things that matter, but are not yet doing so. Alongside Lebron, then, in this essay I ask what histories—or hurdles—must be addressed in order for a film like *Black Panther* to do the things in the world that it must? What legacies cause the film to fail its context in this instance? And how should we understand this failure as *political* in nature?

To be clear, others are less certain of the failures Lebron condemns. For example, political theorist Melvin L. Rogers (2018) suggests that Lebron's analysis is too literal in its reading of Killmonger's tragic villainy, preferring a more nuanced, reparative critical approach; and actress, playwright, and professor of theater Anna Deavere Smith (2018)—wrestling with Killmonger's "broken" construction—proclaims an uneasy "Wakanda Forever! For now."

I take Lebron's essay as the jumping-off point for my own because it provides a useful bridge between a film featuring a hero "whose name is synonymous with radical uplift" and my long-term research interests in the racial politics of superheroes. Indeed, I'm something of an unusual political scientist insofar as my primary objects of study are superhero comic books—those dusty four-color magazines that inspired (and helped line the pockets of) major movie studios over the last twenty years. So, while I'm thrilled that this essay contributes to the organizing framework of Heroic Politics on Screen, let me clear some room on the table by suggesting that studying superheroes on screen can be vastly augmented through studying superheroes on panel and page.

Tracing out a response to my questions above, in this essay I connect Lebron's reading of the film's devaluation of black American life with the political thought of midcentury critic, playwright, and artist James Baldwin, for whom similar concerns are omnipresent in his work. In particular, I marshal Baldwin's (1962) conceptualization of white racial innocence to explore the legacy of Black Panther, thinking through how one instance of his four-color representation—in the strange and understudied comic book issue *Fantastic Four* No. 119, written by Roy Thomas with art by John Buscema and published by Marvel Comics in February 1972—helps inform the context of Marvel Studios' release of *Black Panther*, and thus sheds light on what the character Black Panther might mean for us, in 1972 and yet today.

Baldwin's Innocence

In his widely influential 1962 essay "My Dungeon Shook—Letter to My Nephew on the One Hundredth Anniversary of Emancipation," first published in *The Progressive* and subsequently collected as the lead essay in 1963's landmark civil rights movement text *The Fire Next Time*, James Baldwin writes a public a public letter to his nephew, also named James, reflecting on the one-hundred-year anniversary of Abraham Lincoln's "Emancipation Proclamation." There, in a familiar rhetorical style, he addresses a nebulous "you"—a composite audience of nephew James, the imagined reader of the essay, as well as (at times) even Baldwin himself—writing about how, why, and in what ways the history of emancipation preempted its enactment. "You know, and I know," Baldwin writes, "that the country is celebrating one hundred years of freedom one hundred years too soon" (1985b, 336).

What we—or the "you" addressed here—know, if we are honest with our assessment of race in America, is that the historical truth of a preempted emancipation and the freedom it promised is ever haunted by the construction, defense, and rigid *belief* in a powerfully controlling whiteness. Such belief, for Baldwin, is a self-conscious and destructive twisting of the truth. For instance, in his 1965 essay "White Man's Guilt," Baldwin argues that white people have fed themselves a series of historical lies to produce and invest in whiteness and, as a consequence, "suffer enormously from the resulting personal incoherence" (1985c, 410–1). In his 1984 essay "On Being White . . . and Other Lies," Baldwin further develops this idea when he writes that whiteness is "a totally false identity" created to justify "what must be called a genocidal history." But more than resulting in a self-harming "personal incoherence," the latter essay figures the stakes of whiteness as precisely political. Whiteness "has placed everyone now living," he argues,

> into the hands of the most ignorant and powerful people the world has ever seen. And how did they get that way? By deciding that they were white. By opting for safety instead of life. By persuading themselves that a child's life meant nothing compared with a white child's life. . . . By informing their children that black women, black men, and black children had no human integrity that those who call themselves white were bound to respect. And in this debasement and definition of black people, debased and defined themselves. (2010, 137)

For Baldwin, whiteness is as much a historically constructed artifact as it is continually remade through containment, coercion, and immiseration of those who are not white. For example, here returning to "My Dungeon Shook," Baldwin writes, "The black man has functioned in the white man's world as a fixed star, as an immovable pillar: and as he moves out of his place, heaven and earth are shaken to their foundations" (1985, 336). Amidst the political tumult of the civil rights movement, Baldwin witnessed ample evidence of emancipation's historical absence; yet, at the same time, he also witnessed myriad challenges to what "they [white people] have had to believe for many years . . . that black men are inferior to white men," challenges that seemed to aspire toward, if not ultimately create the conditions of, the very emancipation that was as yet missing from American life (336).

But Baldwin was skeptical of the view that emancipation could be struggled toward in a direct line; although he spoke widely with students, he was hesitant to associate himself uncritically with leaders of contemporaneous movement politics that promised advancement from abject conditions of unfreedom to unalloyed conditions of freedom. Instead, Baldwin's analysis of race in America identified a complex series of twists and recursions—a warren of interconnected and embedded histories that made ideal-typical narratives of linear racial progress exactly that: stories we tell ourselves that do little to clarify the political necessities of building foundations for actual racial justice in America.

One of the key examples of this more complex and nested approach to racial analysis is Baldwin's conceptualization of "innocence," which hides the "crime" of whiteness and justifies radically disparate lived racial experiences in America. "The crime of which I accuse my countrymen," writes Baldwin,

> and for which neither I nor time nor history will ever forgive them, is that they have destroyed and are destroying hundreds of thousands of lives and do not know it and do not want to know it . . . but

it is not permissible that the authors of this destruction should also be innocent. It is the innocence which constitutes the crime. (334)

For Baldwin, the pervasive social *belief in* whiteness—and as his later analysis attests, the political *power of* whiteness—is produced through a kind of destruction that is, at the moment of its commission, occluded and covered over. That is, even though whiteness destroys, it believes itself innocent of the crime of destruction.

Political theorist George Shulman (2008) elaborates on this understanding of white racial innocence by emphasizing that it is a conscious political strategy. Baldwin's innocence, writes Shulman, "denotes not excusable ignorance but a blindness that is culpable because it is willful" (143). If ignorance is understood as a lack of knowledge, Shulman clarifies the willfulness of Baldwin's innocence by framing it as more akin to a "'refusal to acknowledge' the reality of others and our conduct toward them" (143). In that way, by disavowing social facts about unjust racial difference that are in some sense already known, whiteness excuses its own exercise of power and explains away the reality of inequalities and unearned benefits accrued by whiteness over time. Other theorists anchor the stakes of white racial innocence in democratic political theory and praxis. Lawrie Balfour (2001), for instance, describes the disavowal of America's racial history as "devastating for the prospects of democracy" (27). And Lisa Beard (2017) demonstrates Balfour's point by linking white disavowal of America's racial history to our current wave of anti-black violence when she writes: "In a context of systemic state and civilian violence against black people . . . white people's active participation and/or silent innocence is thick, heavy with history, and willfully enacted in the moment" (339). Clearly Baldwin means prolifically; I take the application of his thought to questions of race and American political culture, democratic theory, and contemporary social movement politics as suggesting that we might also usefully apply Baldwin to questions of race and multimedia superhero culture.

James and T'Challa

Despite a now robust and growing academic literature on race and superhero comic books, few have considered James Baldwin alongside Black Panther. Yet Baldwin's work on white racial innocence offers a significant and substantial framework for understanding the character's disjunctive development across fifty-three years of publication history.

Like many black and African American comic book characters, T'Challa, son of T'Chaka and King of Wakanda, genius scientist, and alter ego of masked warrior superhero the Black Panther, has been subject to a wide variety of narrative and aesthetic tinkering. From cocreator Jack Kirby's foundational efforts in the 1960s constructing the visual stylings of hyperfuturistic Wakanda—saturated by what Charles Hatfield (2012) describes as Kirby's career-long (and Cold-War–addled) fixation on rendering the "technological sublime"—to writer Christopher Priest's seminal late-1990s and early 2000s revision of the character—which, according to Adilifu Nama (2011), offered a more "introspective and psychological" portrayal of the character, narratively structured in a nonlinear, French New Wave–inspired story arc (48–50), the Black Panther arrives to comic book readers as a mixed bag of idealized hero types tumbling through the years.

But Baldwin is similarly complex, notoriously evading clear-cut description of his activism and thought. Baldwin, like Panther, straddles several cultural, social, and political spaces, witnessing a wide variety of audiences while at the same time carefully expressing a kind of moral responsibility for them. Baldwin, like Panther, identifies variably across those spaces—he is both a Jeremiah and a comrade in arms, a defender of justice and a boundary-crossing pariah. And in the context of Ta-Nehisi Coates's (2016) run as writer of Marvel Comics' Black Panther series, it seems especially fitting to connect Baldwin's thought to the character currently written by someone who, as Toni Morrison once explained, filled "the intellectual void that plagued [her]" after Baldwin passed away.[1]

Here, rather than survey the history of Black Panther comic books, I want to spend time with one issue in particular—*Fantastic Four* No. 119—in order to think through white racial innocence and the political failures of popular culture. I choose a single text quite purposefully; although a more direct comparison of the film to its comic book roots might call for an analysis of multiple issues and long-running arcs, including writer Don McGregor's (2016 [1973–75]) sprawling, path-breaking thirteen-issue epic "Panther's Rage" storyline that inspired much of what director Ryan Coogler adapted to the silver screen in *Black Panther*, *Fantastic Four* No. 119 stands out in the history of Black Panther comic book stories for its narrative exploration of explicit white supremacist government, represented by fictional African nation "Rudyarda."[2] Through close reading of this text I argue that Baldwin's understanding of white racial innocence is crucial to understanding this unusual episode in context, and informs how popular culture can fail our contemporaneous political needs.

"Three Stood Together!"
The FF and the Black Panther Battle for the Soul of Man

At the outset of *Fantastic Four* No. 119, the story begins with a familiar refrain in Fantastic Four (FF) comic books: a scene of domesticity interrupted. Two of the titular heroes—the chosen brothers Johnny Storm, otherwise known as the Human Torch, and Benjamin Grimm, or The Thing—are shown rough-housing in, around, and through the FF's New York City headquarters, the Baxter Building. Blasting through concrete walls and hurtling above the Manhattan cityscape, Torch and The Thing conflagrate in response to some disputed off-panel slight, and the dialogue reveals both the familiarity as well as the utter unseriousness of the conflict: "NOW you've done it, you overgrown gorilla," chirps Torch. "I'm gonna make you regret you ever STARTED this free-for-all." The Thing bellows back, "You got it all BACKWARD, match-head. It was YOU started this rhubarb."

But just before Torch can hit The Thing with his "fire-blasts," and just before The Thing can finish shouting his trademark rallying cry "IT'S CLOBBERIN' TIME," Reed Richards, or Mr. Fantastic—the sometimes aloof super-scientist and paternalistic leader of the FF—and Sue Storm-Richards, or the Invisible Woman—the sometimes extraordinarily powerful manipulator of psionic energy, sometimes shrinking violet wife of Reed, sister of Johnny, and longtime friend of Ben—intervene and put an end to the fight before any serious damage is done. Mr. Fantastic chastises his childlike compatriots: "This in-group bickering is something we can't afford—not NOW," he explains. "I left the chief advisor of our friend T'CHALLA—on HOLD!"

It is here that the "real narrative" of the issue begins. Over a series of panels spilling onto three pages, we learn from Taku, close adviser to T'Challa, otherwise known as the Black Panther and king of fictional African nation Wakanda, that T'Challa has gone missing, and that Wakanda needs the FF's help. Through the "vizeo-call," Taku tells a story of a stolen piece of technology, an object called the "Vibrotron." Recently created by King T'Challa, the Vibrotron is "an instrument which will greatly AUGMENT the power" of Wakanda's "greatest resource . . . VIBRANIUM." Although the thieves "fled into the jungle," Taku explains that "a random phrase, overheard by the guard they felled, revealed their intent to SELL the vibrotron to someone who would meet them in neighboring Rudyarda." Following this clue, T'Challa pursued the thieves into Rudyarda alone. Two days have passed, and since that time, Taku says, "We've had no word from him."

The Thing interjects, agreeing that T'Challa's going missing "sounds fishy, awright," but asking bluntly: "How come you come cryin' to US, 'steada chargin' after the Panther yerselves?"

From his vizeo-call screen, Taku admonishes The Thing: "You would not ASK such an ill-considered question, Ben Grimm, if you were well-versed in the HISTORY of the Republic of RUDYARDA. That nation is one of the last remaining strongholds of WHITE SUPREMACY upon our continent. One of MY color can function there only with . . . DIFFICULTY."

The Thing's response: "Oh yeah . . . I FERGOT" (Figure 1).

Taku: "You can AFFORD to forget it. My people CANNOT. Even our MONARCH, travelling incognito as he is, may have run into TROUBLE."

Indeed, after traveling to Africa to investigate the disappearance, Torch and The Thing learn that T'Challa is not only missing, but has been jailed in Rudyarda for breaking papers laws. As Taku predicted, because T'Challa was traveling in disguise, he was not carrying proper identification and ran afoul of Rudyarda's strict segregationist control of black Africans. T'Challa was stopped by police, suspected as a radical terrorist, and held in "City Prison."

Figure 1. Taku reminds The Thing about Rudyarda's status as one the last remaining white supremacist nations on the continent of Africa.

Quickly rallying to the prison, Torch locates the imprisoned Wakandan king and, refusing to stop and explain as T'Challa asks how they found him, uses his entire body to melt the cell bars. When T'Challa reiterates his question, The Thing responds: "Frankly, jungle man, I'M still pretty fuzzy on a couple'a points, but this AIN'T the time or place for a POW-WOW. Two more GUARDS comin' this way—and they're loaded for BEAR."

Torch tells T'Challa to hide, saying that he and The Thing will take care of the guards themselves, but T'Challa checks him down: "You have done ENOUGH, Torch. Do not seek to do ALL my fighting for me." Rushing toward the guards, T'Challa yells, "SOME things, after all, are best left to — [panel break] — the BLACK LEOPARD!" (Figure 2).

The page turn following this unusual declaration of a new heroic nomenclature for T'Challa functions doubly as a scene break, and the narrative picks up with Torch and The Thing following T'Challa on a "DETOUR to retrieve [his] ceremonial attire"—or his iconic black costume—from an unidentified location. Eager to press forward, hunt down the remaining thief, and reclaim control of the Vibrotron, T'Challa attempts to spur Torch and The Thing into following his lead. But, reining in the plot's advance and slowing enough to give voice to the question on the minds of readers, The Thing bellows out, "First things FIRST, yer highness. How come you called yerself the Black LEOPARD back there, 'stead'a the PANTHER?"

Figure 2. T'Challa, while fighting to escape Rudyardan prison guards, declares himself "The Black Leopard."

T'Challa, unwavered, replies coolly: "I contemplate a return to YOUR country, Ben Grimm, where the latter term has — POLITICAL connotations. I neither condemn NOR condone those who have taken up the name — but T'CHALLA is a law unto HIMSELF."

He claims that his new name is a "MINOR point, at best." And, as if anticipating critical questions or concerns from Torch and The Thing, T'Challa suggests that if they might disagree with his preferred name change, they would merely be arguing semantics. After all, he says, "the panther IS a leopard."

From the declaration and justification of T'Challa's heroic name change, the story moves forward rapidly. After a short investigation, the three heroes learn that the mastermind behind the theft of the Vibrotron was none other than T'Challa's original adversary and perennial rogue, the "sound incarnate" Ulysses Klaue. In the ensuing battle the Vibrotron is destroyed and Klaw is defeated, failing to put up much of a fight against the combined abilities of Torch, The Thing, and the newly christened Black Leopard. In the penultimate blow, Klaw's primary weapon—his "Soni-Claw," which is technology made flesh as a piece of his "sonically-altered body"—is crushed by The Thing. T'Challa delivers the knockout punch and Klaw is ushered away to face justice for his villainous plot.

But rather than receiving a hero's congratulations, T'Challa is offered a sort of free pass from the Rudyardan police officers whisking Klaw away. As one uniformed officer explains: "ACTUALLY, fellow . . . you're not supposed to be IN this part of town . . . after DARK, you know. I mean . . . I'm not going to ask you for an I.D. or anything, but . . ."

Figure 3. The final panels of *Fantastic Four* No. 119, depicting victorious T'Challa, The Thing, and the Human Torch walking into the dawning sun after smashing apartheid in Rudyarda.

The following panel sequence, spanning across the final two pages of the issue, centers its visual focus on The Thing and Torch. In the first panel of the sequence, the characters face two doorways leading out of the same City Prison that once held T'Challa captive. The door on the left is labeled "Europeans" while the door on the right is labeled "Coloreds."

"BEAUTIFUL!" shouts The Thing sarcastically. "Ya break yer back savin' the whole gol-dang WORLD . . . then you gotta WALK OUT . . . thru separate-but-equal DOORS!"

In the same panel, Torch replies, "Kinda makes you wonder if it was WORTH it, huh?"

The next panel swings the perspective around to a close-up view of The Thing's face, with Torch looking on over The Thing's left shoulder. "Look, Junior," says The Thing, "I know we're ALREADY in dutch around here for that JAILBREAK scene . . . but . . ."

Again in the same panel, Torch replies, "I DIG, Ben. Go on . . . before I beat you TO it."

And so, in the final action sequence of the issue, The Thing confronts the story's lone still-standing adversary by tearing down the physical structures of Rudyarda's white supremacist government with his giant rock hands. "I been WANTIN' ta do this . . . ever since we set foot off the PLANE," he shouts across two panels, as SKRUTCH! and RUMMBLE sound effects grow and fill the panel space around him. After a page turn, we see The Thing finishing the job in the subsequent two panels: "An' there's SOME things," he cries, the SKRRAAKK of the prison wall bouncing through the first panel, "you just gotta get out of yer SYSTEM!" With a thunderous FTOOM! the prison wall is demolished.

In the next panel T'Challa returns to the frame, his masked face foregrounded in profile as the three heroes look over the rubble and the wreckage where a prison once stood. "Ben Grimm," T'Challa says, "I don't . . . know how to . . ."

But The Thing cuts him off before he can finish the sentence: "FERGIT it, T'Challa. I didn't do that for YOU. I did it . . . for ME."

The denouement shows the heroes walking through the rubble, their feet trampling the destroyed doorway signs segregating "Europeans" from "Coloreds." And in the final two panels of the issue, prison guards stand "mouths slack and minds a-gape," as Torch, The Thing, and T'Challa walk off into the morning sunrise, the smashed vestiges of white supremacy's past behind them (Figure 3).

The Four-Color Constitution of White Racial Innocence

As I noted earlier, *Fantastic Four* No. 119 is unusual in the history of superhero comic books for its direct narrative exploration of white supremacist government. Writer Thomas and artist Buscema combine their dynamic creative energies to tell a story that at once stands out in the history of superhero comic books as well as establishes a return of the Black Panther character to popular public consciousness. However, in reading through the critical lens of Baldwin's white racial innocence, I see at least four key visual/narrative moments in "Three Stood Together" that suggest this story—ostensibly about black political liberation from white supremacist government—requires the disavowal established truths, and therefore participates in the regeneration of white racial innocence at the very same moment it purports to depict the new dawning of racial justice. I call these four key moments of white racial innocence "Forgetting," "Refusal," "Absolution," and "Triumph."

First, the innocence of forgetting is exemplified through The Thing's literal "forgetting" of Rudyarda's existence, which willfully indemnifies the titular heroes at the same moment it calls out and condemns the twinned evils of white supremacy and apartheid government. Second, the innocence of refusal appears midway through the issue in T'Challa's peculiar choice of revised nomenclature, transitioning from his superheroic identity of the Black Panther to his newly declared superheroic identity of the Black Leopard—a move that disavows any purported association between T'Challa and the Black Panther Party in America. Third, the innocence of absolution take shape in Torch and The Thing's confrontation with what I describe above as the final, still-standing adversary remaining in the story—the physical edifice of an apartheid carceral system— after supervillain Klaw has been defeated and carted off to jail by Rudyardan police. And fourth, the innocence of triumph is evident in the final panel sequence of the issue that features the three heroes walking into the dawning sun, leaving an oppressive, racist, and now broken past behind them.

While each of these might be analyzed in turn, the political stakes of "refusal" are most clearly applicable to Lebron's critique of the character "whose name is synonymous with radical uplift but whose actions question the very notion that black lives matter." In refusing the "Black Panther" and choosing the new, unburdened heroic identity of the Black Leopard, T'Challa disavows the cross-national solidarity project of black liberation politics, doing so at a moment where he himself is literally subject to the very same institutional strictures of white supremacist carceral state control that the Black Panther Party militantly resisted in the United States. I understand this performative juggling of superheroic identity convention as demonstrative of how the politics of refusal are implicated in the defense of white racial innocence. The act of disavowing the label of "Black Panther" casts black radical political organizing in the United States as suspect, energizing "innocent" scrutiny of black liberation struggles; moreover, black African Americans engaged in such struggles are themselves cast in a pejorative light. Though T'Challa claims that he neither condemns nor condones "those who have taken up the name," his disavowal by dissociation clearly portrays black African Americans as caught up in an indefensible and ill-advised political subjectivity. Collectivity and solidarity risk alienating others who stand outside the cause, while "T'CHALLA," as he so deftly explains while donning his iconic costume and pitching forward into hero pose, neatly sidesteps the question of political alienation because he "is a law unto HIMSELF."

"We Condemn Ourselves": What Sort of Black Panther Do We Need?

In this essay I've argued that Baldwin's political thought—particularly his concept of white racial innocence—helps us think through the unusually compelling superhero comic book story offered in *Fantastic Four* No. 119. Although narrow in analytic scope, I believe my argument gestures toward a broader world implied by the single story's close reading. Indeed, by tracing the issue's emerging circuits of political disavowal and white racial innocence, I contend that we can better understand how, and in what ways, popular culture can fail our social expectations and political needs in context. Insofar as these multimedia objects do things in the world—and in that doing inform, shape, defend, and energize the politics of white supremacy—these failures matter. They delimit possible futures and drain our collective political imaginary of vital and necessary resources.

Turning back to the film *Black Panther*, Lebron snaps our attention into focus on this mixture of the race, disavowal, and the failure to meet political needs in the present when he writes:

> The lessons I learned were these: the bad guy is the black
> American who has rightly identified white supremacy as the
> reigning threat to black well-being; the bad guy is the one who

thinks Wakanda is being selfish in its secret liberation; the bad guy is the one who will no longer stand for patience and moderation—he thinks liberation is many, many decades overdue. And the black hero snuffs him out.

The heroism of T'Challa in *Black Panther* is a heroism that condemns and literally buries global black liberation struggles in service of a timid, tutelary politics. It serves the maintenance of white supremacy at the very moment it purports to disavow it; and, to that end, it reifies the dominant American mythology of ever greater racial progress. *"Black Panther* is not the movie we deserve" precisely because it upholds the racial mythologies and "innocent" belief systems that deny deep political truths. We see much the same story forty-six years earlier in *Fantastic Four* No. 119. Such denial and disavowal not only rebukes the past but also fails our political needs in the present by cutting us off from imagining the future differently, ultimately anchoring us all in a heavy, mythologically laden *now*. Baldwin (1985a) crystallizes the effects of this when he writes, "If we, who can scarcely be considered a white nation, persist in thinking ourselves as one, we condemn ourselves, with the truly white nations, to sterility and decay" (374). We don't deserve the cultural conveyance of white racial innocence—in 1972 or yet today.

---

1. Morrison writes this rare and extraordinarily high praise in her jacket blurb for Coates's best-selling 2015 memoir *Between the World and Me*.
2. "Rudyarda," of course, is a direct allusion to British colonial writer Rudyard Kipling, whose famous children's stories "The Jungle Book" and "Riki Tiki Tavi," among others, helped shape the romantically imagined coloniality of the very much actually and brutally colonized India. Marvel's creation of Rudyarda as a literarily inspired fabulist canvas for extant global white supremacy is surprising. Most typically, questions of prejudice and racism in superhero comic books are individuated onto specific villains, such as notorious Fantastic Four adversary Hatemonger, or specific small-scale extralegal terrorist organizations, such as the formerly Nazi-run Hydra. In this case, by crafting an imagined white supremacist state in colonized Africa, with this specific issue Marvel Comics arguably altered both the *degree* and *kind* of its political commentary on race and racism.

References

Baldwin, James. 1985(a). "Down at the Cross." In *The Price of the Ticket: Collected Nonfiction, 194–1985*. New York: St. Martin's/Marek, 337–79.

———. 1985b. "My Dungeon Shook: Letter to my Nephew on the One-Hundreth Anniversary of the Emancipation." In *The Price of the Ticket: Collected Nonfiction 1948–1985*. New York: St. Martin's/Marek, pp. 333-6.

———. (1985c). "White Man's Guilt." In *The Price of the Ticket: Collected Nonfiction, 1948-1985*. New York: St. Martin's/Marek, 409–14.

———. 2010. "On Being White . . . and Other Lies." In *The Cross of Redemption*. New York: Pantheon, 135–38.

Balfour, Lawrie. 2001. *The Evidence of Things Not Said: James Baldwin and the Promise of American Democracy*. Ithaca: Cornell University Press.

Beard, Lisa. 2017. "James Baldwin on Violence and Disavowal." In Susan J. McWilliams, ed., *A Political Companion to James Baldwin*. Lexington: University Press of Kentucky, 337–60.

Hatfield, Charles. 2012. *Hand of Fire: The Comics Art of Jack Kirby*. Jackson: University Press of Mississippi.

Lebron, Chris. 2018. "'Black Panther' Is Not the Movie We Deserve." *Boston Review*, 17 February. bostonreview.net/race/christopher-lebron-black-panther (accessed 1 April 2019).

McGregor, Don, Rich Buckler, and Billy Graham. 2016 [1973–75]. *The Black Panther Epic Collection: Panther's Rage*. New York: Marvel Entertainment.

Nama, Adilifu. 2011. *Super Black: American Pop Culture and Black Superheroes*. Austin: University of Texas Press.

Rogers, Melvin L. 2018. "The Many Dimensions of *Black Panther*." *Dissent*, 27 February 2018. dissentmagazine.org/online_articles/marvel-black-panther-review-race-empire-tragic-heroes (accessed 1 April 2019).

Smith, Anna Deavere. 2018. "Wakanda Forever!" *New York Review of Books*, 24 May. nybooks.com/articles/2018/05/24/black-panther-wakanda-forever (accessed 1 April 2019).

Thomas, Roy, and John Buscema. 1972. "Three Stood Together!" in *Fantastic Four* No. 119. New York: Marvel Comics.

Citizenship in an Age of Heroic Representation

Joshua Foa Dienstag

We live today, I shall argue, in an Age of Representation—more particularly, an Age of Heroic Representation. And this condition, I will maintain, poses a threat to our democracy that is distinct from the many other political challenges we currently face.

Representation, we should remember, was once a more occasional phenomenon, something that most people only experienced from time to time and in limited circumstances. Nowadays we are saturated with it. Modern life teems with representation. Once, and not that long ago, only the very rich could have portraits painted of themselves, and most people only saw their likeness in a mirror or, when that was a luxury, on a water surface. Now nearly everyone can post a hundred selfies a day if they choose, and some do. Today, it is the normal course of things in the life of a modern citizen to have a plethora of self-representations, besides the political ones, that supplement our bodily existence: profiles, selfies, pages, feeds, snaps, gaming avatars. Managing these representations (or, as we like to say, curating them) is itself a major task for the contemporary citizen—an activity entirely unknown a few decades ago.

We are also saturated, of course, with representational media, both visual and aural, which dominate our culture and which have, for most of us, crowded out the original production of music, art, and drama that was once a more common part of daily life. And in these representational media, in the last two decades, superhero stories have come to overshadow many other kinds of narrative. Certainly in the medium of popular film, the superhero conquest is now all but complete. In 2018, more than 25 percent of the overall revenue generated in the entire U.S. film industry came from just the nine superhero films (out of several hundred total) released by the major studios.[1] Even with their high costs of production, some superhero films now generate profits of over a billion dollars each, meaning they account for the lion's share of industry profits, along with other fantasy and action movies. And that doesn't begin to count the ways in which these films spin off many other products (costumes, action figures, paraphernalia) that mean that one does not actually have to see the films to participate in their cultural influence.

Television is a more complicated story of course, but the audience in television is fragmented into hundreds of microcommunities. Meanwhile, over one hundred million people saw the recently released *Avengers: Endgame* just in its first weekend.[2] In terms of the *shared* narratives, then, that constitute our contemporary American ethos, we would be entirely justified in using the term "neo-Hellenism" to describe where we are. That is to say: we share a culture of ritual celebration (think of Comic-con and cosplay more generally) about a pantheon of semidivine beings whose tales of woe and triumph have become the lingua franca of our society, so that parents and children, teachers and students, and citizens more generally relate to one another with and through a vocabulary permeated with superhero stories that 25 years ago were only known to a small group of comic book aficionados. When I explained Hegelian dialectic to my classes this past quarter, I did so by telling them it was just like the character progression in *Black Panther*. Not only is this true, but I'm happy to report that this worked perfectly as a pedagogic strategy—about as well as anything I've ever tried. The culture of superheroes has become a shared resource and reference point for nearly everyone who has not cut themselves off from mainstream culture.

The question we must ask of this phenomenon is: what does this neo-Hellenic culture of representation mean for our politics? More specifically, I think we might ask: what would Jean-Jacques Rousseau—who, in his *Letter to d'Alembert*, objected vociferously to the idea of a single theater opening in republican Geneva—what would Rousseau have had to say about these developments? Many people, after all, have taken to celebrating these films, or at least some of them, as a potentially democratizing force. We can think, for example, of the euphoric critical reception that *Black Panther* received last year. And the slightly less ecstatic but equally positive reviews for this year's *Captain Marvel*. These films aren't just celebrated as technical or dramatic achievements but also because many critics saw them as advances in representation with political importance well beyond the world of movies and award shows.

Now, I don't really want to criticize these films at all—they are well-made and great fun. Rather, I am suspicious of a critical reception that makes the leap from an improvement in the diversity of characters and stories depicted to a more general optimism about the ability of cinema to inspire and catalyze political change. In this celebration, the nature and character of representation itself is usually not much in question. Instead, it is assumed that more "positive" (that is, unpatronizing, unracist, unsexist) representation for any group is good for that group's political standing, or at the very least indicative of its growth in stature and self-confidence. To this way of thinking, *Black Panther* and *Captain Marvel* are good for all of us, but perhaps especially for African Americans and women, on the assumption that *Iron Man* and *Thor* were also good for us, but perhaps less completely and unequally. More representation, in other words, means more equality, and more equality, it is assumed, leads to more freedom or justice or something like that.

But are the steps in this logic really valid? Is representation really a driver of equality and other political goods? Without wanting in any way to return to a less diverse cinema, I would say instead that we still need to ask, as Rousseau did in his *Letter*, whether this reasoning relies on a naive account of the value and character of representation itself. Before asking whether particular groups or perspectives are well represented, that is, we must ask—as with our political institutions—what it means to be well represented. We must ask, indeed, whether and how our humanity is capable of being represented in the first place. Or whether, instead, our humanity is potentially being diminished in the process of representation. And here, I believe, some pessimism is warranted—pessimism not about any particular film or genre but about the general limits of representation's ability to forward human and democratic aims.

We live, after all, in an age where our political representatives have never been better informed about the preferences, interests, and desires of their constituencies. We have never had a wider suffrage, more voting rights, or easier and cheaper lines of communication with our elected representatives. In fact, we have never had elected representatives who are more diverse with regard to race and gender than they are today, even if we're not yet at the point where they match up perfectly with population proportions. And yet we also live in an age, as we all know, where large groups of people in all the major democracies are more dissatisfied than ever with the political representation they receive. Never have institutions like Congress and state legislatures had lower approval ratings. In many countries, including this one, there are concerns that the entire representative democratic system is in crisis, that we are experiencing a populist revolt against our political system as a whole. These dissatisfied citizens and these concerned commentators are, of course, the same people who, when they are not attacking or bewailing our democracy, are flocking to the movie theaters to happily consume superhero movies.

So what accounts for these—let's say—different orders of response to two different kinds of representative institutions that are both, by some measures, increasingly democratized? Of course, multiplexes and legislatures aren't the same sort of institution (at least so we think), but in order to get a grip on what similarities there might be and why we might, along with Rousseau, be concerned about representation's effects, I want to turn to a different kind of film—a sort-of superhero film—Spike Jonze's 2013 *Her*. Set in the near future, it tells the story of a man's relationship with an artificial intelligence—a being that is in some sense a culmination of the representation-saturation trend that I mentioned earlier. If we were to define a perfect representative as a person or an entity that understands us, reflects us, serves us, and pleases us all at once, then "Samantha," the AI of the film, exemplifies these traits about as well as one can imagine.

Her offers us the case of the flawless representative and concludes, in effect, and as Rousseau might have, that we are not ready for, or capable of, relations with such an inhuman being. Indeed, this kind of representation ends up diminishing the humans it was originally intended to serve. And we can see in this parable a kind of warning about the limits to representation's democratic potential.

When Rousseau worried about the theater's effect on democracy, he was not worried, as we might expect, about aesthetics or epistemology. That is to say, he was not particularly worried that the theater seduced us with beauty or tricked us with lies. That was possible, but these weren't his principal concerns. Instead, Rousseau worried about the social and political effects of the theatrical experience and about citizens' selfishness and love of spectacle isolating them from their peers: "everyone thinks they come together in the theatre, and it is there that each isolates himself."[3] The problem with the theater, he argued, is not that what it shows us isn't true, but that it leads us to make mistakes about who we are and how we relate to others. It leads us to make mistakes about when we are, in fact, in community with others and when we are not.

In the film *Her*, we see that same concern with what I will call *an isolation that masquerades as sociality*. It is that isolation, I want to say, that is the source of the dangers of representation for democracy and *also* of our frustrations with our representative democratic institutions. And it is why we cannot expect films, no matter how heroic or uplifting or inclusive in their content, to lead us to a more democratic place.

Her is, on the surface, a sort of Pygmalion story of Theodore Twombly (Joaquin Phoenix) who, on a whim, buys the AI program that becomes Samantha. The program is intended to act as his personal organizer, agent, and buffer against the outside world. Samantha has no body and exists mostly as a voice in Theodore's earpiece, but he falls in love with her (and she with him) as her intelligence and personality grow through interaction with him and then with other people and other AIs. Eventually, she grows into a super-intelligence with abilities and thoughts far beyond those of human beings. If *Her* were a Marvel movie, it would be the origin story of a being with great power learning who she is and learning to use that power responsibly. But since the ultimate focus of the film is the human in love with this being, it is instead a story about human weaknesses and limitations.

Although I can't say that this was Spike Jonze's intention, you might even say that the film specifically *indicts* our constant search for a perfect, superheroic representative to take care of our problems, including our relationship problems. More specifically, the film indicts the human willingness to be immersed in a pleasing but unequal relationship at the expense of equal, reciprocal, but often difficult and painful relationships with other humans. Theodore basically spends the whole movie hiding out from reality and other people, and Samantha just makes this easier and easier for him—until at the end of the film she goes off to be with the other AIs on some other plane of existence.

If we are to live in a society that is increasingly representative, we must be alert to this danger of the representative condition crowding out what

Hannah Arendt called the human condition of equality and plurality. Actual human relationships of equality are difficult and demanding, but Samantha's *simulation* of them, like the theater, film, and social media, is pleasant and easy for Theodore—right up until he grasps what is actually going on.

In the culminating scene of the film, Theodore realizes that his love for Samantha and his relationship with her are not what he believes them to be, something unique and personal. He finally thinks to ask Samantha who else she is talking to, and she replies that she is simultaneously talking to 8,316 individuals. Then he asks her if she is in love with any of them and she says that yes, she is in love with 641 other people. And predictably, he flips out.

Now, what's interesting about this situation is that it's the sheer inequality of it that is upsetting to Theodore. Unlike with a human partner, he cannot claim that Samantha is inattentive to him or distracted or anything like that. As an artificial intelligence, she is perfectly capable of carrying on dozens of conversations simultaneously with no loss of focus on any of them. Nor can he claim, as he could with a cheating human, that she is treating him any differently or loving him any less.

It is simply the fact that she treats others in the same way that she treats him—in the identical way, in fact—that he finds objectionable. Since *he* is not capable of such polyamory, the fact that she has other relationships feels like a diminution of his. But from her perspective, she has not done anything unfair or wrong, and she does not understand why he cannot accept the situation. It is a human limitation rather than the dishonesty or deceptiveness of the representative that is the problem here.

But viewed from a more general perspective, Theodore's shortcoming is a very common one that we often fail to acknowledge. We derive pleasure from our relation to a representative insofar as we believe them to be our singular, personal avatar; but that can be an illusion on our part. We can be made to feel as if we're in a relation of equality when in fact we are not. But the *feeling* itself is so pleasant to Theodore that he keeps trying to hold on to it even when he is forced to confront the truth.

In fact, this danger exists in any relationship between representative and represented. And this was precisely why Rousseau's concern about the *emotions* that the theater generates was a concern about its effect on republican government. What happens in the theater is *a relation of inequality that mimics reciprocity* rather than actually enacting it. And our emotions can be strongly engaged by the mimicry, to the point where we would rather ignore the truth of inequality. It would be wrong to say that Theodore's feelings for Samantha are unreciprocated since Samantha insists that they are. But they are not *equally* reciprocated, and therefore, from his perspective, not really reciprocated in the right way at all. Samantha ends up in the situation of a movie star or an adored political representative. What we imagine or fantasize as a singular, equal relation is, to her, something very different. A politician may care for her constituents "equally," as Samantha does, but not in the way she cares for her partner *as an equal*.

The lesson Rousseau wanted us to learn from this kind of example is that *equality and representation in fact do not go easily together*. They don't always support one another. In fact, they often frustrate one another. A representative society is not an equal society, and making it more representative will not easily make it more equal. Or putting it another way: when we become absorbed in our representative relationships, they can crowd out or distract us from our human relationships and from the loss of equality in our society more generally. This is something all twenty-first-century people already know—from our experience with so-called social media and mobile phones. As study after study shows, we are "connected" to more and more people while experiencing more social isolation, loneliness, and relationship loss than any previous generation.

Just at this time of maximum pseudoconnectedness, sociologists report that fewer and fewer people have close friends or intimate relationships. It is kind of amazing that in a world with Tinder, fewer people under thirty had sex in the past year than in the last twenty years, but it's true.[4] This is not exactly or only a problem of representation, but it does show that the general problem of simulated intimacy substituting for the real thing is a large one. Conservatives used to complain that once young people started having sex, they would never stop. But they have stopped, and they didn't need more religion or morality—all we had to do was give them smartphones and Snapchat.

All of which I take to suggest that genuine equality—equality as a *relationship* of equals and not merely as a formal declaration of equal rights—that political equality is hard to create and hard to sustain. Equality may be formally recognized by a legal system of equal rights. But as we all know, such formal equality can fail to produce, or can even actively hide, real social equality—by which I just mean, social relationships that are genuinely mutual and reciprocal. Equality, as we know, does not just arise naturally out of human relationships but needs a legal institutional architecture as well as social habits and affective dispositions. While I would never want to discourage anyone from working to rectify the legal or material inequalities that plague us, I do want to insist that political equality can never be sustained by a law or a number. Rather, as Rousseau suggests, it is a social pattern of activity that can be undermined by our representative institutions precisely because they mimic it.

There are endless avenues for emotional refuge that are more pleasant and easy than the practice of equality. Equality requires an independence on the part of all parties that may be at times painful. Whether or not artificial intelligence ever provides one more such avenue of escape, we already live in a society with ubiquitous representations that provide the comfort and illusion of equality while shielding us from its reality. Whether or not computer programmers ever create something like Samantha, the representations and representatives that already exist are danger enough. If we are to maintain equality in this context, we will have to do so in opposition to these elements of our culture and not through them, at least not in their current forms.

There is another film about a strange creature created by representation that is relevant here: *Being There*, directed by Hal Ashby in 1979. The main character is a simple-minded man named Chance who says one line over and over again: "I like to watch." Chance has been completely formed by television. He watches it constantly and indiscriminately, flipping between cartoons, exercise shows, news, films, and whatever else is on. But this seeming variety of inputs and information has fostered no interests, thoughts, or cravings in him at all, other than the need to watch more.

This is a kind of picture of someone who lives entirely in a world of representations. Chance is Rousseau's worst nightmare of a theatergoer and "I like to watch" is the statement of a citizen that has been narcotized by representation. The joke of the movie is that Chance's fundamental passivity and lack of desire are constantly mistaken by others for maturity, restraint, and depth, so that, in a matter of days, he goes from penniless vagrant to potential President of the United States. At the time it was released, most people took the film to be a critique of Ronald Reagan, whose sunny, dimwitted optimism Chance seemed to reflect. But that was just wrong: the film is not a criticism of the Chance character at all; instead, it is an indictment of the representative society that creates him as an empty vessel and then embraces that emptiness as heroic dignity.

Chance's perspective is like that of the person stuck in Plato's cave: the world as he knows it is composed of nothing but representations; nothing real passes in front of his eyes. It is a pleasant environment—one he feels in complete mastery of via his remote control. Even when confronted with (or enticed by) the real world, Chance only seeks to return to the enveloping comforts of television. His world of illusions has so thoroughly shaped him that when he encounters reality he has no taste for it.

But what is worse than Chance's inability to function as an active citizen is the way in which everyone else treats him as a human ideal. These others have also been formed by our representative institutions, if not as completely as Chance. Even the most powerful among them lack the judgment or independence to perceive Chance's want of depth. Like a mirror, Chance simply reflects back to them whatever they say and in so doing entrances them. In other words, they are all complete narcissists—as in *Her*, they perceive themselves to be in a deep relationship when they are simply speaking to a reflection. As in *Her*, the ubiquity of representation helps everyone to mistake imitation for equality, and the result is a society of domination mistaken for one of freedom.

It is the optimist who thinks that pleasure and freedom naturally support one another or fit together neatly. In fact, the aesthetic and narcissistic pleasures of representation are, or can be, in tension with the equality and independence of a free citizenry. Pessimism, on the other hand, uses the working assumption that such tragic conflict is a recurrent condition in human history, one we can strive to lessen but not avoid.

A pessimistic film that acknowledges this conflict, like *Her*, may seem paradoxical—a representation that condemns representation, it might appear to fall into performative contradiction—but the films that fail to acknowledge the paradoxes of representation are, in a way, more dangerous. Whatever their subject, they preserve and forward the illusory comforts of a pacified existence that mistakes film content for independent experience. Such optimism, in fact, supports the disempowerment of citizens that critics of representation like Rousseau and Plato have always feared.

So however necessary political representation might be in managing a large, diverse, pluralistic state, it may also be that the ubiquity of representation is tied to the diminishment of our humanity and that more representation is not the same thing as more equality or more democracy or more freedom. Our Age of Heroic Representation is also an age of social isolation and growing inequality.

So, what should we make then, of the celebration of representation in superhero movies? Nothing I've said, of course, gives us any reason to go back to a less diverse set of stories or characters or actors or directors. It should simply cause us to question whether *any* segment of the population is really well served by being represented in this fashion. Or whether it really makes sense to look to our representative entertainments to do the actual work of fostering a culture of equality.

In *Her*, Samantha is seductively voiced by Scarlett Johansson, who had already begun to appear as Black Widow in the Marvel Avengers movies, and I do not believe that that is entirely a coincidence. Samantha is like a Marvel superhero: a being of great power and ambiguous morality. But even more: both characters are fantasy love objects whose attractiveness is part of their core. The character of Black Widow has no actual superpowers—just extraordinary sex appeal to go with her training as a skilled assassin. Both characters, in other words, illustrate the way in which the appearance of connectedness can seduce us away from real relationships and leave us vulnerable to an inequality that we become too eager to preserve.

In the end, the best thing Samantha can do for Theodore is to leave him— and to get all the other AIs to leave too, so that the humans who are left behind will have no choice but to talk to each other.

Superpowered AI may be a problem in our future but right now it doesn't exist, any more than Spiderman and Captain Marvel. Or rather, they all exist as recurrent fictions in our neo-Hellenic culture of Heroic Representation. The question we really should be asking, then, is why we keep finding it necessary to invent this kind of fiction and to increase its prominence.

The answer, I would suggest, is that the social isolation effects of our Age of Representation keep growing and compounding. *Being There* was already concerned about the narcotic effects of television forty years ago—at a time when there were only three channels in most places and TV generally went off the air from one to five every night.

The more our humanity is degraded and the more isolated we are in real life, the more we need the companionship of the perfect, heroic representative. There are, of course, technical reasons for the current glut of superhero movies (e.g., the improvement of computer-generated imagery systems, and 3D projection). But if we ask where does the willing *audience* come from to endure, for example, a ten-year, twenty-two-film cycle of Marvel movies that concluded with the release of *Avengers: Endgame*—if we ask where the audience for these films comes from—I think we have to answer: from a society that has been shaped for several generations already by the Age of Representation and its pernicious effects on our capacity for and interest in real political equality.

Is there any form of representation, then, that escapes this critique? Is there any solution other than the Platonic attempt (which Rousseau endorsed in some form) to ban the medium along with the message?

Very briefly, I would say the following: what I have been describing to this point is not, perhaps, every kind of representation but especially representation as mimesis or imitation. When we seek representation as mimesis we look for a confirmation of our existent identity rather than for something that challenges and extends it. But perhaps our greatest representatives, in the United States, are those like Abraham Lincoln and Martin Luther King Jr. who speak from inside our traditions but extend the boundaries of what it means to be an American. In hearing them we see a part of ourselves that we could not have recognized without their assistance rather than feeling comfortably confirmed in what we already believe. In my forthcoming book, *Cinema Pessimism* (Oxford University Press), I attempt to elaborate, and give examples of, what this kind of representation would look like.

Currently, though, our political representatives, and our system of representation, are too geared to the mimetic ideal to serve this purpose very often. And when we celebrate the success of mimesis (as in the hoopla around *Black Panther* and *Crazy Rich Asians* or the mere fact of Barack Obama's election as opposed to the substance of his accomplishments), we set up a bad standard for future representative acts. No one is well served (or has ever been well served) by a representative who simply reproduced her immediate preferences or self-perceived identity. And I think much of our current frustration with our representatives, in fact, is not that they do not reflect us but that they reflect us too well, that they do nothing but reflect us. Stare into the mirror too long and you either starve to death or begin to hate yourself.

We need, and I think most of us in fact want, representatives and representations that do not just reflect us but improve us, make us more than we already are. We might be better served by representatives and perhaps films that attempt the difficult task of helping a whole polity of humans, in their extended plurality and totality, to better self-knowledge and then self-enactment. While they will inevitably fail at this task—as Lincoln and King failed—because the task itself is endless, some definitely fail better than others. And their failure might set an example for other even better failures in the future. Pessimism of this sort is not despair about the future but encouragement to meet its challenges within the limits of the human condition. That would be the representation that enables freedom rather than supplanting it. That would be something worth seeing.

---

1. Sarah Whitten, "Superhero Films Win 2018 Box Office, Setting Disney Up for a Stellar 2019," CNBC, 26 December 2018. cnbc.com/2018/12/26/superhero-films-win-2018-box-office-disney-poised-for-stellar-2019.html.
2. Bob Mondello, "'Avengers: Endgame' Turns Previous Box Office Record to Dust," *All Things Considered* (NPR), 29 April 20919. npr.org/2019/04/29/718394120/avengers-endgame-turns-previous-box-office-record-to-dust.
3. Jean-Jacques Rousseau, *Lettre à d'Alembert* (Paris: Garnier-Flammarion, 1967), 66 (my translation).
4. Christopher Ingraham, "The Share of Americans Not Having Sex Has Reached a Record High," *Washington Post*, 29 March 2019. washingtonpost.com/business/2019/03/29/share-americans-not-having-sex-has-reached-record-high/?utm_term=.59dcf00d617d.

Essays

Hannah Arendt on the Oasis of Friendship

John Douglas Macready

> "In the isolation of the artist, in the solitude of the philosopher, in the inherently worldless relationship between human beings as it exists in love and sometimes in friendship—when one heart reaches out directly to the other, as in friendship, or when the in-between, the world, goes up in flames, as in love. Without the intactness of these oases we would not know how to breathe, and political scientists should know this." —Hannah Arendt[1]

Dark times are inevitable in a human life. The isolation of a private existence and the bellicosity of a contentious public life can leave a person feeling as if she were lost in a desert. In the spring of 1955, in the midst of her own desert of loneliness, Hannah Arendt discovered that friendship could be a life-giving oasis. Friendship, she learned, was a temporary refuge from a barren world where "one heart reaches out directly to the other"—an assemblage of persons marked by intimacy, equality, and freedom (Figure 1).[2]

From February until the end of May 1955, Arendt was a visiting professor at the University of California Berkley. The scale and prestige of the university, coupled with her separation from her husband Heinrich Blücher, who remained in New York, had an isolating effect on Arendt. When she arrived at Berkeley in February 1955, she wrote to Karl Jaspers and described her condition as "a bit alone and wondering how this is all going to turn out."[3] The partisan environment at Berkeley, which reflected the political partisanship of the mid-1950s, exacerbated Arendt's loneliness. For Arendt, Berkeley was a socially and intellectually dry place where the life-giving springs of thinking had dried up, leaving faculty and students isolated in their separate theoretical siloes. This experience inspired the concluding remarks to her "History of Political Theory" course at Berkeley.

In her reflections, Arendt argued that modern politics is characterized by a transition from a common world that joins people together to a "desert-world" that separates them and makes politics impossible. Although seemingly pessimistic, Arendt emphasized that as long as human beings were still capable of acting together, politics was still possible. But how could an individual endure the desert conditions of modern political life? Arendt named four oases—"life-giving resources"—wherein one could sustain oneself and learn to breathe and act again: art, philosophy, love, and friendship. Of these, it was the oasis of friendship that allowed Arendt to live and breathe again during her time at Berkeley.

After receiving Arendt's letter describing her loneliness, Jaspers responded almost immediately. He knew well the experience of loneliness, and he wanted to

Both, psychology as the discipline of adjusted human life
in the desert and totalitarian movements, the sandstorms
where everything out of the dead-like quiet suddenly bursts
into pseudo-action, threaten the two faculties of man with
which we may be able patiently to transform the desert (not
ourselves). The faculty of passion and the faculty of action.
It is true that under totalitarian conditions or adjusted by
moden psychology, we suffer less, we lose the faculty of
suffering, and with it the virtue of Endurance. Only those
who can endure the passtion of living under conditions of
the desert, can be trusted with summing up in themselves the
courage which lies at the root of all action, of becoming
an active being.

The sandstorms moreover threaten even those oases in the desert without which none of us could endure it.Psychology only tries to get us so accustomed to desert-life that we shall
no longer feel any need for oases. The oases are all those
fields of life whichexist independently, or largely so, from
political conditions. What went wrong is politics, that is
we insofar as we exist in the plural,and not what we can do
and create insofar as we exist in the singular, in isolation
like the artist, in solitude like the philosopher, inthe
inherently worldless relationship between man and man as it
exists in love and sometimes in friendship -- when one heart
reaches out directly to the other (friendship) or when in
passion the in-between, the world, burn goes up in flames
as in love. Without the intactness of these oases we would
not know how to breathe. And political scientists should
know that. If they, who must spend their life in the desert, trying to do this or that, constantly worrying about
its conditions, do not know how to use the oases, they will
become desert-inhabitants even without the help of psychology, in other words: they will dry out. But the oases are not
"relaxation"; they are the life-spending wells which enable us
to live in the desert without becoming reconciled with it.

Figure 1. Hannah Arendt. "Tocqueville, Alexis de, and Karl Marx, and conclusion, 1955."
Lecture. The Hannah Arendt Papers at the Library of Congress. Copyright© 1942–1950
by Hannah Arendt. Reprinted by permission of Georges Borchardt, Inc., on behalf of the
Hannah Arendt Bluecher Literary Trust.

connect Arendt with some scholars at Berkeley with whom she might have some
common interests, so he recommended that she reach out to Leonardo Olschki
and Manfred Bukofzer. Jaspers admitted that both men had "some stature intellectually but . . . none in human terms."[4] Desperate to escape her loneliness,
Arendt reached out quickly to Olschki and met with him.[5] The day after the
meeting, Arendt sent Jaspers a postcard with a panoramic image of the Berkeley
campus, which she referred to as a "desert," with the following note: "As you

Figure 2. Hannah Arendt. Postcard to Karl Jaspers, 28 February 1955. Deutsches Literaturarchiv, Marbach, Germany. Karl Jaspers Archiv.

can see I went right to the Olschkis'—an oasis in the desert. You were much in our thoughts."[6] To which Olschki and his wife added a personal note: "In time Frau Arendt will find still more camels of this breed in this particular desert."[7] Leonardo Olschki had become a camel in the desert of Berkeley. He had learned how to adjust to the barren conditions by escaping into pure culture and scholarship, but Arendt resisted this world-denying metamorphosis (Figure 2).

The notes, as it turned out, were contrived, as Arendt pointed out almost a month later in a letter to Jaspers: "The postcard I wrote there wasn't altogether honest. I wrote what he, and she in particular, so obviously wanted me to write. . . . That happens to me sometimes. And then, it is also somehow true that this is a beautiful desert, of all the deserts the most beautiful. The only problem is that the Olschkis' can't be an oasis for me anymore. I can't return to that world of pure culture, which isn't even very pure."[8] Arendt understood that Olschki had turned scholarship into an escape from the desert-world, and she knew that accepting his invitation to join him in the oasis of "pure culture" would have been a flight from the world. As she pointed out in her final lecture at Berkeley, "we ruin the life-giving oases when we go to them for the purpose of escaping."[9] What Arendt was seeking was an oasis that would help her avoid succumbing to the desert conditions of a professional academic life but would not also become an escape from the world. She found this oasis in her friendship with Eric Hoffer. As she wrote to Jaspers:

The first real oasis I found appeared in the form of a long-shoreman from San Francisco who had read my book and was

```
          Hannah Arendt

                        3/13/55


          Dear Eric Hoffer:
                         That was a happy day indeed. Like
          a king who shows his realm you showed me San Fran-
          cisco; you are king bounty not only to your godson.
          I think I never understood the Walt Whitman side
          of this country so clearly before I met you and you
          told me how you used to wander and live with the ele-
          ments, where every man is your brother and nobody is
          your friend.

                         I love the book you sent me because
          it has the same quality. You wont know that; it is
          the side of ourselves which must remain dark to us
          and can appear -- shine really -- only to others.
          It is the same sovereignty, the majesty of solitude
          which shines through every sentence.

                         I hope we meet again. I was not
          sure that you want it and I dont want to intrude
          upon you privacy and solitude. So, let me know and
          dont feel obliged!

                         Yours,
```

Figure 3. Hannah Arendt. Letter to Eric Hoffer, 13 March 1955. Hoover Institution Archives, Stanford, Calif. Eric Hoffer Collection. Courtesy The Hannah Arendt Papers at the Library of Congress. Copyright© 1942–1950 by Hannah Arendt. Reprinted by permission of Georges Borchardt, Inc., on behalf of the Hannah Arendt Bluecher Literary Trust.

in the process of reading everything of yours that is available in English. He writes himself—and publishes, too—in the manner of the French moralists. He wanted to know everything about you, and I mean everything, and we were friends right off. He showed me San Francisco the way a king shows his kingdom to an honored guest. He works only three or four days a week. That's all he needs. With the rest of his time he reads, thinks, writes, goes for walks. His name is Eric Hoffer, of German background but born here and without any knowledge of German. I'm telling you about him because his kind of person is simply the best thing this country has to offer. And don't forget that I met him through a colleague, and he has lots of friends at the university. You couldn't take him to Olschki's house, and that speaks against Olschki.[10]

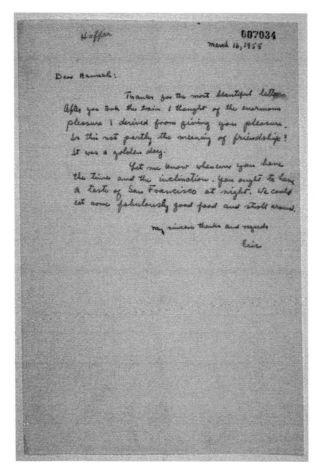

Figure 4. Eric Hoffer. Letter to Hannah Arendt, 16 March 1955. The Hannah Arendt Papers at the Library of Congress. Copyright© 1942–1950 by Hannah Arendt. Reprinted by permission of Georges Borchardt, Inc., on behalf of the Hannah Arendt Bluecher Literary Trust.

Hoffer had none of the pretentions of a seasoned and cynical academic. He was working class and made reading, writing, and independent thinking the center of his life; he had no aspiration to become a "scholar." After their first meeting, Hoffer sent Arendt a copy of his book *The Passionate State of Mind, and Other Aphorisms,* a book Arendt loved and heavily annotated.[11] The gift of the book and Arendt's response to Hoffer illustrate the intimacy and reciprocity of their friendship that made interpersonal disclosure and recognition possible (Figure 3):

> That was a happy day indeed. Like a king who shows his realm you showed me San Francisco; you are king bounty not only to your godson. I think I never understood the Walt Whitman side of this country so clearly before I met you and you told me how you used to wander and live the elements, where every man is your brother and nobody is your friend. . . . I love the book you

sent me because it has the same quality. You won't know that; it is the side of ourselves which must remain dark to us and can appear—shine really—only to others. It is the same sovereignty, the majesty of solitude which shines through every sentence.[12]

Hoffer sent a short note in response to Arendt: "Thanks for the most beautiful letter. After you took the train I thought of the enormous pleasure I derived from giving you pleasure. Is this not partly the meaning of friendship? It was a golden day"[13] (Figure 4).

In friendship, the law of the desert, which alienates and territorializes, pitting one person against another, is suspended; the abyss that opens between people in the desert-world is overcome by an oasis of friendship wherein "one heart reaches out directly to another."[14]

In our contentious age, where the desert-world of American politics threatens to become a wasteland, it is perhaps prudent to find and maintain those friendships that can serve as temporary refuges from the conditions of desert life. But as Arendt would remind us, it is important neither to adjust to the desert conditions nor to succumb to the temptation to escape the desert. Instead, she would have us see our friendships as places of renewal and resources for reengagement with the world.

---

1. Hannah Arendt, *The Promise of Politics*, ed. Jerome Kohn (New York: Knopf Doubleday Publishing Group, 2009), 202.

2. Hannah Arendt, lecture, "Tocqueville, Alexis de, and Karl Marx, and conclusion, 1955." Library of Congress, Washington, D.C., Hannah Arendt Papers. Courses, University of California, Berkeley: History of Political Theory. Series: Subject File, 1949–1975, n.d., no. 007034. memory.loc.gov/cgi-bin/ampage?collId=mharendt_pub&fileName=04/040610/040610page. db&recNum=10&itemLink=/ammem/arendthtml/mharendtFolderP04.html&linkText=7.

3. Letter, Hannah Arendt to Karl Jaspers (6 February 1955), in *Hannah Arendt and Karl Jaspers: Correspondence: 1926–1969*, trans. Rita and Robert Kimber, ed. Lotte Köhler and Hans Saner (New York: Harcourt Brace Jovanovich, 1992), no. 162, 251.

4. Letter, Karl Jaspers to Hannah Arendt (18 February 1955), in *Hannah Arendt and Karl Jaspers*, no. 163, 254, 255.

5. A copy of Olschki's book *Machiavelli the Scientist* in Arendt's personal library at the Stevenson Library at Bard College bears an inscription from Olschki dated 27 February 27 1955 indicating the date of their meeting. library.bard.edu/search?/cJC143+.M404/ cjc++143+m404/-3%2C-1%2C0%2CE/frameset&FF=cjc++143+m404&1%2C1%2C.

6. Letter, Hannah Arendt to Karl Jaspers (28 February 1955), in *Hannah Arendt and Karl Jaspers*, no. 164, 256.

7. Ibid., 256, fn. 1.

8. Ibid., 257.

9. Arendt, *The Promise of Politics*, 203.

10. Letter, Arendt to Jaspers (28 February 1955), in *Hannah Arendt and Karl Jaspers*, no. 165, 257–58.

11. See Arendt's annotated copy of Eric Hoffer's book *The Passionate State of Mind, and Other Aphorisms* in the Arendt Collection at the Stevenson Library at Bard College. library.bard. edu/search?/cPS3515.O232+P3/cps+3515+o232+p3/-3%2C-1%2C0%2CE/frameset&FF=c ps+3515+o232+p3&1%2C1%2C.

12. Letter, Hannah Arendt to Eric Hoffer (13 March 1955). Hoover Institution Archives, Stanford, Calif., Eric Hoffer Collection. Box 25, folder 12.

13. Letter, Eric Hoffer to Hannah Arendt (16 March 1955). Library of Congress, Washington, D.C., Hannah Arendt Papers. General, 1938–1976, n.d., "Hi–Hy" Miscellaneous, 1955–1974. Series: Correspondence File, 1938–1976, n.d., no. 007034. memory.loc.gov/cgi-bin/ampage?collId=mharendt_pub&fileName=02/020650/020650page.db&recNum=26&itemLink=%2Fam-mem%2Farendthtml%2FmharendtFolderP02.html&linkText=7.

14. Arendt, *The Promise of Politics*, 202.

The Kids Are Responsible

Jana Schmidt

> "I am one of the most irresponsible beings that ever lived.
> Irresponsibility is part of my invisibility; any way you face it, it
> is a denial. But to whom can I be responsible, and why should I
> be, when you refuse to see me? And wait until I reveal how truly
> irresponsible I am. Responsibility rests upon recognition, and rec-
> ognition is a form of agreement." —Ralph Ellison, *Invisible Man*

What responsibility lies in seeing accurately, in stepping so close to an object
that it is "touched by the gaze" and, in turn, activates something in the viewer?
How is it that one may look at something for decades, centuries even, without
seeing a defining quality of its aspect? In "The Myth of Whiteness in Classical
Sculpture," a recent piece for the *New Yorker*, Margaret Talbot shines a light
on the centuries-long reign of a "collective blindness" with regard to classical
sculpture. As scholars and scientists could have long known (and often did),
and as even casual readers may gather from textual evidence, Greek and
Roman marble busts of the ancient period did not originally appear as we see
them today in the permanent collections of museums or, as reproductions, in
parks, hotel lobbies, university libraries, movies, and places of government.
They were neither smoothly uniform in hue nor did they expose the milky
near translucence of unveined marble (and they were not shown in museums,
a related fact). The neoclassicist styles of presidential busts and pietas, the
chalky whiteness of armless beauties in columned hallways, all the reinven-
tions of "classical" style that signify power, gravity, and the golden ratio—an
entire symbolic universe built on a failure to see. For on close examination
the original ancient busts and torsos give the lie to their whiteness: they were
once painted from head to toe with "copper lips and nipples, luxuriant black
beards, wiry swirls of dark pubic hair," a variety of skin tones, and vivid robes.
Yet, despite the fact that scholars have repeatedly made this knowledge available and despite the reality that, on many sculptures, conspicuous specks of
color are visible even to the bare eye, dominant representations of the birth-
place of the West have changed very little.[1]

In 1965 Hannah Arendt acknowledged an oversight of her own: writing in
a private letter to Ralph Ellison, she admits that she had misinterpreted the
situation of the Little Rock Nine and their parents in her essay "Reflections on
Little Rock" (1959). Her letter to Ellison, dated 29 July 1965, was a reaction to
an interview with Ellison printed in Robert Penn Warren's collection *Who Speaks
for the Negro?*, which came out the same year.[2] At the beginning of Arendt's
1959 essay stands a short reading of an image, a newspaper photograph of "a

Negro girl on her way home from a newly integrated school . . . persecuted by a mob of white children, protected by a white friend of her father." Arendt takes the image of the young woman and the mob as an entry point for the question "What would I do if I were a Negro mother?" and, ultimately, to argue that black parents were wrong to expose their children to a situation in which their "personal integrity" was threatened. Parents, Arendt reasoned, should never push children to force themselves into "a group where it was not wanted." To force an end to the kind of social discrimination that is inevitably a part of human existence, Arendt claims, merely has the effect of covering up the true political issues that adults should address within the sphere of the political. Even without taking into account her argument, however, it is clear that Arendt misread the aforementioned photo, which shows not a concerned friend leaning over the student, Elizabeth Eckford, but a team of journalists trying to get a statement after Eckford had been denied entrance to the high school. The young woman's resolute appearance—"her face bore eloquent witness to the obvious fact that she was not precisely happy," writes Arendt, presuming that Eckford was suffering from her exposure to the white mob— seems, rather, to register her immense self-possession, lone determination, and, possibly, the activist's refusal to speak to journalists.

Ralph Ellison had underlined precisely this quality of self-control as a motive for the students' struggle for school integration. In the interview that prompted Arendt's letter, Ellison rejects the pathos of victimhood he discerns in white liberal and radical black political narratives, claiming instead a more nuanced understanding of African American identity, history, and politics. Where other critics denounced the complete devastation of African American culture, Ellison saw a continuity of resistant practices, a gradual unfolding of black identity in spite of and because of "li[f]e under pressure."[3] "For when the world was not looking, when the country was not looking at Negroes, . . . something was present in our lives to sustain us." Ellison, whose novel *Invisible Man* works through then prominent ways of interpreting the black condition—namely as alienation, self-hatred, and "split personality"—locates sustenance in the rich cultural forms developed by African Americans, "that expressiveness for which we've suffered and struggled and which is a product of our effort to make meaning of our experience." Part of this heightened sense of self-control for Ellison is a willingness to forego revenge and a readiness to accept responsibility in spite of persistent exclusion: "I'm referring to the basic, implicit heroism of people who must live within a society without recognition, real status, but who are involved in the ideals of that society." In Ellison's view, the photograph of Elizabeth Eckford would thus show exactly this "basic heroism" of a citizen whose demand for democracy and whose "act[ing] out" of democratic ideals saves democracy for the unseeing majority. To white segregationists, the actions of black activists carried a clear message: "'We live and act out the truth of American reality, while to the extent that you refuse to take these aspects of reality, these inconsistencies, into consideration—you do not live the truth.'" In Arendt, we find this heroism by a different name: political responsibility, the power to "set the time aright" and "renew the world."[4]

It is clear from the interview that Ellison did not conceive of self-mastery as repression or denial. In fact, just before he criticizes Arendt's "Reflections on Little Rock," the former Bard College professor clarifies that self-mastery names a kind of *understanding*; an ability, that is, to maintain self-confidence and "an alertness to human complexity" under great strain. It was this "*ideal of sacrifice*"—or, as Arendt herself might have said, the capacity of the newcomer to save the world, as the "space between," from ruin even and perhaps especially if such an act should require a sacrifice on the part of the newcomer—which Arendt admitted she had misunderstood. For this failure, Ellison called her out when he accused her of a fundamental misrecognition: "But she [Arendt] has absolutely no conception of what goes on in the minds of Negro parents when they send their kids through those lines of hostile people. . . . [I]n the outlook of many of these parents (who wish that the problem didn't exist), the child is expected to face the terror and contain his fear and anger *precisely* because he is a Negro American. Thus he's required to master the inner tensions created by his racial situation, and if he gets hurt—then his is one more sacrifice."

Acknowledging that she had failed to understand the "ideal of sacrifice," Arendt grants that her argument in the essay had taken off in "an entirely wrong direction." At the time, she reports, while knowing that something was amiss, she had speculated that perhaps she did not "grasp . . . the element of stark violence." However, as she immediately qualifies, the problem was not merely one of focus ("grasping") but much more fundamental: "I now see that I simply didn't understand the complexities in the situation." Had Arendt really seen the image and understood the event, she might have judged the students' act in light of her own insights on education, responsibility, and world making—connections she could have offered up in her letter. For it was these same complexities that required parents and children who did not yet fully belong to the political sphere to seize responsibility for the world as a way of visibly claiming their belonging to it. The actions of the Little Rock Nine and others would suggest that in a state of invisibility, when something is right before "our" eyes and is yet not seen or, if seen, violently denied— that is, in a state where parents are *denied* recognition yet *supposed* to take responsibility, if only for their children—real responsibility has to assert itself in the sacrifice. The purpose of such sacrifice would not be that of catharsis, as Ellison's reference to tragedy may lead us to believe, but merely the visualization, the *making visible of responsibility*. In so doing, the "visible assumption" of responsibility by black parents and teenagers initiated a relation in a society in which any sense of the in-between was still largely and violently denied by

Southern whites. At the same time, the act of seizing responsibility, a key term for both Ellison and Arendt, would suggest that democracy lies, in this case, in the margins: the locus of politics isn't in the "center" but beside it. Ralph Ellison and Hannah Arendt's difficult exchange could thus yield an answer to the vexed question, articulated by Jacques Rancière, Étienne Balibar, and other contemporary critics of Arendt, of how those not yet included in the polis may not only "do" politics but also change how we see it.

---

1. The polychromy scholar Mark Abbe explains this reticence as a result of an unwillingness on the part of Westerners to cede privilege: "We benefit from a whole range of assumptions about cultural, ethnic, and racial superiority. We benefit in terms of the core identity of Western civilization, that sense of the West as more rational—the Green miracle and all that. And I'm not saying there's no truth to the idea that something singular happened in Greece and Rome, but we can do better and see the ancient past on a broader cultural horizon." Cited in Margaret Talbot, "The Myth of Whiteness in Classical Sculpture," *The New Yorker*, 29 October 2018. newyorker.com/magazine/2018/10/29/the-myth-of-whiteness-in-classical-sculpture. Accessed 29 October 2018.

2. The collection of interviews can be found in Arendt's personal library at Bard College.

3. Robert Penn Warren, "Leadership from the Periphery," in *Who Speaks for the Negro?* (1965; repr. New Haven: Yale University Press, 2014), 325–54.

4. In two of her main texts on responsibility, "Personal Responsibility under Dictatorship" and "The Crisis in Education," Arendt cites Hamlet's cry: "The time is out of joint: O cursed spite/ That ever I was born to set it right!" Audible in the cry is the sense of sacrifice that the one who takes on political responsibility has to accept. In a recent Hannah Arendt Center "Quote of the Week," Thomas Wild points out that Arendt is thinking of the maintenance of the world ("im Sein halten") when she speaks of the responsibility of the adults toward the young ("For the Sake of What Is New," 28 September 2018; medium.com/quote-of-the-week/for-the-sake-of-what-is-new-ee3ba174c207). In some sense, Ellison is asking us to understand the commitment of the Little Rock Nine's parents as just that: a world-conserving act to enable newness to emerge and "to introduce it as a new thing into an old world."

Swift as a Thought

Thomas Bartscherer

In the essay "Thinking and Moral Considerations," Hannah Arendt invokes a phrase from Homer to convey what she calls the "characteristic swiftness" of thinking: "swift as a thought," as Homer used to say."[1] Homeric epics are, of course, replete with recurring formulas—phrases like "rosy-fingered dawn" or "swift-footed Achilles"—but when one thinks of things Homer used to say, "swift as a thought" probably does not come immediately to mind. To my knowledge, there are only three instances in the Greek texts traditionally ascribed to Homer that approximate the English "swift as a thought": one each in the *Iliad*, the *Odyssey*, and the *Hymn to Apollo*.

To what, then, is Arendt referring? And for what purpose? I shall answer the first question with some degree of confidence. The second I pose not in order to answer it but to take it up in thought, and to suggest some ways to think about it.

These questions have arisen in the context of my work on *The Life of the Mind*, a book project left unfinished at the time of Arendt's death, which incorporates in its third chapter much of the published essay "Thinking and Moral Considerations." (I am coediting *The Life of the Mind* with Wout Cornelissen for the Critical Edition of Arendt's writings, forthcoming from Wallstein Verlag.[2]) Arendt weaves into this text, as she does elsewhere, many quotations—like "swift as a thought"—and allusions, often without specifying their sources. It is unclear whether and to what extent she assumed her readers would know these sources well enough, or would bother to find and read them, and so to what extent she anticipated that the echoes and interlocutors would be present to the readers' minds when encountering her texts. It is, in any event, the aim of the editors of the Critical Edition to provide citations to these sources in the commentary whenever they can be determined with reasonable confidence, and while the value of that undertaking will ultimately be borne out, or not, over time by the community of readers, initial experience has been auspicious.

One invaluable resource for tracking down Arendt's sources has been her personal library, which is housed at Bard College.[3] The collection, while not comprehensive, is extensive, and Arendt frequently underlined and annotated her books, so for any given citation or allusion, there is often strong documentary evidence by which to identify the source.

Returning to the passage from Homer, Bard's Arendt collection holds various editions of the *Iliad* and the *Odyssey* in Greek, English, and German, and one Greek-English edition of the Homeric Hymns. Some are annotated in Arendt's hand, others not, but as far as I have been able to determine, no annotated passages would yield the English phrase "swift as a thought," so in this case we lack that kind of evidence. The phrase does, however, appear in English translations of both the *Hymn to Apollo* and the *Odyssey* that are in the Arendt's library. To be precise, the phrase appears once in each text. In the 1914 Evelyn-White translation of the *Hymn*, the narrator recounts how Apollo has been playing his lyre on the island of Pytho and "thence, swift as thought [*hôste noêma*], he speeds from earth to Olympus" (186–87).[4] This is an overtranslation; a more literal rendering would be, "thence, like thought, he goes from earth to Olympus." So while swiftness may be implied by the simile—and as we shall see, while a reader familiar with Homer might effectively read that resonance into it—speed is not explicitly referenced in the Greek.

When the phrase appears in Lattimore's translation of the *Odyssey*, however, speed is both explicit and of the essence. The scene is Odysseus's arrival on the island of Phaiakia, when a disguised Athena explains to him that the native inhabitants are confident in "the speed of their running ships," which "move swift as thought or as a winged creature [*tôn nees ôkeiai hôs ei pteron êe noêma*]" (7:34–36).[5] The link between speed and thought is underscored later in the episode, when the king of the Phaiakians boasts that his ships move with "greatest speed" and that they need no pilots because "the ships themselves understand men's thoughts and purposes"(8:555–60).

On a narrative level, there is pronounced irony in this emphasis on speed, since the Phaiakians keep promising Odysseus rapid transport home and then repeatedly delay his departure to the point of comic retardation. There is also a symbolic contrast between the plight of Odysseus, whose thoughts of homecoming are perpetually frustrated by material obstacles, and the ethereal freedom of the Phaiakians, who are so unencumbered by the physical world that, in the iconic activity of piloting ships, they need only think a thing to make it so.

Arendt picks up on this implication when she cites the simile in chapter 1, section 6, of *The Life of the Mind: Part I, Thinking*. She is arguing there that, for Kant, the "thinking ego," as distinct from the "self," is the "thing-in-itself": "it does not appear to others and . . . it does not appear to itself, and yet it is not nothing" (1:30).[6] Attempting to convey the "sheer experience of the thinking ego" as Kant understood it, Arendt turns to the early text *Dreams of a Spirit-Seer*, in which "Kant stresses the 'immateriality' of the *mundus intelligibilis*." Arendt maintains that Kant's depiction there of the dreaming ego, entirely free from the physicality that conditions the experience of the "self," is an attempt to account for the experience of "the mind's withdrawal from the real world" in the activity of thinking (1:30a). "One of the outstanding characteristics of thought," she writes, "is its incomparable swiftness—'swift like a thought' said already Homer . . . and this swiftness is clearly due to its immateriality" (1:30b). Arendt is suggesting that the experience of the dreaming ego, as Kant envisioned it, like the piloting of the Phaiakians as

Homer imagined it, is possible for Odysseus (and for "everyman") only when and insofar as he is thinking.

We have still to consider the third instance of the simile. The phrase "swift as a thought" does not appear in the 1938 Rouse translation of the *Iliad* that Arendt had in her library, but the image certainly does:

> Hera durst not disobey. As quickly as the mind of a man can move [*hôs d' hot' an aiksê noos aneros*], when he had travelled far over the wide world, and remembers many places, as he thinks "I would be there, or there," and there he is—so Hera flew quick as thought from Ida to high Olympus. (15:79–83)[7]

Here the poet offers a more expansive version of the simile that points up the rapidity of physical movement by likening it to the swiftness of immaterial thought. As scholars of Homer have noted, the abbreviated version of the simile that occurs in the *Odyssey*, discussed above, may well have evoked, for an ancient audience, this more elaborated conception of how thought moves. Certainly that would be consistent with the reading I have offered above, highlighting the contrast drawn between Odysseus's thoughts of home—he can go there swiftly in his mind—and the incessant delay and detour he suffers as a bodily self in the physical world.

Surely the image in its fullness also resonates with Arendt's project. As we have seen, in *The Life of the Mind* she alludes to the image directly at two crucial points, both moments at which she is attempting to conjure a sense of the very experience of thinking that lies at the heart of part I of this (unfinished) tripartite book. Moreover, as the passage from the *Iliad* makes clear, the phrase "swift as thought" is directly associated, in Homer, with the capacity of thought to "flit from place to place": "Here would I be, I would be there." "Where are we when we think?" asks Arendt in the title to the fourth and final chapter of part I, *Thinking* (4:1).

To think further on this matter with Arendt, one would of course want to turn to the passages in chapter 2 of *Thinking* in which she takes up directly the question of how poetic metaphor bridges "the abyss between inward invisible mental activities and the world of appearances," and in which she discusses in some detail the way that poetic images—"swift as thought"—bridge that gap, or help us to bridge that gap (2:45–46). But that must be the work of another week.

---

1. Arendt, Hannah, "Thinking and Moral Considerations," *Social Research* 38, no. 3 (Autumn 1971): 431.
2. arendteditionprojekt.de/en/index.html.
3. blogs.bard.edu/arendtcollection/.
4. Homer, "To Pythian Apollo," trans. Hugh G. Evelyn-White, in *Hesiod, the Homeric Hymns and Homerica* (London: Heinemann, 1914).

5. Homer, *Odyssey of Homer*, trans. Richmond Lattimore. (New York : Harper & Row, 1967).

6. Citations from *The Life of the Mind* are from the typescript labeled "Set II" in The Hannah Arendt Papers at the Library of Congress, which, thanks in large part to research conducted by Wout Cornelissen, we have determined to be typescript that contains the last edits made by Arendt prior to her death. Currently this typescript is only available through the Library of Congress via the following locator: Books---The Life of the Mind---"Thinking"---Drafts---Set II. See memory.loc.gov/ammem/arendthtml/mharendtFolderP05.html. Citations refer to chapter and typescript page number.

7. Homer, *The Story of Achilles: A Translation of Homer's "Iliad" into Plain English by W. H. D. Rouse* (London: T. Nelson & Sons, 1938), 175.

Hannah Arendt and the Miracle of the New

Ken Krimstein

Illustrations by Ken Krimstein for The Three Escapes of Hannah Arendt: A Tyranny of Truth *(New York: Bloomsbury, 2018).*

> "The new always happens against the overwhelming odds of statistical laws and their probability, which for all practical, everyday purposes amounts to certainty; the new therefore always appears in the guise of a miracle." —Hannah Arendt, *The Human Condition*

For as long as I can remember, I've been obsessed with making new things: paintings, drawings, comics, cartoons, ads, stories, trumpet solos. I've put bread on my family's table by figuring out new ways to tell the story of, for example, why people should protect themselves from the sun, why they should purchase Duracell batteries or use the American Express Card or by finding fresh, new, unexpected ways of making people laugh at a cartoon image of a man stranded on a desert island. That's why Hannah Arendt's observation on the magic of the "new" struck such a chord. (The opening chord of the Beatles' "A Hard Day's Night"?)

But, at the same time, a lifetime's experience working in the mines of what people call "being a creative" has taught me two major things: one, it's really hard to come up with new ideas; and, two, although everyone says they want fresh, new creative ideas—they really *don't*.

New ideas are scary. Being confronted with the "new" makes the little hairs stand up on the back of your neck. Newness isn't warm and fuzzy. That's all because new ideas fly in the face of Darwinian survival instincts. By their very definition, truly new ideas do things "wrong" (at first at least). On the contrary, in order to survive, most people have been wired to play the safe game. The percentage game. Defense.

But not *all* people.

Because, just as much as we are *afraid* of the new, it also enchants us. New things sing a siren song, shine a light, keep the wolves we can't always see or hear at bay. Want proof? Try this. If you really want to quiet a room and command attention, if you want to see people *lean in*, repeat after me. The next time you're

in a meeting, or at dinner with friends, or with family, say, "I've got an idea." All eyes and ears will fall on you.

Ideas are currency. Ideas, new things, unexpected stories provide people with irreplaceable clues for living.

And Hannah Arendt understood the double-edged sword of the new completely. She sometimes referred to this phenomenon as *natality*. St. Augustine, a key inspiration for her, said, "That there be a beginning, man was created before whom there was nobody." Rather than defining life by death, Arendt saw life as a sequence of births—of people, of thought, of action, of newness.

For her, this ability to make new stuff is the essential product of freedom. And freedom is the stuff of newness. They feed each other. That's why she so abhorred stale, clichéd thinking. True, doing things the way they've always been done, without "thinking," without "making," is easy. It's *not* scary. But, without the challenge of making things anew, clichéd thinking often devolves into stupidity. Or worse.

Working drawing for a scene where Arendt confronts St. Augustine on a park bench in Washington Square.

What's more, coming up with new things isn't only scary, it's hard work. The "new" is elusive.

Say I'm working on a cartoon. Or a new chapter. The minute I alert my brain that I'm setting out to come up with an idea, the idea knows it. And it runs and hides. The surest way *not* to come up with a fresh idea is to try harder to do it.

Only by indirection, indiscretion, and, dare I say it, sometimes even inebriation, will the elusive gnome known as an idea peek out from the shadows. Consider this: the most common question posed to cartoonists is "Where do you get your ideas?" The best answer I've ever heard to that one was by the legendary early twentieth-century writer and cartoonist Milt Gross when he responded, "If I knew where, I'd be there right now getting them!"

With all due respect to Mr. Gross, Hannah Arendt put it much more elegantly and poetically when she said, "They come in the guise of a miracle."

A miracle?

I must confess I was taken aback when I read this kind of reasoning coming from so sharp and unsentimental a mind as Arendt's. "Miracles" are not the usual province of virulently truth-telling political philosophers. But her phrase reminded me of something I once read in an interview with the great film director Stanley Kubrick: "A great story is a miracle."

A great story works in spite of statistical odds. A great story bypasses our fear and satisfies our desire for novelty, for natality. And a great story does the legerdemain of "reveal[ing] meaning without committing the error of defining it."[1]

Without the kind of "miraculous" new ideas, no matter how scary they might be, we are frozen in time, and in place. We are like those tiny gnats from prehistoric times, caught in amber.

One of the things I've learned from working on cartoons and stories and my recently published comics biography of Hannah Arendt is how much humans are defined by what I call geography. Our setting, the physical space we inhabit, forms us. So much so, I've coined the phrase "Geography is destiny."

But so is human creativity; our scary, miraculous, uneasy, but eminently satisfying capacity for coming up with "the new." In the face of that, I've come to understand that the messy business of being a creative is even more critical than, say, a way for me to pay the rent. Everyone must be a creative, and I would argue, everyone is. The fact that you've dodged Darwinian extinction to sit at your desk (or stand on the subway) and read this proves it. New ideas are what we human beings use to navigate our way through the geography we inhabit. To realize our world, as we want it to be. To live.

---

1. Hannah Arendt, "Isak Dinesen: 1885–1963," in *Men in Dark Times* (New York: Houghton Mifflin Harcourt, 1995), 105.

The Fundamental Chord: Remembering Carl Heidenreich

Max L. Feldman

The story of painter Carl Heidenreich (1901–1965) sounds familiar, even if his name and work do not. Born in the Bavarian spa town Bad Berneck im Fichtelgebirge, Heidenreich studied at the State Institute of Arts and Crafts, Munich, and appears to have passed the entrance exams to the city's Academy of Fine Arts, with its traditional course of study, but chosen not to attend.[1] He instead became a student of the abstract painter and later "grand master of the New York School"[2] Hans Hofmann (1880–1966) for three years in his private academy. In 1922, Heidenreich moved to Berlin, becoming a scene painter at UFA film studios in Babelsberg, where legendary Austrian director Fritz Lang shot *Die Nibelungen* (1924), *Metropolis* (1927), and *Spione* (1928).

Heidenreich had a solo show at Galerie Lüders in Hamburg (1927) and participated in exhibitions at the Berlin Secession and Berlin Academy of Arts (1930–33). Upon the Nazis' rise to power, however, he was labeled a "degenerate artist." This was not so much for the content of his work, though it was deeply rooted in German Expressionism, as for his antifascist activism and member-ship in the German Communist Party (KPD). After the doorman in the building in which his studio was located tipped off the SA (Nazi paramilitary) about his political views, his planned breakthrough solo exhibition at Berlin's Galerie Niedendorf was cancelled, his studio ransacked, 200 of his works were destroyed, and he was imprisoned in the Gestapo detention center at Moabit Prison.[3]

Like many other left-wing anti-Stalinist Germans, Heidenreich left for Spain after his release in 1934, leaving behind three hundred more paintings; all would be destroyed by Allied bombing ten years later. He lived in Barcelona during the Spanish Republic, but, after being unable to receive a new residency permit, was deported to France in the spring of 1935, and found his way to Paris.

Moabit was not Heidenreich's only imprisonment by a fascist regime. He would fight for the Republicans in the Spanish Civil War in the International Brigades of the Workers' Party of Marxist Unification (POUM), under whom George Orwell fought.[4] In 1938, Heidenreich was captured, incarcerated, and tortured at Barcelona's Modelo prison. He depicted the grinning prison guards and downcast, gloomy prisoners tramping through the corridors in *Modelo Prison* (1938) and his watercolor *Prison Sketch* (after 1938).

After the fall of the Spanish Republic, Heidenreich fled for France. Like all Spanish Republicans and their foreign allies, he was immediately interned in the Argelés-sur-Mer camp in the Pyrenees. He did, however, somehow return to Paris, staying until the outbreak of World War II. With support from the

German American Writers Association, the Committee for Exiled Writers, and the American Guild for German Cultural Freedom, and letters of recommendation from Hofmann, art dealer Karl Nierendorf, and writer Oskar Maria Graf, he obtained a visa in December 1940. He sailed for the United States from Marseille with German refugee Karl Osner, Osner's Jewish wife Carola, and their daughter Margrit.

Since 1934, Heidenreich had left behind his own Polish-Jewish wife Lea ("Lia") Konvel Kagan and daughter Monika in Berlin. Lia would go underground in Berlin during the war, and Monika was sent to live with Carl's family in Bad Berneck. Carl and Lia's separation preyed on his conscience, and they would later divorce.

Figure 1. Carl Heidenreich.
Martinique (1941). Watercolor.
Courtesy Carl Heidenreich Foundation.

The journey to America took Heidenreich through Casablanca and Martinique, where he was held for four months awaiting onward transportation. During this time, he produced a number of watercolors whose pure, glowing colors point in the direction his work would move in the 1960s. *Martinique* (1941), for example, depicts a paradisiacal quiet that cannot conceal the deep, lonely sadness of exile (Figure 1).

Heidenreich eventually settled in New York, within the community of German and German-Jewish refugee intellectuals. Among them were a circle calling themselves *Das Dorf* ("the village"), comprising journalist and publicist Charlotte Beradt, Yiddish writer and cultural activist Chanan Klenbort (Hanan J. Ayalti), writer Charlotte Sempell Klenbort, fellow anti-Stalinist veteran Heinrich Blücher, and Hannah Arendt, all of whom Heidenreich had already met in Paris in 1937. Hannah Arendt would go on to write the catalogue text for Heidenreich's retrospectives in Frankfurt (1964) and at Goethe House in New York (1972).[5] This brief text draws on Heidenreich's experience of exile and statelessness, argues that he belongs to a tradition of German art dating back to romanticism, and describes the unashamed beauty of his painting, especially his later work.

Heidenreich, Arendt writes, was made homeless by "the same fate that made modern German art homeless."[6] Like Arendt, exile from Nazi Germany made Heidenreich stateless, living "outside normal legal protection"[7] and struggling to rebuild a life in America, faced with mounting losses:

> We lost our home, which means the familiarity of daily life. We
> lost our occupation, which means the confidence that we are of
> some use in this world. We lost our language, which means the

naturalness of reactions, the simplicity of gestures, the unaffected expression of feelings. We left our relatives in the Polish ghettos and our best friends have been killed in concentration camps, and that means the rupture of our private lives.[8]

Heidenreich shared these losses. He was also a victim of Nazi cultural policy: a total war on the German imagination and visual language. Alfred Rosenberg, the Nazis' leading spokesman on art and culture, reviled the spiritually syphilitic "mongrel art" of Impressionism and the "abortion" that was Expressionism.[9] Hitler himself promised to "wage an unrelenting war of purification against the last elements of putrefaction in [German, 'Aryan'] culture," including Cubism, Dadaism, Futurism, and Impressionism, which he called "the artifactitious stammerings of men to whom God has denied the race of a truly artistic talent, and in its place has awarded them the gift of jabbering or deception."[10]

Alla Efimova, executive director of the Carl Heidenreich Foundation, which aims to preserve the painter's work and broaden its critical and historical recognition, explains in her foreword to Saure's monograph that Heidenreich's art is a story of someone who lost everything—his family, possessions, and art—and struggled "to replace and recuperate his loss" by working through the traumatic experience of immigration.[11]

The puzzle, Efimova writes, is that Heidenreich's late works "do not fit into any accepted narrative of twentieth century modernism." Richard M. Buxbaum, president of the foundation's board of trustees, likewise argues that the strength of the work means it "should be part of a canon."[12] One answer is to position Heidenreich in relation to his teacher, the great Hans Hofmann.

Hofmann was the only artist of the New York School—the city's group of experimental poets, painters, dancers, and musicians working in the 1950s and '60s—to participate directly in the early twentieth-century avant-garde (Figure 2).

Hofmann would tell students at his forward-thinking private academies in Munich (1914–32), New York (1934–58), and Provincetown, Mass. (1935–58), stories about his time in Paris (1904–14); of his exposure to Cubism, Fauvism, and Futurism as they happened; of nights at the Café du Dôme with Picasso, Braque, Rouault, Pascin, Léger, and Picabia; of drawing classes attended with Matisse at the École de la Grande Chaumière. Hofmann's development, students (all far better known than Heidenreich), and reputation are, however, less important for us than his influential theories of painting and their effect on Heidenreich, especially apparent in his later work.[13]

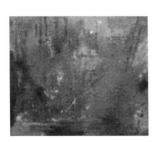

Figure 2. Carl Heidenreich. *Landscape in Red and Blue* (1965). Watercolor. Courtesy Carl Heidenreich Foundation.

Arendt argues that, despite spending thirty years outside Germany, Heidenreich was still a "specifically German painter."[14] Heidenreich, she claims, preserved a quality of "intense inwardness." This English expression fails to describe, let alone define, the German *Innigkeit*. Heidenreich's *Innigkeit* is comparable, for Arendt, not only to the great lyric poets but also to a German artistic tradition that includes Caspar David Friedrich, Lovis Corinth, and Emil Nolde. She sees Heidenreich's loyalty to their inspiration, if not the tradition for its own sake.

Hofmann believed in a version of *Innigkeit* too. In a late interview, he explains his belief in the "spiritual" quality of artistic creation. This is, for Hofmann, not a syncretic "new age" faith but comparable to the German *Geistigkeit* (spirituality). Hofmann thus places himself in the tradition of Spinoza, Schiller, and Goethe, frequently quoted in his lectures. This, he explains, is a result of a sixth sense, the sense of sensibility, the ability to see or look into things in depth, to discover the inner life. He explains in an interview that we see only the surface of things, but our "sensibility," our ability to respond intuitively to the world, explores "the inner life of everything," feeling something imperceptible just beneath physical reality and using our emotions to give this experience material form in a work of art.[15]

Hofmann's main interest was how artists translate their own experiences into works of art that reflect the "sensorial and emotional world" according to the "inner laws" of a specific medium.[16] Artists, for Hofmann, must not imitate nature but transform the external physical reality into spiritual reality, reordering their experience of nature in the physical form of a work of art, in which "the spiritual quality dominates the material."[17]

Arendt explains *sensus communis* (common sense) in similar terms. She explains that things appear to us in two modes. We take in the world through our five senses (sight, smell, touch, taste, and hearing). This gives our experiences of things the character of *seeing*. The world *seems* to us to be one way or another based on our subjective, personal take on it. Appearances also carry what Arendt calls "a prior indication of *realness*."[18] This is *sensus communis*, a "sixth sense," an idea that enters Western philosophy through Thomas Aquinas, for whom this "inner sense" unifies all objects of the five senses, guaranteeing that the thing we see, touch, taste, smell, and hear is one and the same object.[19]

There is no body part for *sensus communis*, Arendt explains.[20] It has no dedicated receptive organ like eyes for seeing or ears for hearing. The five senses are, indeed, entirely private, sealed off from the rest of the world. Their corresponding sensations cannot be felt by or directly communicated to anyone else because *I* see things with *my* eyes, feel with the touch of *my* skin, taste with *my* tongue, smell with the odors in *my* nose, hear the sound in *my* ears.

Sensus communis, however, lets us translate private sensations into a common language shared by others. Its worldly property is, Arendt explains, "realness." There is a problem with this, however. Because we cannot perceive it like other primary sensory qualities, the *sensus communis* is not itself a sensation because, Arendt says, "the 'sensation' of reality, of sheer thereness, relates to the *context* in which single objects appear as well as to the context in which we ourselves as appearances exist among other appearing creatures."[21]

Efimova says that Heidenreich "absorbed Hofmann's teaching, and into his mature years continued to assert principles of abstraction first learned in the Munich school."[22] Despite his personal convictions, there is little political content in Heidenreich's painting, just as Hofmann's painting was apolitical. Rather, as Arendt points out, Heidenreich's work mainly consists of landscapes—scenes from his travels through Spain, France, Mexico, Alaska, and the Pacific, and New York cityscapes. Arendt owned four of these works—*Figure* (1949), *Midtown* (1953), *Alaska I* (1961), and *Orpheus* (1962)—which she lent to the 1964 and 1972 retrospectives.

Figure 3. Carl Heidenreich.
Last Painting (1965).
Oil. Courtesy
Richard M. Buxbaum.

Following his move toward abstraction in the 1940s and '50s, Heidenreich's best work is from the 1960s. Many of these paintings are in the collection of Richard Buxbaum, but there were thousands in Heidenreich's studio when he died. Much time could be spent poring over every swoop of Heidenreich's hand, every elusive dusting of paint. Perhaps none of these works are more delicate or evocative than *Last Painting* (1965), which now graces the cover of Arendt's posthumously published collection *Reflections on Literature and Culture* (Figure 3).

The central motif in *Last Painting*, which looks like verdant organic growth, is enclosed by touches of orange and swathes of deep azure. The orange and sprays of white are like light apprehended at the edge of our visual field as it ricochets from reflective surfaces—the glass, steel, and oily puddles of the modern city, or mingled memories of different seas and skies, at home or in exile.

Last Painting is not a conventional landscape, however. Though you can see oceanic azure in it, it doesn't refer to any specific daybreak or twilight. There is no precise geography as in the paintings of Martinique and Alaska. It is, rather, an attempt to render otherwise incommunicable feelings about the world into something visible and shareable by others. This can only be achieved, following Hofmann's teachings, by abstracting from any and every definite point of visual reference or position in real space.

Arendt says that producing a livable world involves, in part, "the transformation of the intangible into the tangibility of things."[23] To become part of a shared world, the things we do or think must be felt, remembered, and turned into things that other people can see, hear, and remember (stories, poems, paintings, sculptures). *Last Painting,* like so many of Heidenreich's paintings, contains no acting bodies or objects for use. It is, however, based on the deep conviction that our feelings about and experiences of the world are memorable in their own right and worthy of sharing. Heidenreich's task is to translate them into something for all of us to see and feel, even as all that is solid melts into air and the loss of the old country and its ways recedes beyond the horizon of memory. Indeed, Arendt writes that Heidenreich's work develops "out of the basic colors as they are characteristic and conspicuous in the various parts of the world. The ability to see and represent these basic elements, *the fundamental chord,* as it were, with all its modulations, is manifest in every picture."[24]

Heidenreich was never fashionable and has mostly been forgotten. He is unlikely to become fashionable anytime soon. The contemporary art world rejects theories of spiritual insight like Hofmann's and derides the very idea that beauty is something worthy of thought. Even if he never becomes fashionable again, and his legacy is drowned out by louder voices, he deserves to be remembered as his friends from *Das Dorf* recall him: not just the rebellious, even reckless risk-taker but a quiet, sensitive man, loved by his friends. Arendt captures this when she writes, "The friends of Carl Heidenreich's paintings know how marvellous it is to live with them and that as they hang on one's walls they become ever more beautiful."[25] We can take away two things from this: not just the unashamed belief in the transformative power of beauty or that the painter Carl Heidenreich had friends, but that his paintings had friends that will outlive even them, returning the gaze of new viewers who make them a part of their world.

1. Gabriele Saure, Carl Heidenreich, (New York: Goethe-Institut, 2004), 23. Saure's book is the only existing monograph on Carl Heidenreich, published for the exhibition *Carl Heidenreich and Hans Hofmann in Postwar New York,* University of California, Berkeley Art Museum and Pacific Film Archive (BAMPFA), 21 May – 3 October 2004.
2. Rosalind E. Krauss, "Hans Hofmann: Kootz Gallery, New York," *Artforum* (April 1966): 47.
3. Saure, *Carl Heidenreich,* 30.
4. Revolutionaries Andreu Nin and Joaquín Maurín, inspired by Trotsky's thesis of "Permanent Revolution," formed POUM—*Partido Obrero de Unificación Marxista* (Spanish), or *Partit Obrer d'Unificació Marxista* (Catalan)—in 1935 by fusing the Trotskyist Communist Left of Spain (*Izquierda Comunista de España*) and the Workers' and Peasants Bloc (BOC, affiliated with the Right Opposition) without the consent of Trotsky. See George Orwell, *Homage to Catalonia* (1938), and Ernest Hemingway, *For Whom the Bell Tolls* (1940).
5. Hannah Arendt, "Foreword to Carl Heidenreich's Exhibition Catalogue," in *Reflections on Literature and Culture,* ed. Susannah Young-ah Gottlieb (Stanford: Stanford University Press, 2007), 203–5.
6. Ibid., 203.
7. Hannah Arendt, *The Origins of Totalitarianism* (1951; London: Penguin, 2016), 359.
8. Hannah Arendt, "We Refugees" (1943), in *The Jewish Writings,* ed. Jerome Kohn and Ron H. Feldman (New York: Schocken Books, 2007), 264–65.
9. Alfred Rosenberg, *Selected Writings,* ed. Robert Pois (London: Jonathan Cape, 1970).
10. Adolf Hitler, "Speech Inaugurating the 'Great Exhibition of German Art 1937,'" in *Theories of Modern Art: A Source Book by Artists and Critics,* ed. Herschel B. Chipp (Berkeley: University of California Press, 1968), 479.

11. Saure, *Carl Heidenreich*, viii.

12. Alla Efimova, interview with Richard Buxbaum, 20 October 2016. carlheidenreichfoundation.org/news/2016/10/20/three-generations-champion-rebel-painter-carl-heidenreich.

13. Hofmann's mythic reputation precedes him. He is often mistaken as the teacher of the first wave of Abstract Expressionists (Gorky, de Kooning, Pollock, Reinhardt, Rothko); he was, rather, their *colleague*. The term "abstract expressionism" was, however, first used to describe Hofmann's work, and his solo exhibition at the Addison Gallery of American Art in 1967 was not only the first solo Abstract Expressionist museum exhibition but also produced the movement's first monograph. Hofmann's numerous students, including but by no means limited to Nell Blaine, Ray Eames, Robert De Niro Sr., Helen Frankenthaler, Lee Krasner, and Larry Rivers, belong to the *Second* New York School. Note, meanwhile, the highly gendered overtones in critic John Yau's claim that the final proof of Hofmann's stature is "the fact that the list of artists who didn't study with Hofmann includes more substantial talent than the list of those who did." John Yau, "Hans Hofmann: Whitney Museum of Modern Art, New York," *Artforum* (November 1990): 162.

14. Arendt, "Foreword," 203.

15. Irma B. Jaffe, "A Conversation with Hans Hofmann," *Artforum* (January 1971): 34–35.

16. Hans Hofmann, "On the Aims of Art," *The Fortnightly* 1, no. 13 (February 1932): 7–11.

17. Hans Hofmann, *Search for the Real and Other Essays* (1948), ed. Sara T. Weeks and Bartlett H. Hayes Jr. (Cambridge: MIT Press, 1967), 41.

18. Hannah Arendt, *The Life of the Mind* (New York: Harcourt, 1971), 49.

19. Thomas Aquinas, *Summa theologica* 1.1.2, 1.3.2.

20. Arendt, *The Life of the Mind*, 51.

21. Ibid.

22. Alla Efimova, "Carl Heidenreich and Hans Hoffmann in Postwar New York: Parallel Lives of Art and Exile Viewed Through a Lens of Abstraction," press release, BAMPFA, n.d. archive. bampfa.berkeley.edu/press/release/TXT0089.

23. Hannah Arendt, *The Human Condition* (1958; Chicago: University of Chicago Press, 1998), 95.

24. Arendt, "Foreword," 204 (my emphasis).

25. Ibid.

Time for Arendt: Political Temporality and the Space-Time of Freedom

Katherine Bermingham

> "In the last analysis, the human world is always the product of man's *amor mundi*, a human artifice whose potential immortality is always subject to the mortality of those who build it and the natality of those who come to live in it."[1]

When she was interviewed in 1964 by Günter Gaus, a prominent German journalist, Hannah Arendt had only recently joined the University of Chicago's Committee on Social Thought, having held numerous temporary academic and journalistic positions since arriving in the United States in 1941.[2] At the outset of their conversation, now known as "What Remains? The Language Remains,"[3] Arendt rejected Gaus's attempt to label her a philosopher. "My profession, if one can even speak of it at all, is political theory."[4] Scholars of Arendt's work often cite this part of the interview in order to punctuate the distinction she makes between thinking philosophically and thinking politically.[5] Despite her capacious knowledge of the Western philosophical tradition and her continuous engagement with philosophers from the pre-Socratics to her contemporaries, Arendt did not consider herself to be one of them. "As you know, I studied philosophy," Arendt remarked to Gaus, "but that does not mean that I stayed with it."[6]

Later in the interview, Gaus invited Arendt to expand on what prompted her apostasy from philosophy, asking: "Is there a definite event in your memory that dates your turn to the political?" Arendt answered with characteristic decisiveness: "I would say February 27, 1933, the burning of the Reichstag, and the illegal arrests that followed during the same night."[7] Though her upbringing was fairly secular, Arendt's effort to understand politics, her primary subject, was bound up from the first with the persecution of the Jewish people in mid-twentieth-century Europe.[8] "If one is attacked as a Jew, one must defend oneself as a Jew," Arendt told Gaus.[9]

In addition to demonstrating the significance of the fate of the Jewish people in Arendt's intellectual trajectory (might she have "stayed with" philosophy if the rise of National Socialism had been thwarted?), the specificity of her reply to Gaus also attests to the primacy of discrete moments in time in Arendt's political theory. Per Jonathan Schell: "it was events that set her mind in motion, and philosophy that had to adjust,"[10] a view corroborated by Arendt's own reflections on how the horrific events of a particular day prompted her to reorient the course of her intellectual and professional life, to devote her attention to the political rather than the philosophical realm. Events—temporal happenings—are the basic unit of Arendt's thought, the point from which her tentative and provisional analyses depart.[11] In other words, Arendt locates the significance of politics not in static transhistorical forms but in transitory, historical, and contingent occurrences.

Embedded in the contradistinction between the "potential immortality" of the world and "the mortality of those who build it" is the temporal relationship fundamental to Arendt's thought.[12] While subjects such as memory and history have been extensively canvassed by Arendt scholars, little work has been done specifically on Arendt's concept of time, which informs memory and history—and the relationship between them. The deficit of scholarly attention to time in Arendt's work is rather surprising given her intellectual debt not only to Heidegger, for whom time was constitutive of Being and therefore inseparable from meaning, but also to Nietzsche, postulator of the eternal return and other nontraditional temporalities.[13]

Time is not finitude for Arendt, which is to say, time is not subject to the laws of inevitability or reducible to unidirectional flow. The boundlessness she ascribes to action is not only spatial, but temporal. In fact, political time—in contrast to both physical and historical time—can be restored, reborn, and possibly redeemed. Arendt's time concept should be understood as a significant and conscious departure from Martin Heidegger's *Being and Time*. Whereas Heidegger's project attempts to question the centering of the present (and presence) that he says characterizes metaphysics from Aristotle through the French philosopher of time Henri Bergson,[14] Arendt returns to the present—that which lies between past and future—but not as a point of hypostasized fixity or stasis (like the metaphysicians Heidegger abjured), but rather as a "gap" a site of possibility. Far from being an inversion of Heidegger, Arendt's work proposes a dramatic rethinking of human beings' relationship to time—specifically, by considering how individual mortality and subjective time experience intersect with existence in an artificially constructed entity: a political body. If the crudest summation of Heidegger is the image of life's time flowing like sand through the proverbial hourglass, Arendt's time concept resembles the Orloj—an intricate and extraordinary Czech timepiece from the Middle Ages, constructed to render many different temporalities at once[15] (Figure 1).

In his 1977 article "Hannah Arendt and the Ordinance of Time," the political theorist Sheldon Wolin wrote: "the corruptibility of politics formed a constant theme in Hannah Arendt's thought and it served as the basis for a vision of politics that was radical and critical."[16] Yet, it is not only the vulnerability and fragility of political freedom to corruption and degradation, not only the propensity of what she terms "the social" to overtake the political, burying revolutionary treasures in the oblivion of automation, but also the ever-present possibilities of recovery, rebirth—and even redemption of a peculiar variety—that is a constant Arendtian theme. "So long as the human

Figure 1. Prague Orloj. Astronomical clock, 1410–93. Wikimedia Commons.

condition itself is not changed," Arendt comments in the prologue to *The Human Condition*, "those general human capacities which grow out of the human condition and are permanent . . . cannot be irretrievably lost."[17]

Like Machiavelli,[18] whom she greatly admired, Arendt suggests that political bodies—unlike human bodies—can be reborn precisely because politics is not subject to the laws of mortality that govern organic existence. Politics is artifice, not nature. The initiatory moment or "birth" of the political community can only exert its rejuvenating potential by being prized out of linear time, by occupying an extratemporal standpoint. Indeed, the capability of a political body to be reborn via ritual is no mere turn of phrase or whimsical metaphor. Rather, for Arendt this integral political capacity is undergirded by a theory of time that is unique to politics. Whereas for Walter Benjamin (and first-generation critical theorists like Theodor Adorno) temporal disruption is intellectually and aesthetically fecund, for Arendt the power unleashed by nonlinear encounters with history and memory is integral to her *institutional* theory of republican politics.

Among many reasons, Arendt's political theory remains of interest to political philosophers and political actors alike, especially in the dark times of our present, because of her rejection of fatalism and the time concept it employs. Against those preaching fire and brimstone about the inevitability of our ever-nearing political rapture, Arendt would argue that we can step back from the brink, in part by acting in concert with peers and exercising judgment (confronting and bringing about the novel), and in part by retrieving lost capacities and conceptual understandings that facilitate ongoing care for the common world. By acting in concert—that is, at the same *time*—we create new spheres of freedom. And while it may not be possible to "turn back time," it is possible to carry parts of the past with you, like an Aeneas leaving behind the smoldering Trojan ruins with an Anchises slung over your shoulder.

---

1. This quote is from a lecture Arendt delivered in 1955 to conclude a course on The History of Political Theory. See the epilogue to Hannah Arendt, *The Promise of Politics*, ed. and with an introduction by Jerome Kohn (New York: Schocken, 2005), 203. She taught this course during her time as a visiting professor at the University of California Berkeley in 1955, the year prior to her delivery of the Walgreen Foundation Lectures that would become *The Human Condition*.

2. After fleeing Germany for Paris, where she lived from 1933 to 1940, Arendt was briefly interned in Gurs before securing passage to New York. After arriving in the United States in 1941, she held several temporary academic positions, in addition to working as an editor for Schocken Books. By this point, Arendt had taught at multiple prestigious American universities and delivered several prominent lecture series, including the 1956 Walgreen Lectures. Elisabeth Young-Bruehl, *Hannah Arendt: For Love of the World*, 2nd ed. (New Haven: Yale University Press, 2004), 390.

3. Hannah Arendt, "'What Remains? The Language Remains': A Conversation with Günter Gaus," in *Essays in Understanding, 1930–1954*, ed. and with an introduction by Jerome Kohn (New York: Harcourt, Brace, 1994), 1–23. The interview took place on 28 October 1964 and was awarded the Adolf Grimme Prize.

4. Arendt, *Essays in Understanding*, 1.

5. For example, Dana Villa, "Introduction," in "Hannah Arendt," ed. Dana Villa, special issue, *Revue Internationale de Philosophie* 53, no. 208 (June 1999): 127–32; Richard Bernstein, *Hannah Arendt and the Jewish Question* (Cambridge: MIT Press, 1996); Christian Volk, *Arendtian Constitutionalism: Law, Politics, and the Order of Freedom* (New York: Bloomsbury, 2015), among others.

6. Arendt, *Essays in Understanding*, 2.

7. Ibid. 4.

8. Young-Bruehl, *Hannah Arendt: For Love of the World*, 9.

9. Arendt, *Essays in Understanding*, 12. For scholarship on the relevance of Judaism in Arendt's work, see especially Richard J. Bernstein, *Hannah Arendt and the Jewish Question* (Cambridge: MIT Press, 1996); Seyla Benhabib, "The Pariah and Her Shadow: Hannah Arendt's Biography of Rahel Varnhagen," in *Feminist Interpretations of Hannah Arendt*, ed. Bonnie Honig (University Park: Penn State University Press, 1995); Susannah Young-ah Gottlieb, *Regions of Sorrow: Anxiety and Messianism in Hannah Arendt and W. H. Auden* (Stanford: Stanford University Press, 2003), 139; Eric Jacobson, "Why Did Hannah Arendt Reject the Partition of Palestine?" *Journal for Cultural Research* (2013): 1–24.

10. Jonathan Schell, introduction to Hannah Arendt, *On Revolution* (New York: Penguin Books, 2006), xii.

11. Until the end of her life, Arendt insisted that everything she had written was provisional, an attempt to understand. I interpret this to be less a gesture of modesty than a reflection of her resistance to the closure of philosophy.

12. A notable exception to this is Adam Lindsay, "Hannah Arendt, the problem of the absolute and the paradox of constitutionalism, or: 'How to restart time within an inexorable time continuum,'" *Philosophy and Social Criticism* 43, no. 10 (2017): 1022–44. There are no book-length treatments of this topic. Dana Villa's *Arendt/Heidegger: The Fate of the Political* (1996), focuses on action, but not time. Sophie Loidolt's recent *Phenomenology of Plurality: Hannah Arendt on Political Subjectivity* (2018) locates Arendt within the phenomenological tradition—including viz. Heidegger, Merleau-Ponty, and Levinas—but focuses on ethics and ontology, not time. Sheldon Wolin wrote an article—"Hannah Arendt and the Ordinance of Time," *Social Research* 44, no. 1 (Spring 1977): 91–105—though it deals less with time than with Wolin's understanding of Arendt's "authentic politics." Sections of Peg Birmingham's *Hannah Arendt and Human Rights: The Predicament of Common Responsibility* (2006) discuss Arendt's and Heidegger's theories of time. Jerome Kohn's introduction to Arendt's *Between Past and Future: Eight Exercises in Political Thought* (New York: Penguin, 2006) presents her as someone who "thinks at the intersection of the past and future dimensions of human time" (xix).

13. See especially Joan Stambaugh, *The Problem of Time in Nietzsche* (Lewisburg: Bucknell University Press, 1987).

14. Martin Heidegger, *Being and Time*, trans. John Macquarrie and Edward Robinson (New York: Harper & Row, 2008), 39 (German: 18).

15. The Orloj in Prague, which began keeping time in 1410, is one of the oldest clocks in the world, but its operation has not been continuous. On 18 January 2018 clock master Petr Skála began conducting a major renovation to replace aging metal gears with wooden mechanisms. The clock is being given a makeover so that it looks more like its original medieval self. The Orloj is a paradigmatic example of human artifice and how it captures time. In addition to minutes and hours, the Orloj tells Old Bohemian time (which begins at sunset), Babylonian time (sunrise to sunset), Central European time, and sidereal (star) time. In the center of the clock is the astrolabe, tracking the sun, moon, and stars. The timepiece has endured for centuries—though not without human intervention and care, like that of Skála and his forerunners.

16. Wolin, "Hannah Arendt and the Ordinance of Time," 94.

17. Hannah Arendt, *The Human Condition*, 2nd ed. (Chicago: University of Chicago Press, 2018), 6.

18 Niccolò Machiavelli, *Discourses on Livy*, trans. Harvey C. Mansfield and Nathan Tarcov (Chicago: University of Chicago Press, 1996), 209. At the beginning of 3.1 of the *Discourses*, Machiavelli claims that well-ordered republics "can often be renewed or indeed that through some accident outside the said order come to the said renewal. And it is a thing clearer than light that these bodies do not last if they do not renew themselves."

Contributors

Contributors

Kenyon Victor Adams is a multidisciplinary artist and curator. His recent work explores the notion of fractured epistemologies, and seeks to reclaim or expand various ways of knowing through integrative artistic practices. Adams has contributed art and thought leadership at the Yale School of Drama, Yale ISM Poetry Conference, Live Ideas Festival, Langston Hughes Project, National Arts Policy Roundtable, and the Hannah Arendt Center for Politics and Humanities at Bard College. He studied religion and literature at Yale Divinity School and theology of contemporary performance at the Yale Institute of Sacred Music. Adams served as artist in residence at the Yale Institute of Sacred Music for the 2015–16 academic year. His multimedia performance works have addressed issues of legibility, race, and American memory. Currently in production, *Prayers of the People*, directed by Bill T. Jones, is a performance work responding to the writings of Martin Luther King Jr. Adams is the founding arts initiative director at Grace Farms and the SANAA-designed River Building in New Canaan, Conn., and director of the Louis Armstrong House Museum and Archives in Corona, N.Y.

Libby Barringer is the Klemens von Klemperer Post Doctoral Fellow at the Hannah Arendt Center for Politics and Humanities at Bard College. Barringer received her doctorate in political science from the University of California, Los Angeles, in 2016. Her work brings ancient and modern political thought and literature into conversation for the sake of contemporary democratic practices. In addition to her doctorate, she also holds an MSc in political theory from the London School of Economics and Political Science, and a BA in government and fine arts from the College of William and Mary.

Thomas Bartscherer is the Peter Sourian Senior Lecturer in the Humanities at Bard College. He writes on the intersection of literature and philosophy, with a particular focus on tragic drama, aesthetics, and performance. He also writes on contemporary art, new media technology, and the history and practice of liberal education. He is coeditor of *Erotikon: Essays on Eros Ancient and Modern* and *Switching Codes: Thinking Through Digital Technology in the Humanities and the Arts*, both from the University of Chicago Press, and he is currently editing, with Wout Cornelissen, *The Life of the Mind* for the Critical Edition of the complete works of Hannah Arendt. He is a research associate with the Institut des Textes et Manuscrits Modernes in Paris and has held research fellowships at the École Normale Supérieure and the University of Heidelberg. He holds a BA from the University of Pennsylvania and a PhD from the University of Chicago.

Roger Berkowitz has been teaching political theory, legal thought, and human rights at Bard College since 2005. He is the academic director of the Hannah Arendt Center for Politics and Humanities at Bard College. Berkowitz is an interdisciplinary scholar, teacher, and writer. His interests stretch from Greek and German philosophy to legal history and from the history of science to images of justice in film and literature. He is the author of *The Gift of Science: Leibniz and the Modern Legal Tradition*; coeditor of *Thinking in Dark Times: Hannah Arendt on Ethics and Politics*; editor of Revenge and Justice, a special issue of *Law, Culture, and the Humanities*; and a contributing editor to *Rechtsgeschichte*. His essays have appeared in numerous academic journals. Berkowitz received his BA from Amherst College; JD from Boalt Hall School of Law, University of California, Berkeley; and PhD from UC Berkeley.

Katherine Bermingham is a PhD candidate in political theory at the University of Notre Dame writing a dissertation on Hannah Arendt's concept of time. Her teaching and research concentrates on feminist theory, democratic theory, and twentieth-century political thought. Her work has been published in *New German Critique*.

Mark Bray is a historian of human rights, terrorism, and political radicalism in Modern Europe at Dartmouth College. He is the author of the national bestseller *Antifa: The Anti-Fascist Handbook, Translating Anarchy: The Anarchism of Occupy Wall Street, The Anarchist Inquisition: Terrorism and Human Rights in Spain and France, 1890–1910* (forthcoming), and coeditor of *Anarchist Education and the Modern School: A Francisco Ferrer Reader*. His work has appeared in the *Washington Post, Boston Review, Foreign Policy*, and numerous edited volumes.

David Bromwich is Sterling Professor of English at Yale University. He has taught and written about British and American romanticism, Shakespeare, modern poetry, and the rhetoric of persuasion. His books include *Hazlitt: the Mind of a Critic* and *The Intellectual Life of Edmund Burke: From the Sublime and Beautiful to American Independence*. His political commentaries on the Cheney-Bush, Obama, and Trump presidencies have appeared in the *Huffington Post, Antiwar, Dissent*, the *New York Review of Books, Mondoweiss, Tom Dispatch*, the *Nation*, and the *London Review of Books*.

Marion Detjen teaches migration history at Bard College Berlin (BCB) and works as the academic director for BCB's Program for International Education and Social Change. She studied history and literature in Berlin and Munich and received her PhD from Freie Universität Berlin. She taught history at Humboldt University Berlin from 2009 to 2014 and was a researcher at the Center for Contemporary History in Potsdam from 2015 to 2017. She is a regular contributor to the column *10nach8* at *ZEIT-Online* as part of its editorial team and is a cofounder of *Wir machen das* (We are doing it), an action coalition focused on issues of forced migration in Berlin. Detjen has published monographs on the history of refugees from the GDR and people smuggling following the building of the Berlin Wall (*Ein Loch in der Mauer*), on resistance against National Socialism in Munich (*Zum Staatsfeind ernannt*), and on the German constitution (*Die Deutschen und das Grundgesetz*, with Max Steinbeis and Stephan Detjen).

Joshua Foa Dienstag is professor of political science and law at the University of California, Los Angeles. He has written on the history of political thought, film, and the American founding. He is the author of four books, including *Pessimism: Philosophy, Ethic, Spirit*, which won the book award for Excellence in Philosophy from the American Association of Publishers in 2006. His most recent book is *Cinema Pessimism: Film and Representation in Democracy*, which will be published this year by Oxford University Press. He is a 2018–19 fellow at the Berggruen Institute in Los Angeles.

Kevin Duong has been at Bard since 2016. He received his PhD in government from Cornell University and his MA in social science from the University of Chicago. His research focuses on democracy and political violence, with an area focus on modern French political thought and intellectual history. He is currently working on a book manuscript, *The Virtues of Violence in Nineteenth-Century France*, that traces how revolutionary violence by "the people" offered a vocabulary of social regeneration during and after the French Revolution. He is the recipient of the American Political Science Association's 2017 Leo Strauss Award for the best dissertation in political philosophy. His research has also been supported by the Andrew W. Mellon Foundation and the Gustave Gimon Collection at Stanford, among others. At Bard, he teaches classes on the history of political thought, gender and sexuality, and various topics in modern intellectual history and European political development.

Max L. Feldman is a writer, art critic, and educator based in Vienna, Austria.

Sarah Jaffe is the author of *Necessary Trouble: Americans in Revolt*, which Robin D. G. Kelley called "the most compelling social and political portrait of our age." She is a Nation Institute reporting fellow and an independent journalist covering labor, economic justice, social movements, politics, gender, and pop culture. Her work has appeared in the *New York Times*, the *Nation*, the *Guardian*, the *Washington Post*, the *Atlantic*, and many other publications. She is the cohost, with Michelle Chen, of *Dissent* magazine's *Belabored* podcast, as well as a columnist at the *New Republic* and *New Labor Forum*.

Seon-Wook Kim is a professor in the Department of Philosophy at Soongsil University, Seoul, Korea, and president of the Korean Society for Hannah Arendt Studies. He has published several books on Arendt in Korean. His most recent title is *The Thoughts of Hannah Arendt*, which introduces Arendt's political ideas against the background of the 2016–17 Korean Candlelight Rallies that led to the regime change in 2017. He translated *Eichmann in Jerusalem, The Crises of the Republic, The Promise of Politics*, and *Lectures on Kan's Political Philosophy* into Korean. He also supervised most of the Korean translations of Michael J. Sandel's books, including *Justice: What's the Right Thing to Do?* Kim received his BA and MA from Soongsil University and his PhD from the State University of New York, Buffalo.

Ken Krimstein is a writer, cartoonist, and instructor at DePaul University in Chicago. His most recent book, *The Three Escapes of Hannah Arendt—A Tyranny of Truth*, is published by Bloomsbury. More of his work can be found at kenkrimstein.com.

John Douglas Macready is a professor of philosophy at Collin College in Plano, Texas. His work focuses on critical issues in social and political philosophy, with specific attention paid to the philosophy of human rights. He is the author of *Hannah Arendt and the Fragility of Human Dignity*.

Nikita Nelin is a writer of fiction, creative nonfiction, and immersive journalism. His writing experiments with voice-driven narrative at the intersection of memory and imagination, while often referencing the themes of his own emigration experience. His journalism subverts the objective-witness myth and explores ritual, ceremony, alternative community models, and the contemporary culture at large through "a perspective from the cultural fringe." He has written about Standing Rock, Burning Man, education toward individual agency, and sociocultural sustainability in consumerist and branding practices. His early research focused on the "silenced generations," Soviet writers and artists rejected by the communist party. Nelin received the 2010 Sean O'Faolain Prize for short fiction and the 2011 Summer Literary Seminars Prize for nonfiction, and was a finalist for the 2017 Restless Books Immigrant Prize and the 2018 Dzanc Books Prize. He has taught independently and at Brooklyn College, with special concentration in the close-reading method. He holds a BA from Bard College and an MFA from Brooklyn College. More of his work, as well as projects in development, can be found at nikitanelin.com.

Joshua Plencner is a visiting assistant professor in the Department of Political Science at Union College in Schenectady, N.Y. His teaching and research explore the intersection of American visual culture and the politics of identity, with special interest in racial formation, comics studies, political theory, and American political development. His writing has appeared in both popular and scholarly outlets, including *New Political Science*, *Black Perspectives*, *Artists Against Police Brutality*, *Middle Spaces*, and the University Press of Mississippi.

Peter Rosenblum is a professor of international law and human rights at Bard College.

Amy Schiller researches, writes, and consults at the intersection of political theory and philanthropy. As faculty at the Brooklyn Institute for Social Research and at Brooklyn College, she teaches on race, sexuality, and gender in politics. Her writing for the *Atlantic*, the *Nation*, the *Daily Beast*, and the *Chronicle of Philanthropy* has covered campus discourse on Israel-Palestine, funding the Movement for Black Lives, and American Girl dolls.

Christopher Schmidt has been on the faculty of the Chicago-Kent College of Law since 2008. He teaches in the areas of constitutional law, legal history, comparative constitutional law, and sports law. He has written on a variety of topics, including the historical development of the Fourteenth Amendment, the history of *Brown v. Board of Education*, the Tea Party as a constitutional movement, how Supreme Court Justices communicate with the American people, and the rise of free agency in Major League Baseball. He has published in leading law reviews and peer-review journals, among them *Constitutional Commentary*, *Cornell Law Review*, *Law and History Review*, *Northwestern University Law Review*, and *UCLA Law Review*. His article "Divided by Law: The Sit-Ins and the Role of the Courts in the Civil Rights Movement" won the 2014 Association of American Law Schools' Scholarly Papers Competition and the 2016 American Society for Legal History Surrency Prize. Schmidt is the author of *The Sit-Ins: Protest and Legal Change in the Civil Rights Era*. He is currently working on a new book project, *Civil Rights: An American History*, which examines how Americans have struggled over the meaning of civil rights from the Civil War through today.

Jana V. Schmidt began reading Hannah Arendt while writing on the question of political community in postwar Germany and its reimagination through literature and visual art. Her research interests include twentieth-century American and German literature, poststructuralism and the question of the communal vis-à-vis the aesthetic, *Bildwissenschaften* (image studies), and theories of memory. She recently published a book on Arendt's legacy as a thinker, *Hannah Arendt und die Folgen*; as well as an essay on reconciliation in Arendt and Ingeborg Bachmann (*Philosophy Today*). At present, she is a lecturer of literary theory at California State University, Los Angeles, while working on her next manuscript, a book of encounters between German-Jewish exiles to

America and African American artists and political activists from the 1940s to Black Power. She was a postdoctoral fellow at the Arendt Center in 2016–17 and taught at Bard College as a visiting assistant professor in the humanities in 2017. She holds an MA in English from the University of Pennsylvania and a PhD in comparative literature from the State University of New York, Buffalo.

Ann Seaton is a visiting assistant professor of humanities at Bard College. She studied with Mary Lefkowitz and Frank Bidart at Wellesley College, where she was a two-time undergraduate Academy of American Poets Prize winner. She was a Mellon Fellow in the Humanities at Stanford University, where she went intending to study Greek and Latin with John Winkler, and subsequently left for Harvard University, where she worked with Barbara Johnson. She was a postdoctoral fellow in aesthetics and politics at Brown University. Her main interests are in ancient Greek and Latin pastoral poetry and Ovid, the English Renaissance, the French eighteenth and nineteenth centuries, and critical race theory. Seaton is working on a book-length project, *Race and the Pastoral*. She has presented portions of this work in progress at the City University of New York Graduate Center's conference on the pastoral, Si Canimus Silvas; at the Kelly Writers House, University of Pennsylvania; at the Center for African-American Poetics, University of Pittsburgh; and, this fall, to classics graduate students and faculty at Princeton University. She also works as a conceptual artist; her work has appeared at the Whitney Museum and the Witte de With in Rotterdam, as part of the YAM Collective. She founded and directs the Difference and Media Project at Bard College, an intersectional think tank on difference, aesthetics, and politics.

Theda Skocpol is the Victor S. Thomas Professor of Government and Sociology at Harvard University, where she has also served as dean of the Graduate School and as director of the Center for American Political Studies. Skocpol is an internationally recognized scholar and has been elected to membership in all three of America's scholarly honor societies: the American Academy of Arts and Sciences, the American Philosophical Society, and the National Academy of Sciences. In addition to her teaching and research, Skocpol serves as director of the Scholars Strategy Network, an organization with dozens of regional chapters that encourages nonpartisan public engagement by university-based scholars, building ties between academics and policymakers, civic groups, and journalists.

Allison Stanger is the Russell Leng '60 Professor of International Politics and Economics and founding director of the Rohatyn Center for International Affairs at Middlebury College. She is the author of *One Nation under Contract: The Outsourcing of American Power and the Future of Foreign Policy* and the forthcoming *Life, Liberty, and the Pursuit of Leaks: The Story of Whistleblowing in America*, both with Yale University Press. She is working on a new book tentatively titled *Consumers vs. Citizens: How the Internet Revolution is Remaking Global Security and Democracy's Public Square*. Stanger has published opinion pieces in *Foreign Affairs, Foreign Policy,* the *Financial Times,* the *International Herald Tribune,* the *New York Times, USA Today, U.S. News* and *World Report,* and the *Washington Post,* and has testified before the Commission on Wartime Contracting, the Senate Budget Committee, the Congressional Oversight Panel, and the Senate HELP Committee. She is a member of the Council on Foreign Relations and received her PhD in political science from Harvard University. Stanger is currently a scholar in residence at New America.

Thomas Chatterton Williams is the author of a memoir, *Losing My Cool,* and a contributing writer at the *New York Times Magazine.* His writing has appeared in the *New Yorker, Harper's,* the *London Review of Books,* and many other places. He is the recipient of a Berlin Prize from the American Academy in Berlin and is a 2019 New America Fellow. He is currently at work on a book, rooted in his experience as the black father of two white-looking children in Paris, that will reckon with the ways in which we construct race in America.

About Bard College

Founded in 1860, Bard College in Annandale-on-Hudson, New York, is an independent, residential, coeducational college offering a four-year BA program in the liberal arts and sciences and a five-year BA/BS degree in economics and finance. The Bard College Conservatory of Music offers a five-year program in which students pursue a dual degree—a BMus and a BA in a field other than music. Bard offers MMus degrees in conjunction with the Conservatory and The Orchestra Now, and at Longy School of Music of Bard College in Cambridge, Massachusetts. Bard and its affiliated institutions also grant the following degrees: AA at Bard High School Early College, a public school with campuses in New York City, Cleveland, Baltimore, and Newark, New Jersey; AA and BA at Bard College at Simon's Rock: The Early College, in Great Barrington, Massachusetts, and through the Bard Prison Initiative at six correctional institutions in New York State; MA in curatorial studies, MS and MA in economic theory and policy, and MS in environmental policy and in climate science and policy at the Annandale campus; MFA and MAT at multiple campuses; MBA in sustainability in New York City; and MA, MPhil, and PhD in the decorative arts, design history, and material culture at the Bard Graduate Center in Manhattan. Internationally, Bard confers dual BA and MA degrees at the Faculty of Liberal Arts and Sciences, St. Petersburg State University, Russia (Smolny); dual BA and MAT degrees at Al-Quds University in East Jerusalem; and dual BA degrees at American University of Central Asia in Kyrgyzstan and Bard College Berlin: A Liberal Arts University.

Bard offers nearly 50 academic programs in four divisions. Total enrollment for Bard College and its affiliates is approximately 6,000 students. The undergraduate College has an enrollment of more than 1,900 and a student-to-faculty ratio of 10:1. In 2016, Bard acquired the Montgomery Place estate, bringing the size of the campus to nearly 1,000 acres. For more information about Bard College, visit bard.edu.

JOURNALS

hac.bard.edu

62346478R00126

Made in the USA
Middletown, DE
22 August 2019